AF255496

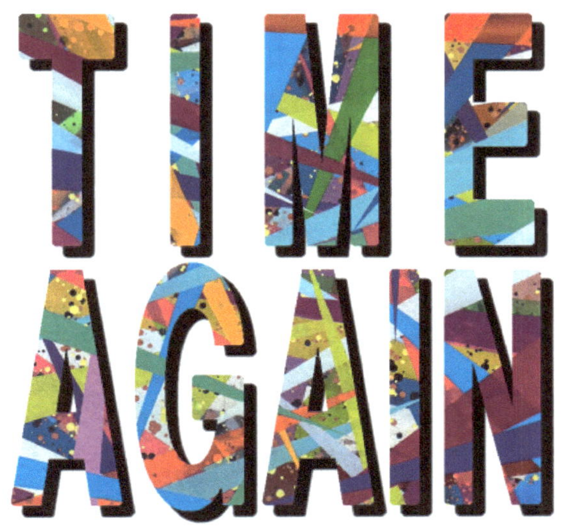

Brent Houzenga

Cover Design & Interior Layout by Brent Houzenga
All artwork © Brent Houzenga

Edited by Karen Cooper

ISBN 978-1-964252-67-4
Printed in the United States of America

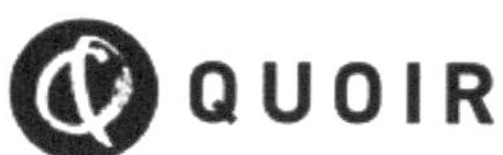

Published by Quoir
Chico, California
www.Quoir.com

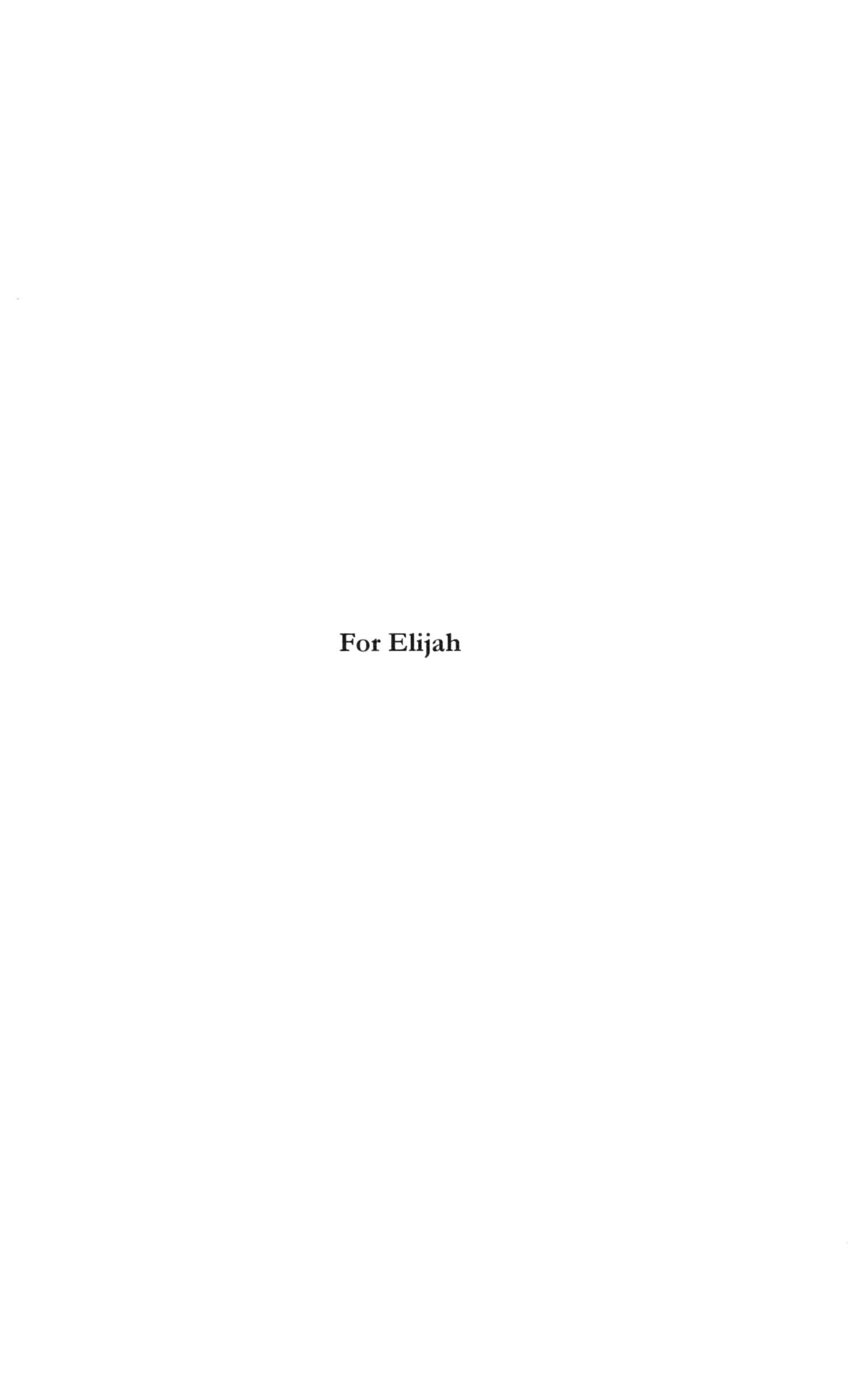

For Elijah

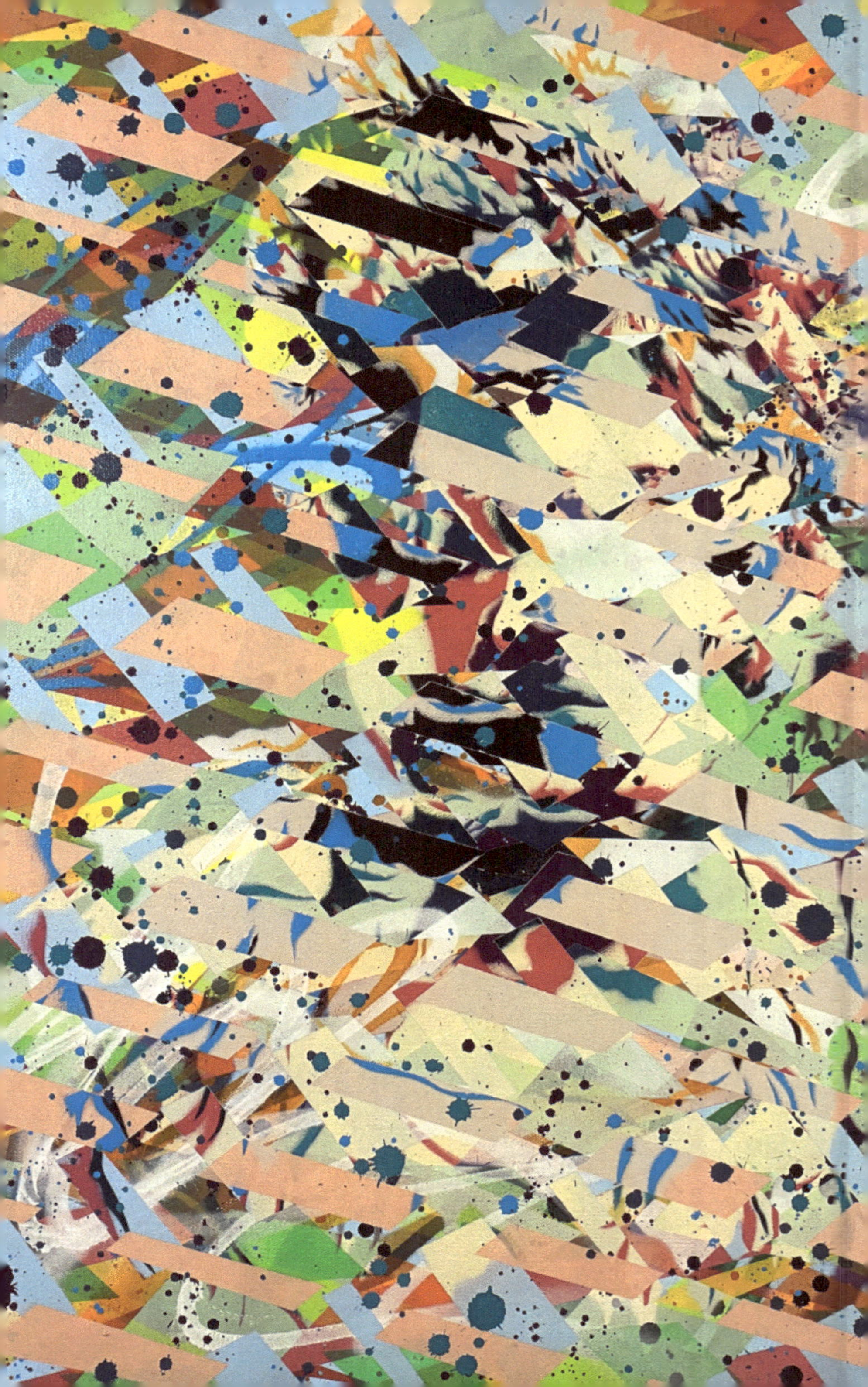

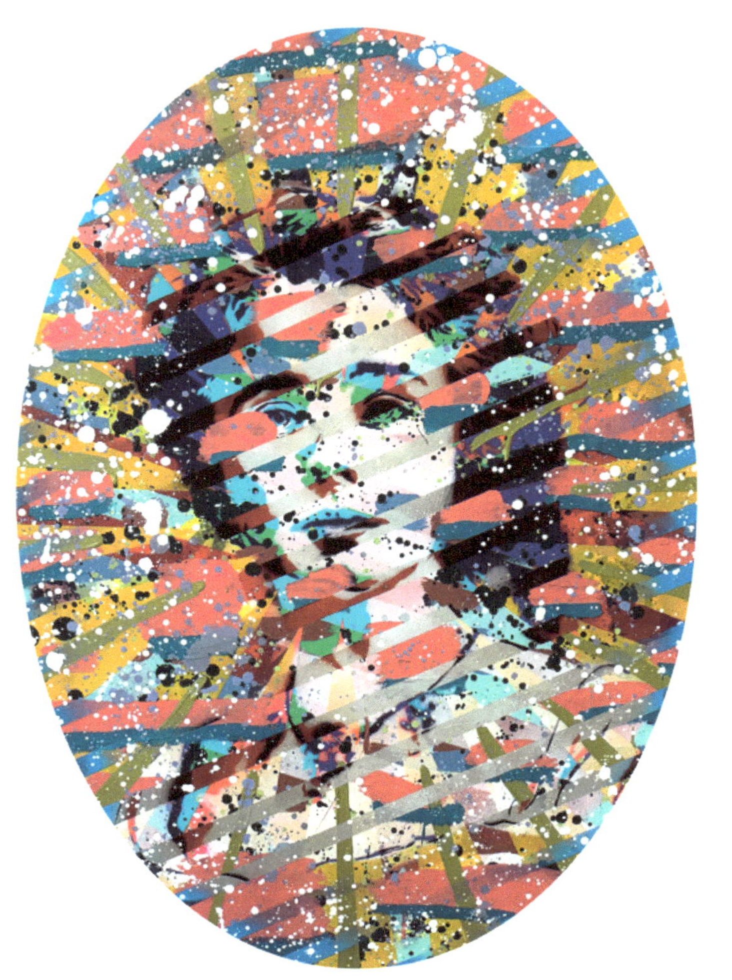

STATEMENT

For the last nineteen years my work has focused on painting found people from the 1890s, whose photos I found in the trash. Although I don't know who these people are, they changed my life.

Initially, what they helped me understand is the finite time we have here on earth. That realization lit a fire underneath me and pushed me to go after what I love, using their visage as my symbol. Most of my work is somehow related to time, whether that be through the idea of time travel and ghosts, or the subjects, layers and objects involved in my process. Some other evident influences include punk rock, street art, comic books, mysticism and psychology. While I'm interested in science, I'm much more interested in mad science and experimentation.

Portraying anonymous people in this pop aesthetic almost one hundred percent of the time urges viewers to ask "who is that?" The viewer wants to jump to conclusions. "Is that Lincoln? Is that Tesla?" This has led me to seek out stories I can actually tell. These stories have often come from local news and causes, historical figures associated with current events, or personal stories taken from my life or the people I encounter. Synchronicity is a very important part of my navigation. Some figures who I believe were drawn to me, or me to them, over the last few years include: James Baldwin, Emmeline Pankhurst, Lucy Parsons, Frederick Douglass, George F. Johnson, Thomas Garrett, Louise Michel, Edward Bellamy, Assata Shakur… and the list continues to grow.

I'm very interested in portraiture, but I'm equally interested in abstraction and the space between representation and the void. My experimentations with process have led me to think about these two premises often: On the microscopic level, everything is made of energy. On the macroscopic level, everything is stardust. My hope is to depict my figures as part of the cosmic consciousness.

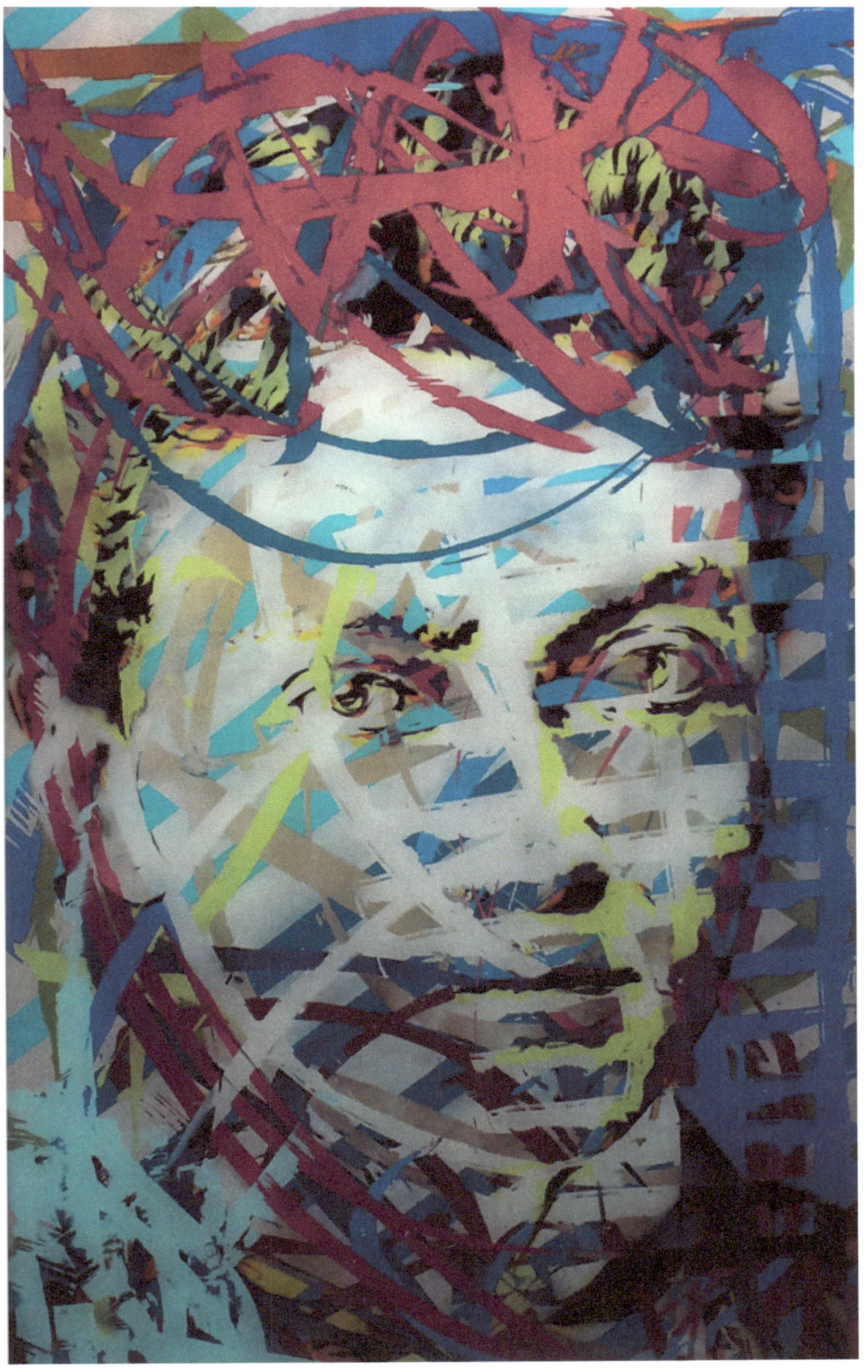

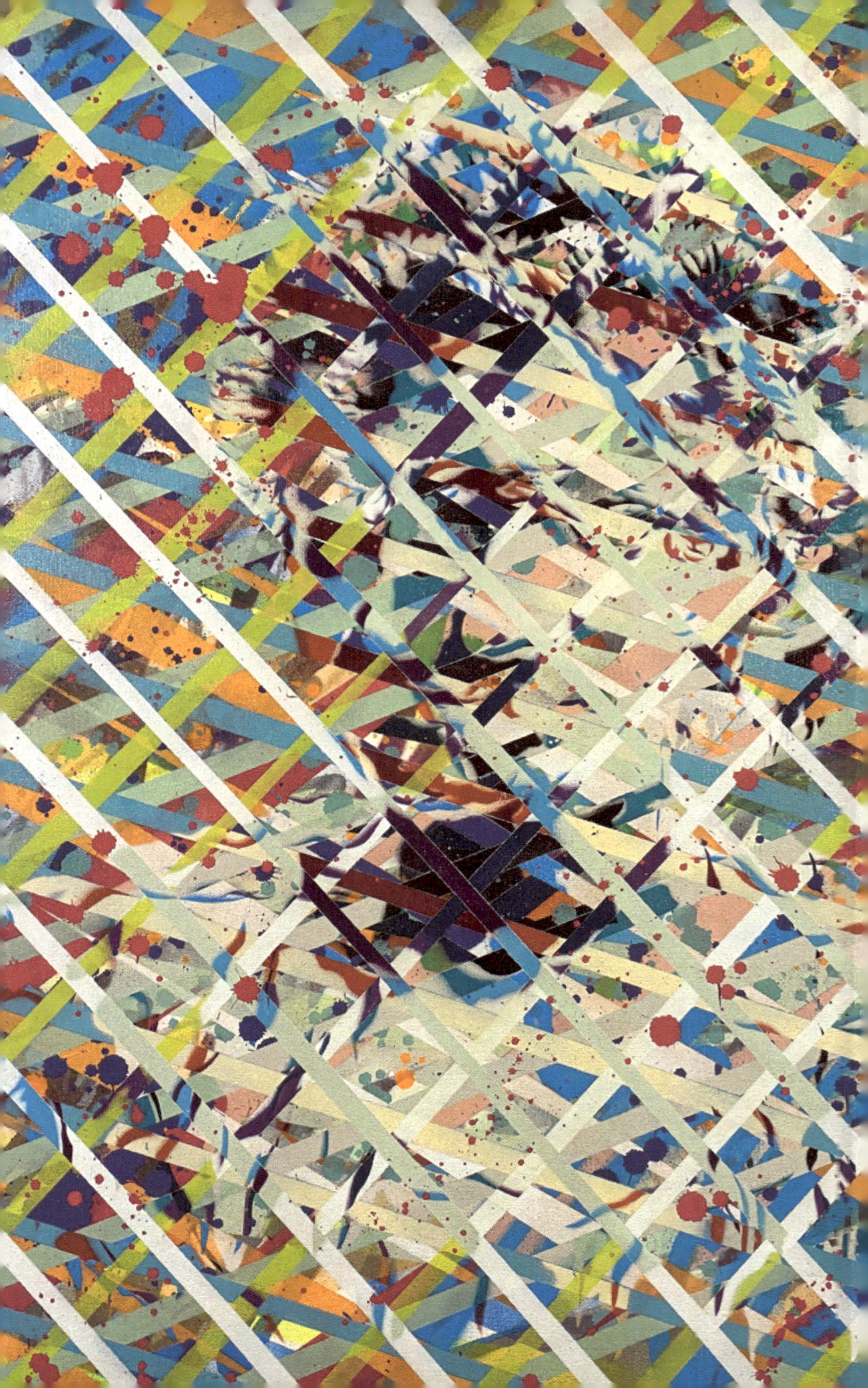

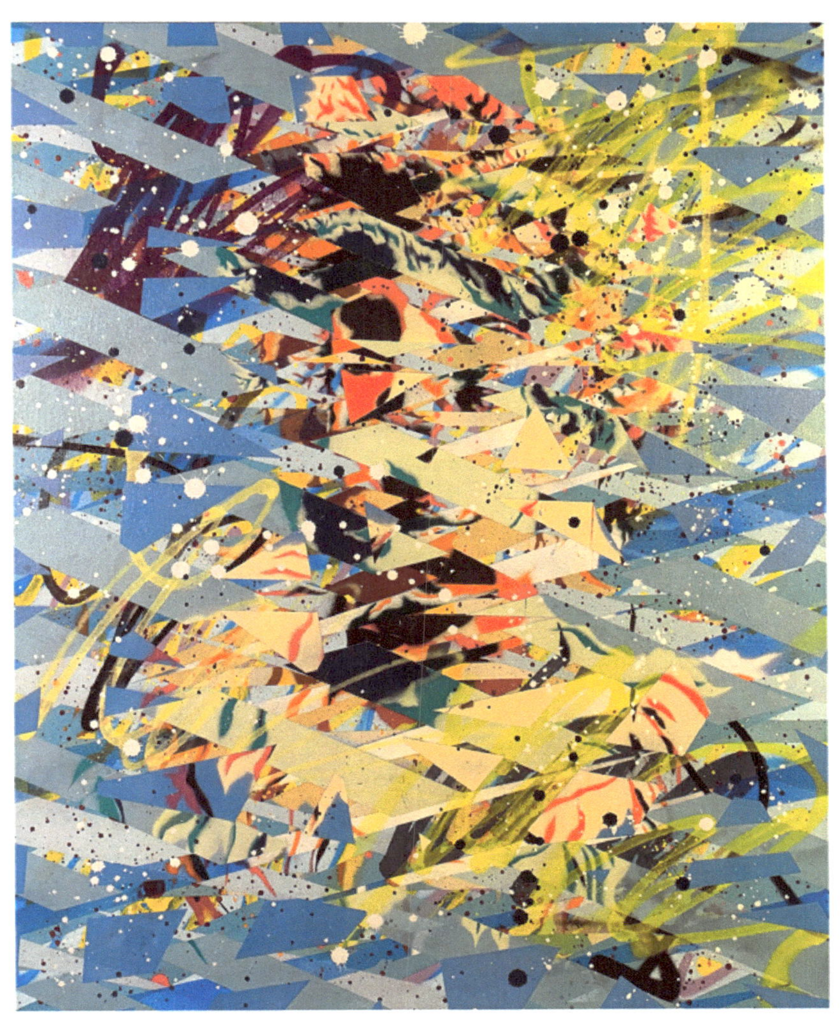

TIME AGAIN

I lead with my heart. I feel my way through things and I make connections intuitively, so in many instances I don't quite understand what I'm doing until it is well under way. That is what happened with this body of work. I didn't notice, or it wasn't quite intentional, that there was a theme evolving. I wanted to tell stories about inspiring people, and it just so happened that the most inspiring stories to me all revolved around revolutionary thinking.

I'm not a fan of the phrase "that's just the way it is" because in essence that means there is nothing that can be done. All of these figures knew that something had to be done and they had no other choice but to be that person.

When I realized what I had already begun to do, and looked around at what's happening today, that's when I decided to dig in a little deeper. Synchronicity and connection got me here and as I take a firmer direction on my path, it continues to guide my research. Open one book and it leads to another. All of these stories are connected. They're connected to you and to me.

I can't tell every story, but I can point to a few and hope that the viewer takes it as an example. I don't know if I still believe in utopia, but I do believe in rebellion.

It's Time Again.

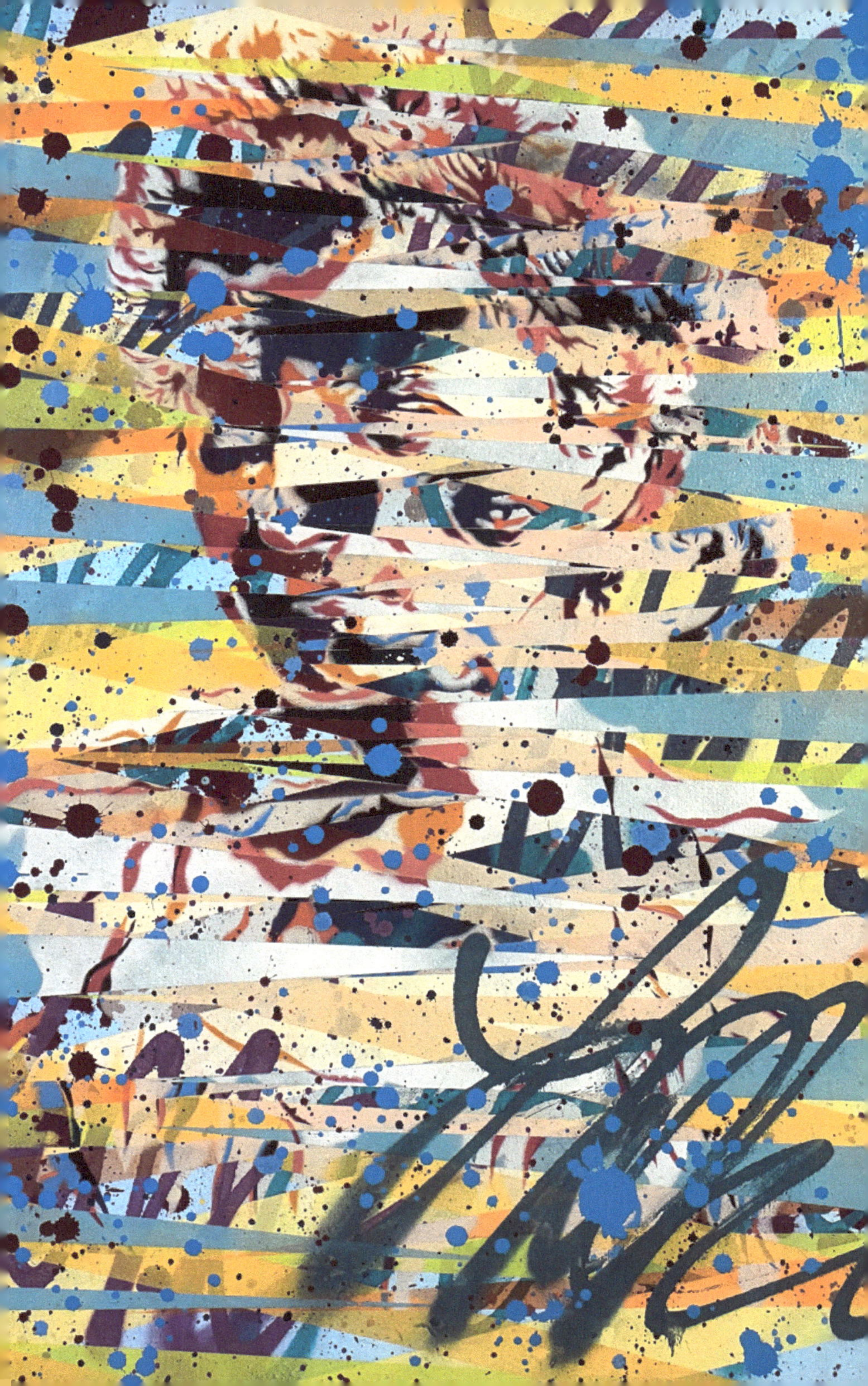

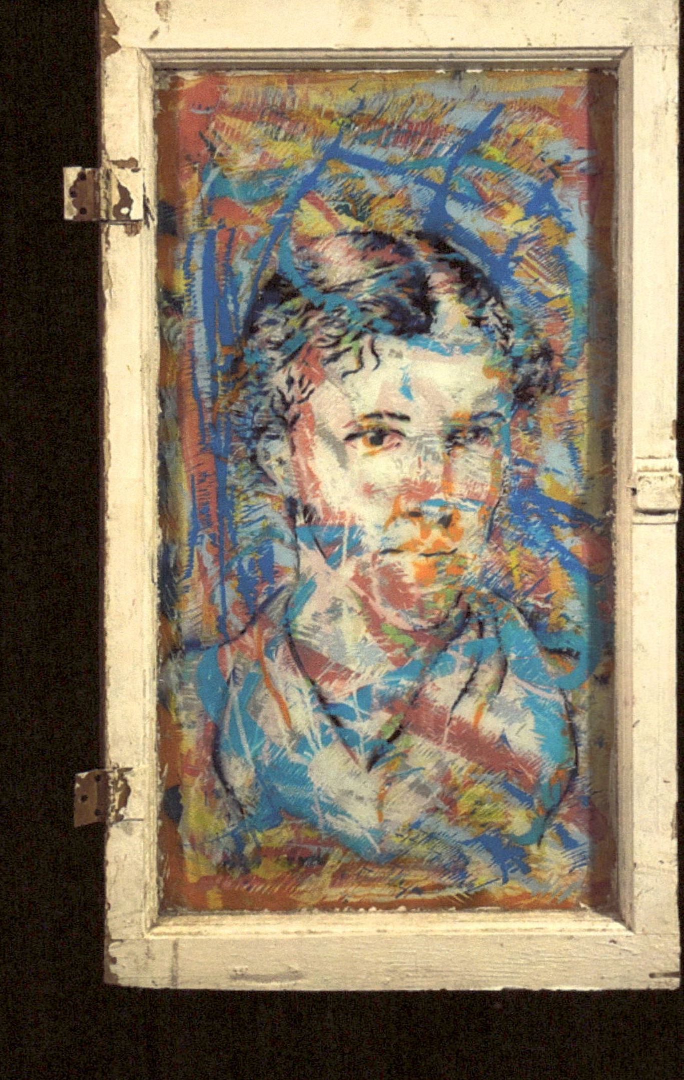

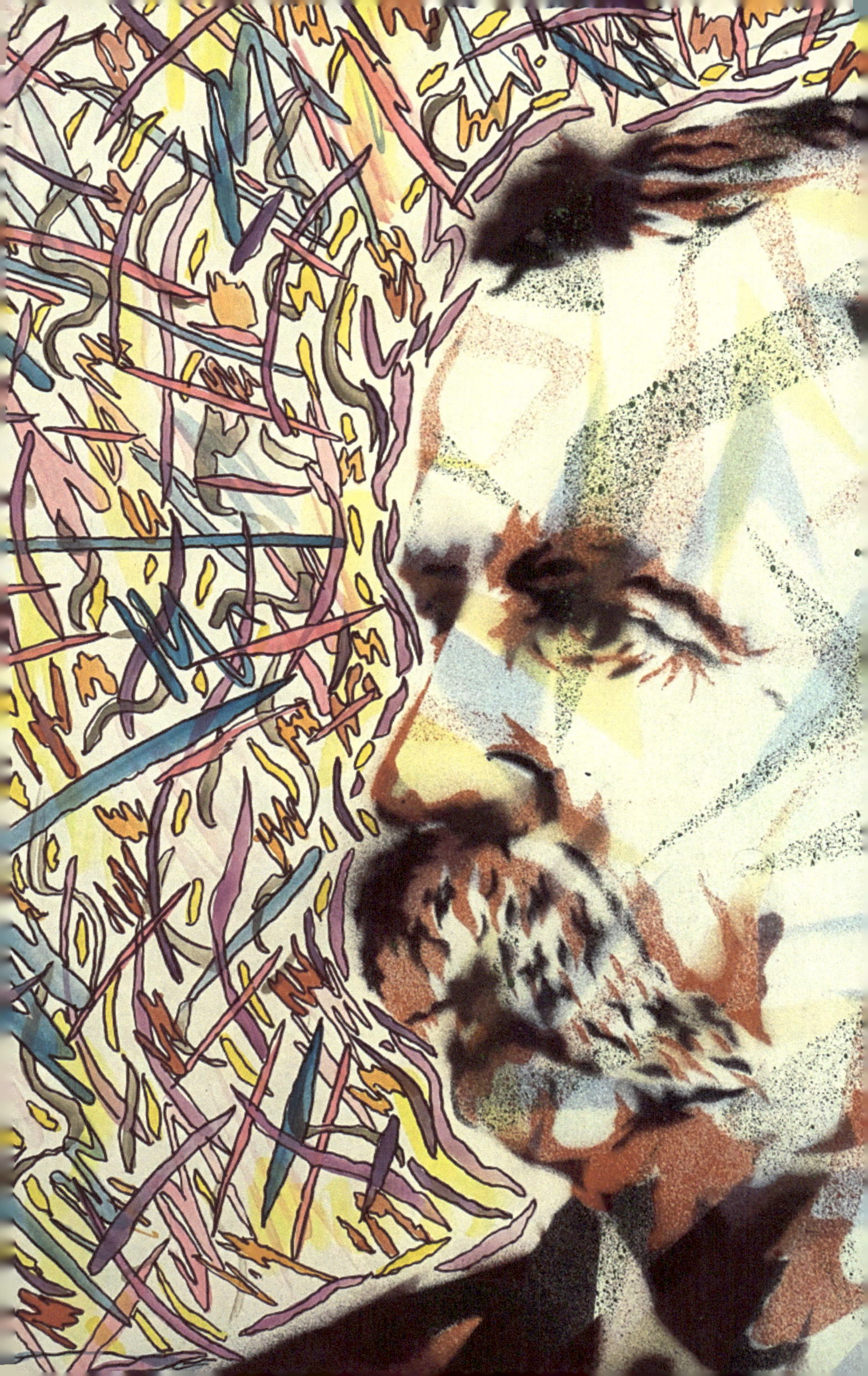

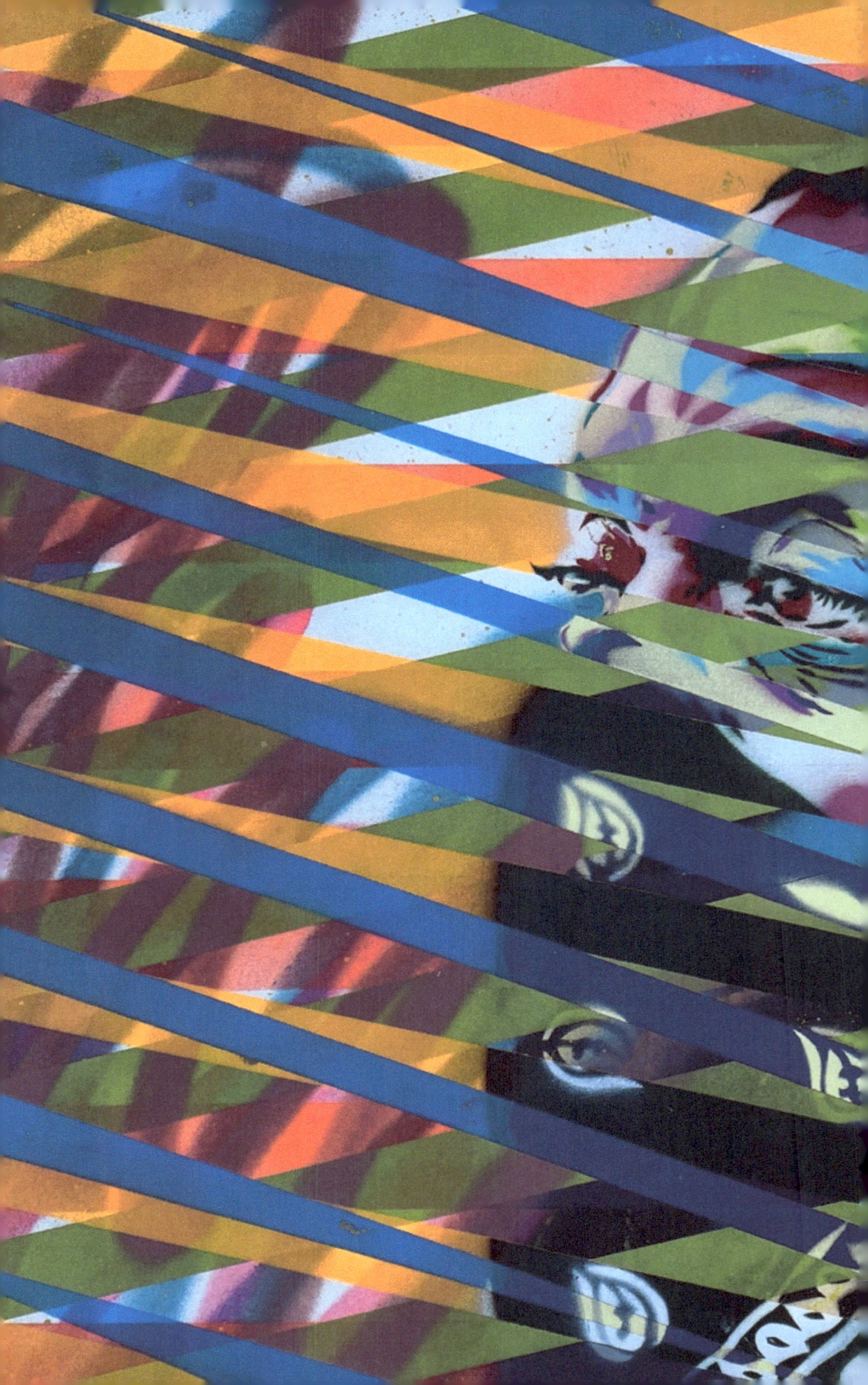

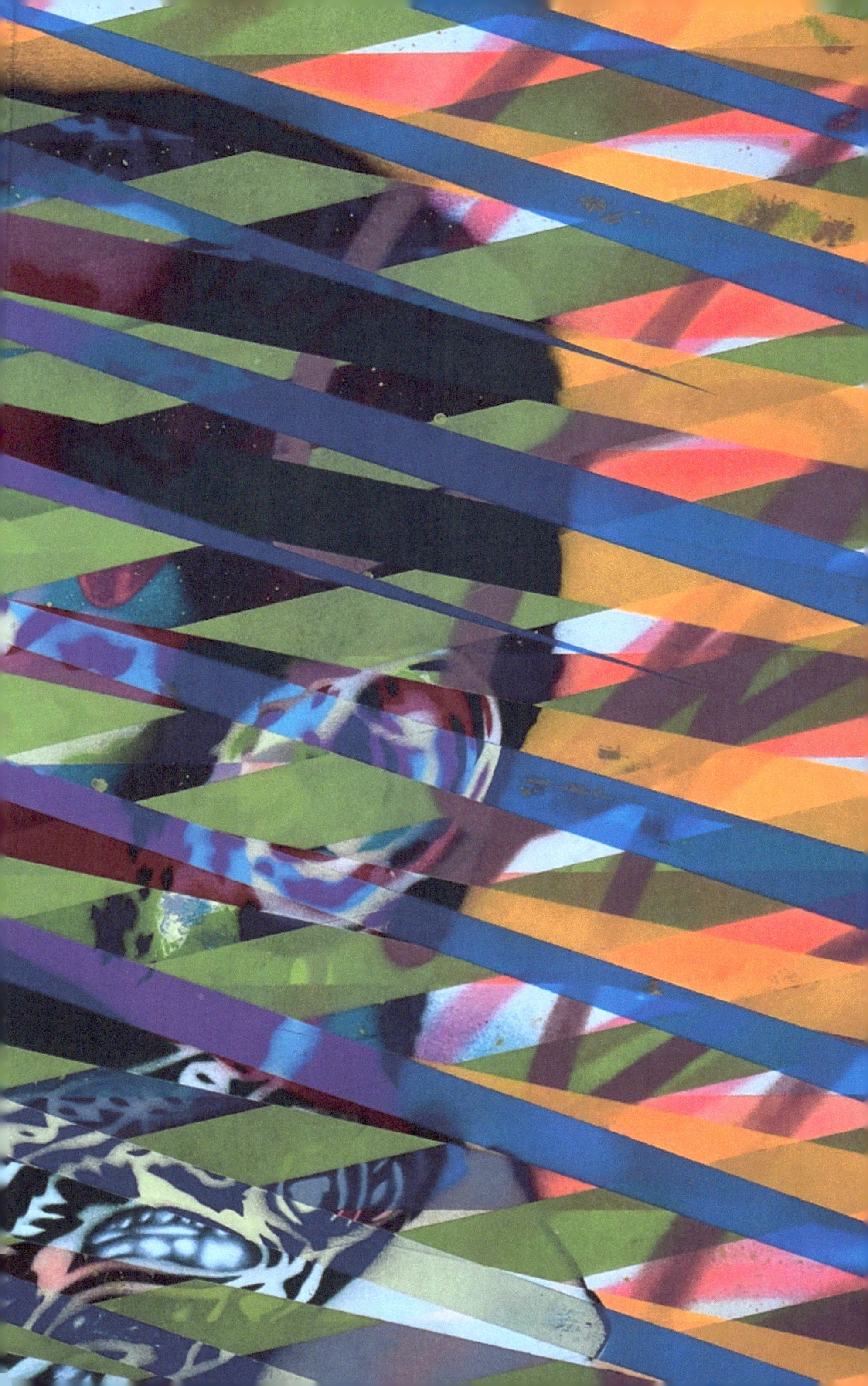

HEROES - JOE STRUMMER

For a long time—a long long time—I would not paint anyone famous. No heroes. No idols. No celebrity worship. No Marilyn Monroe. No Andy Warhol. No Marlon Brando. Whatever. Painting my anonymous people, in a way, was my answer to our culture's (often misguided) worship of celebrities, idols and heroes. I believe we're all meant to shine.

In 2016, I had the idea to do this project, *Left Handed For A Year*, where I would draw a portrait every day with my left hand. By doing so, I believed I would somehow connect an unused or seldomly used part of my brain with a more dominantly used part of my brain. I make art all the time, but I never do it with my left hand. This was supposed to be an experiment in my own psychology, an experiment with my own neurons.

As I had to make a new portrait every day, I used a sort of free association way of finding my subjects. Each day's portrait was chosen in relation to something that came up that day, some music I was listening to, something that was happening in current events, a story I had read, etc., etc. Sometimes I went off on a tangent for a few days… presidents, cowboys, friends, superheroes… Anything was fair game.

I tried to remain open and stay free, yet—as I mentioned—for a long time, I just would not fuck with famous people. It didn't matter if I liked them or not. Well… one night I'm doing a drawing of Joe Strummer. I'm a huge Clash fan and an even bigger fan of Joe himself (especially now after this event). I'm drawing him and my son Elijah—who was very little, maybe just over a year old—wakes up, gets out of bed and comes to sit on my lap as I'm drawing. He asks, "Who's that daddy?" and without skipping a beat I say, "That's Joe Strummer. That's one of daddy's heroes." And I burst into tears. One of daddy's heroes? No heroes. No idols. No celebrity worship…

In that moment, I guess I just realized how important it is to have heroes. I still don't believe you should idolize anyone, but it is really very important to have heroes. It is important to have people to look up to. It is important to have people you wish to aspire to be like. Not because they are famous, but because of the life they chose to lead. What do they represent now that they are gone?

I guess the real importance of this story is how that sentence just came out of my mouth. It was one of the things this project helped me realize: "That's one of daddy's heroes." I was in denial before that moment. And while I still have a very tenuous relationship with celebrities and people who we are told are supposed to be important, I have a much firmer grip on what a hero is, who mine are, and what that means to me.

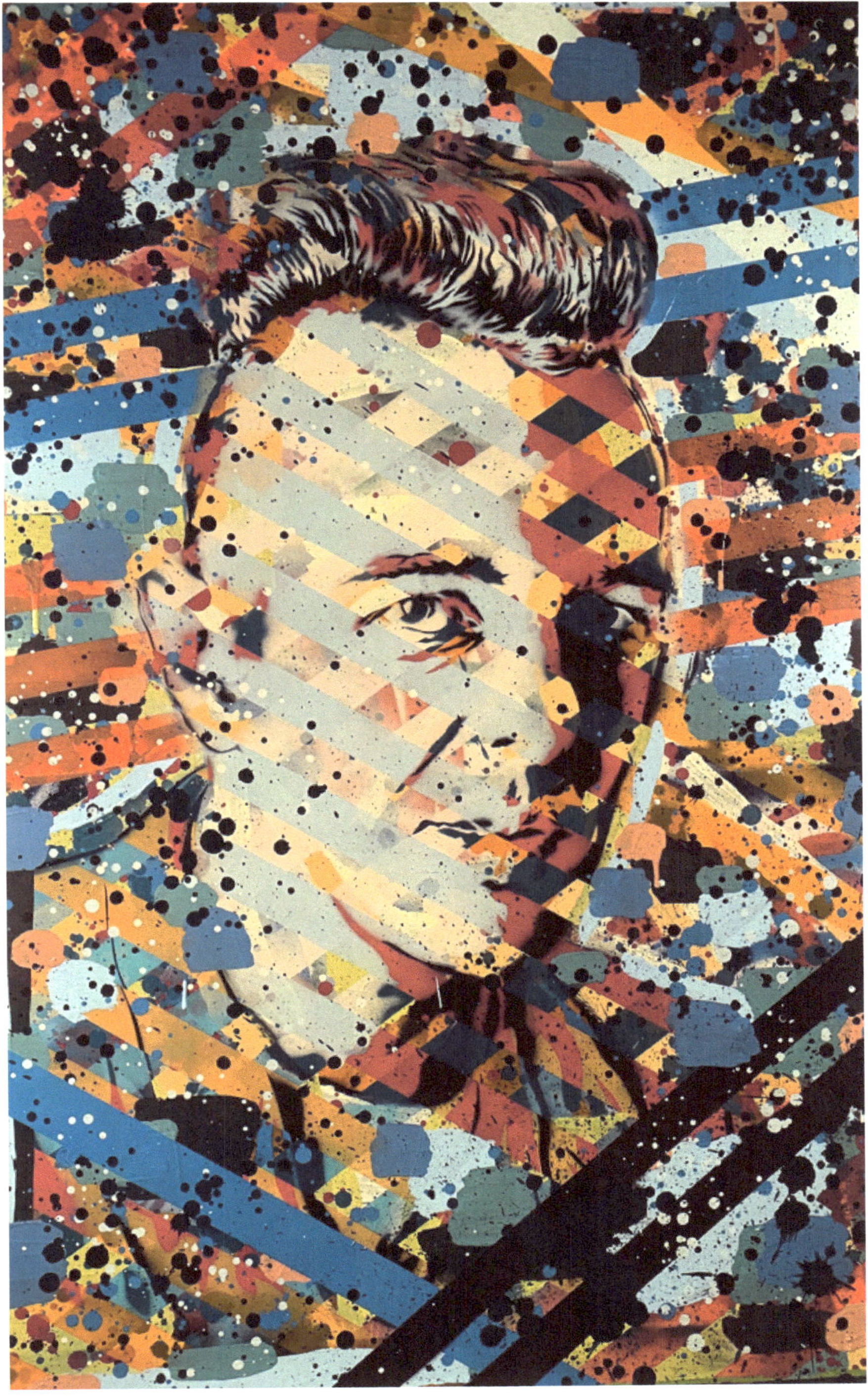

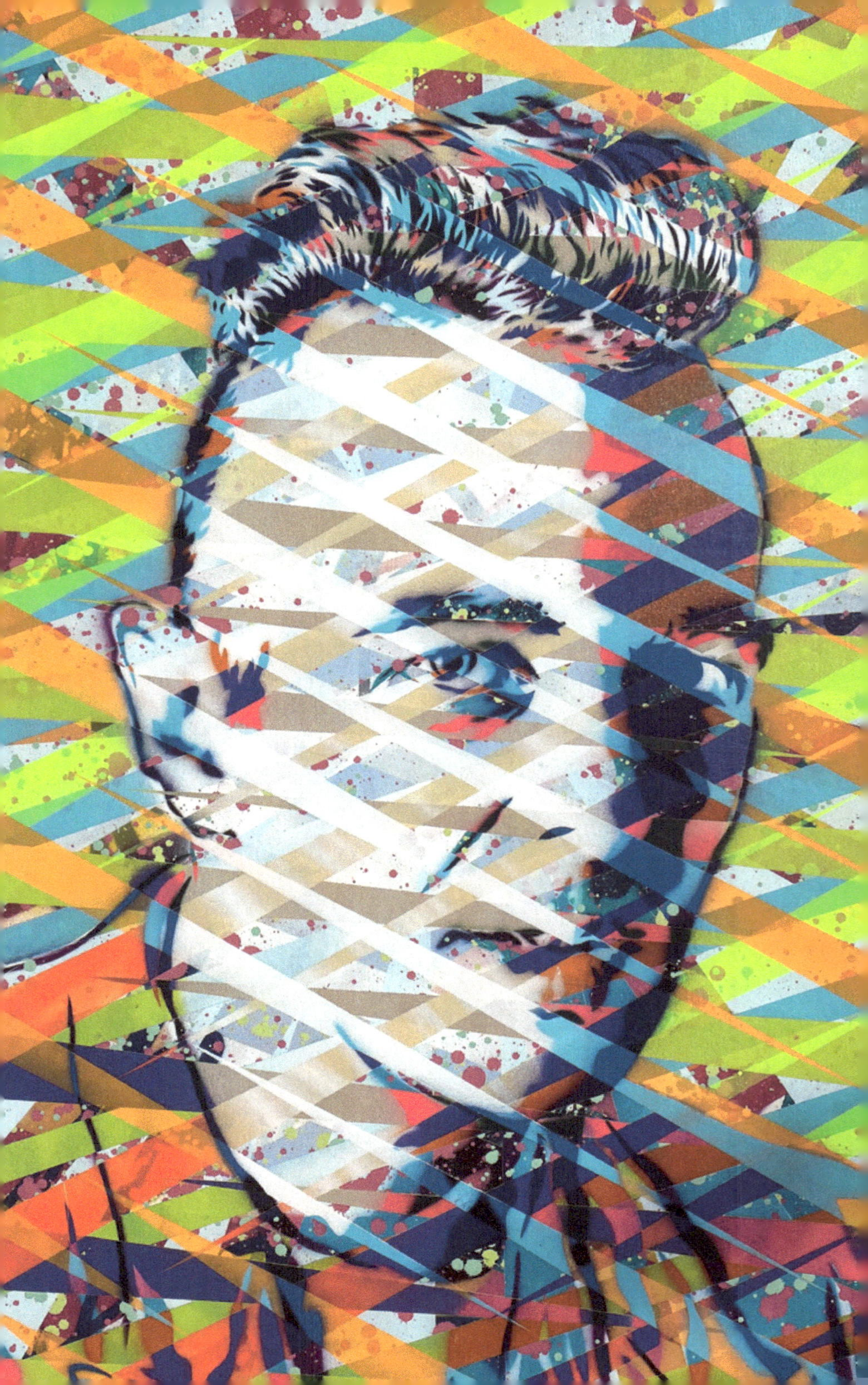

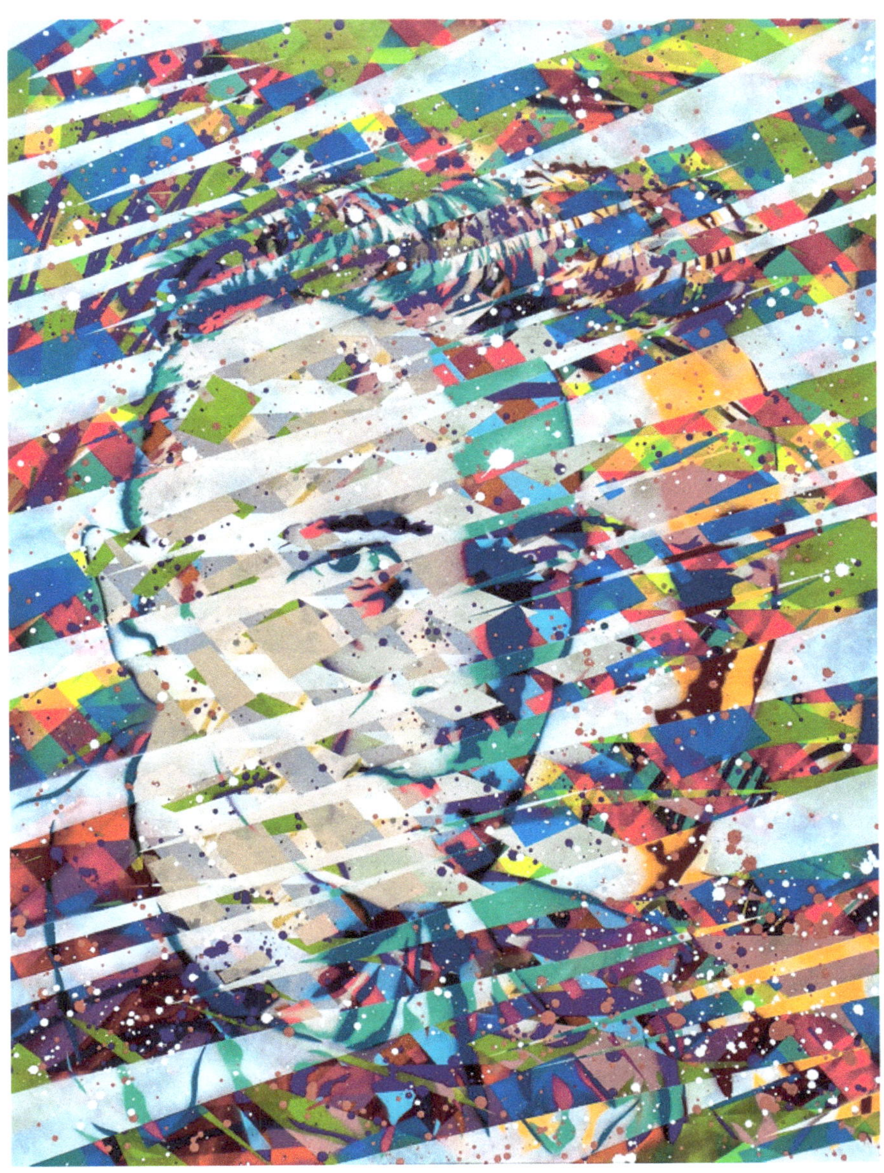

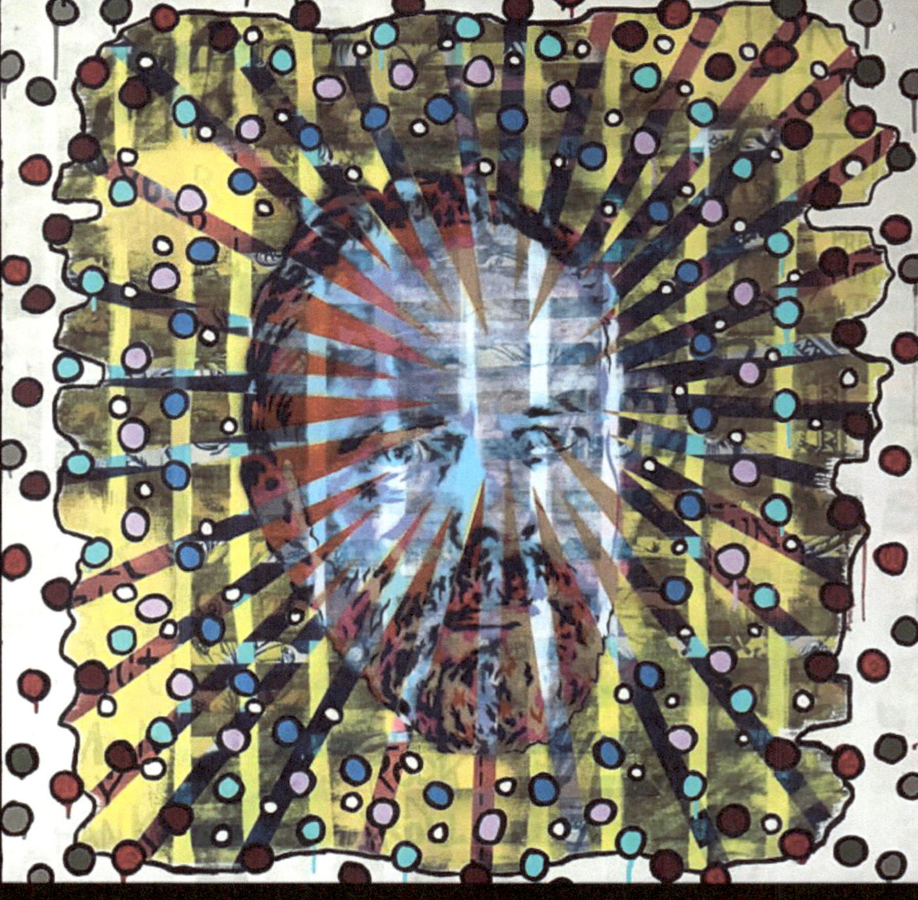

PHILIP K. DICK

I consider myself an independent scholar of the late great author Philip K. Dick. I've been reading and collecting bits of his life and career for about a decade. I'm part of an online and in-person Philip K. Dick community and have even helped plan festivals and parties in his honor. I could write quite a bit about my interest in him, but, for the sake of staying on topic, I will keep this fairly brief.

Dick was not an outspoken revolutionary, but I remember being a young punk kid reading *Time Out of Joint* and *The Man in the High Castle* for the first time and thinking: "He's wrapping these conspiracy theories in science fiction. He's not writing science fiction. He's only using that as a medium to get his message across."

I know enough about him now to know that my initial thoughts were not entirely true, but nothing ever was with him. What I do know about his work is that he used it to convey some major themes that are important to our cause. In every story the main character is just some guy. Novel after novel, the main character is the everyman. It could be me, it could be you, but it's always the average joe who ends up becoming tangled in these confounding situations. He had the great gift of making you empathize with the main character, no matter how foolish. Empathy is a major theme in his work, and the implications of living life empathetically are important for us to consider today.

Dick's characters live within worlds where great technologies exist, but you can bet that in every story those technologies do not benefit the little guy. They do not benefit the everyman. No. Usually they are presented as an obstacle to him while they tend to benefit the wealthy and the powerful. Sound familiar?

What does it mean to be human? This is another major theme in Dick's work, which emerged after seeing the results of the Nuremberg trials, where many Nazi soldiers testified that they were "just doing their jobs." The human vs. the android. Dick said, "Look! Even a human can be robotic. If that's true, then what does that mean?"

Dick got me thinking and he got me reading. A big part of my connection to his work is the synchronicity I find in it. In almost everything I read there's some detail that stands out as being uncanny. These details seem to mirror many of the connections that I make in the world, which are very integral to my practice.

I think it's pretty revolutionary that Dick got these themes of empathy and what it means to be human smuggled out into the world wrapped in science fiction. It's sub-version at its finest. And although many of his protagonists fail against the suppressive systems in his stories, there is no failure in getting these themes out into the world. To get people thinking is to get people changing.

If you study history, it seems to be the same story over and over again throughout time. This is yet another theme in Dick's work. We are always going to be fighting the same fight. It's a story that repeats itself. The empire never ended. It's Time Again.

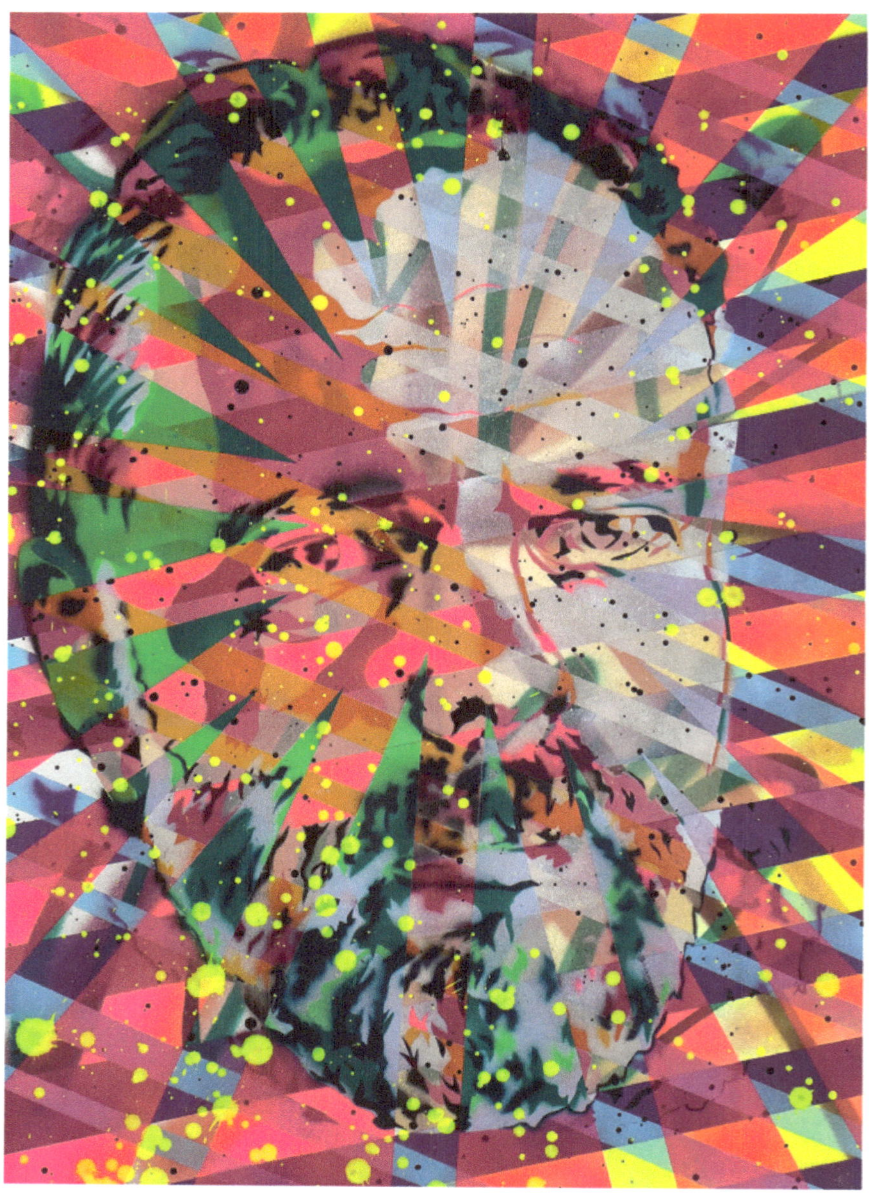

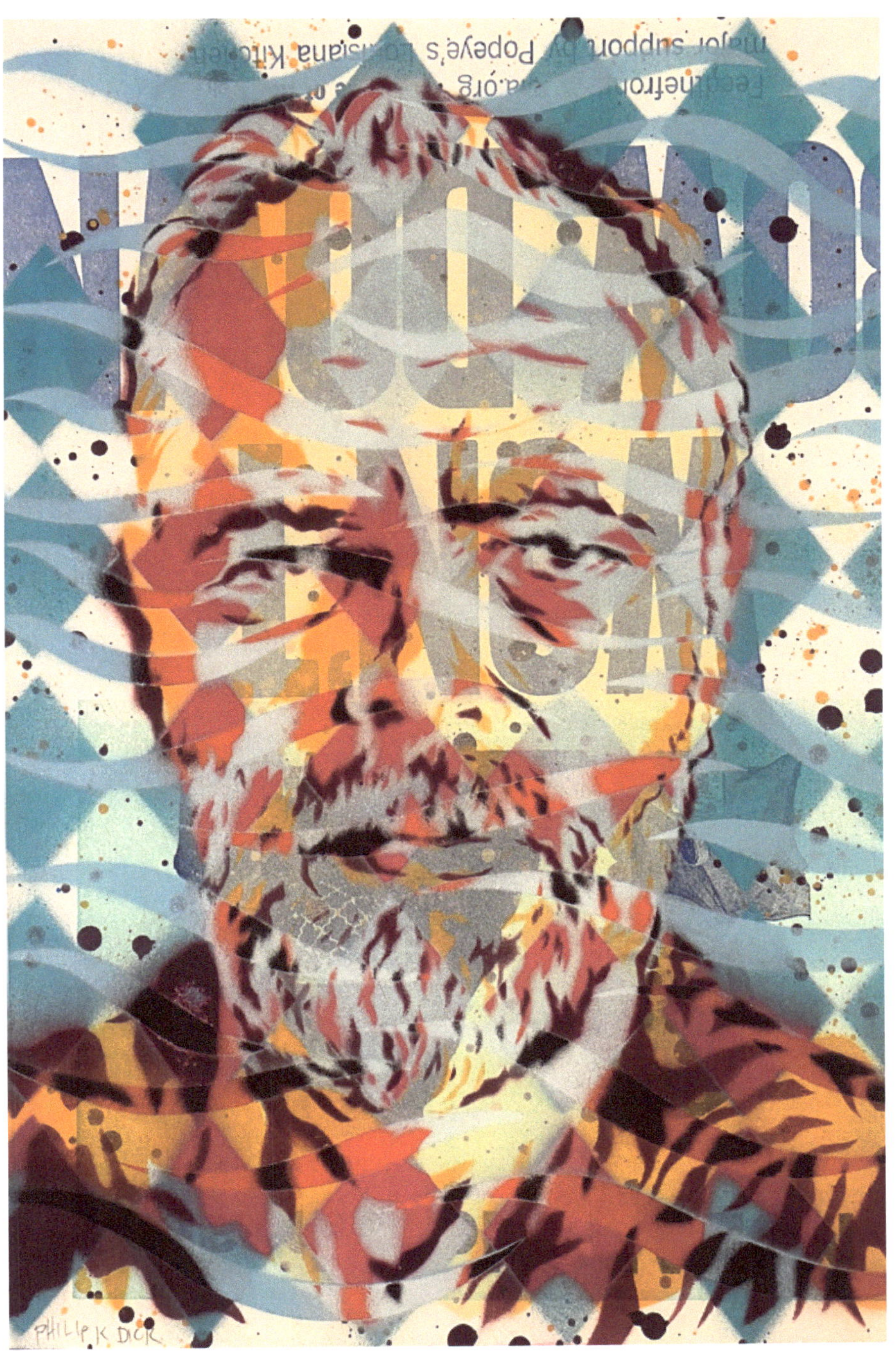

major support by Popeye's Louisiana Kitchen
feed.netfrom...a.org
PHILIP K DICK

FREDERICK DOUGLASS

Subversion and rebelliousness have always been core tenants of who I am, but not because I'm at war with the world. These feelings took root within me at a young age and have persisted into adulthood, not because of an overwhelming tendency to be opposite, but because of my strong conviction that anything is possible and that our time on earth is not meant to be spent in toil and drudgery. I do not believe that it is a utopian vision to find and live out our purpose; I believe it is our birthright. This is my belief and what I strive for, and has always been my message. Everyone is meant to shine.

My story began with finding two photo albums in someone's trash. Discarded images from the 1890s of people who became the symbol for my message. These images enabled me to tell my story about inspiration and the overwhelming feeling that we don't have much time. What do you want to do with that time while you're here? Those people could be me or you. They could be anyone. We can all be someone. Yet, despite all that we do, there will always be those who try to throw you away. There are always opposing forces.

Synchronicity has played a vital role in my life and work. Though I may not always understand what I'm doing, the signposts still clearly read, "you are on the right path," and in many instances I only begin to understand it all much later.

To this day, I still paint anonymous people. It will always be a constant in my work and remains the starting point for what my work has become. The other constant I started to recognize was that viewers had an inherent need to put a name to a face. They would often jump to wild conclusions, exclaiming, "is that Lincoln?" even though the person depicted looked nothing like him. To me it never mattered who they were. They could be anyone. You can be whatever you want to be.

This was also my answer to the celebrity worship I was seeing everywhere around me. Putting people on a pedestal is diminishing. When you realize that your heart carries the same flame as anyone else, that is when you give yourself permission to burn brighter. This "no idols" viewpoint made it difficult for me to understand that heroes are necessary. Heroes give you something to strive towards, and while we should not worship our heroes, we should take them as an example of what we can achieve with our time on earth. This opened me up to incorporating some of my personal heroes in my work.

This need in the viewer to know who they were looking at also gave me an idea. Up until this point, that need had been an excellent instigator for me to tell my story. What if I used the same type of visual subversion to find other stories I could tell? My story is fine and can be inspiring, but at the end of the day the person it is most important to is me… What if I could educate through my art by provoking one very simple question: "Who is that?"

I had already begun to diverge in my work, tapping into my own personal inspirations, psychology and, yes, some of my heroes. I had already begun to be inspired by research. My relationship to those found photographs gave me a personal interest in the 1800s and the studies I did on the history of photography itself led me to Frederick Douglass. Did you know he was the most photographed man of his century? Did you know he wrote many incredible essays about art and the power of the image? He led an absolutely extraordinary life. He escaped from slavery, taught himself how to read and write and became one of the most influential people of his time.

These are the types of stories we should know. The question is, why didn't I know this already?

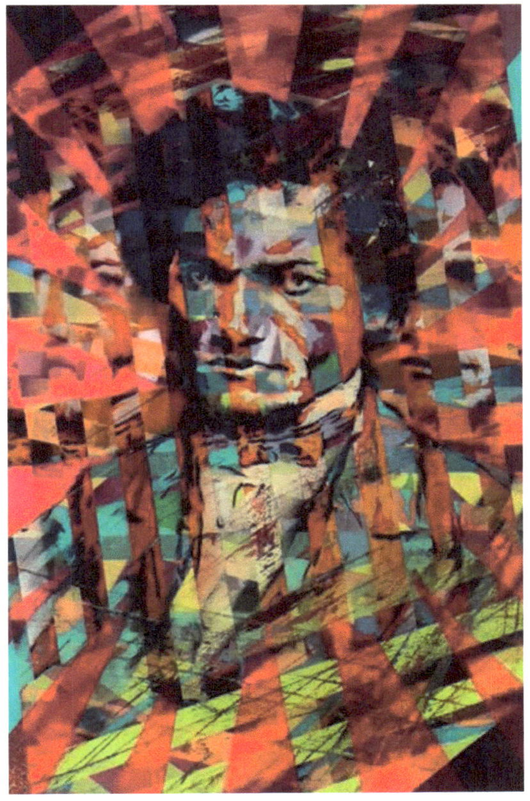

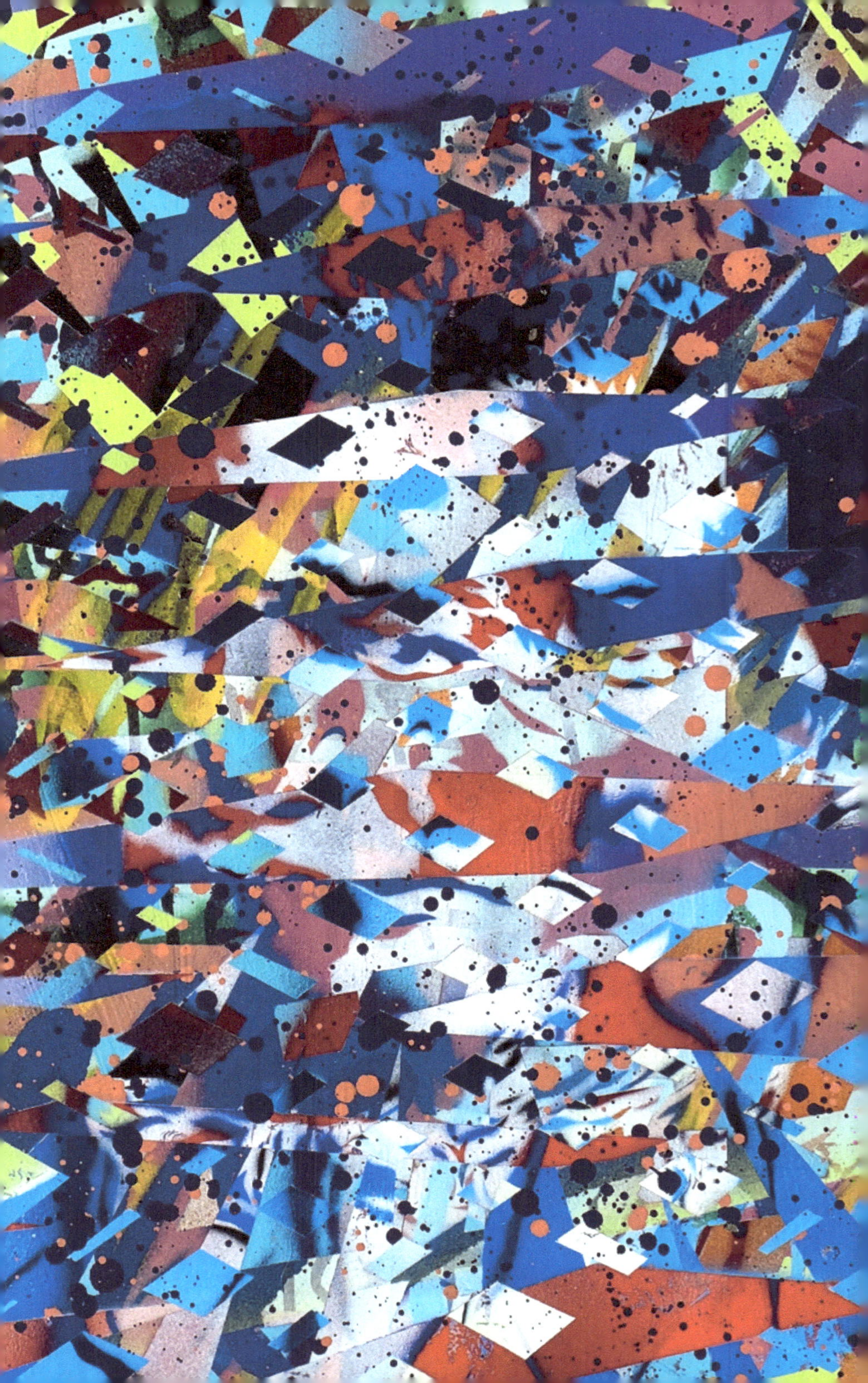

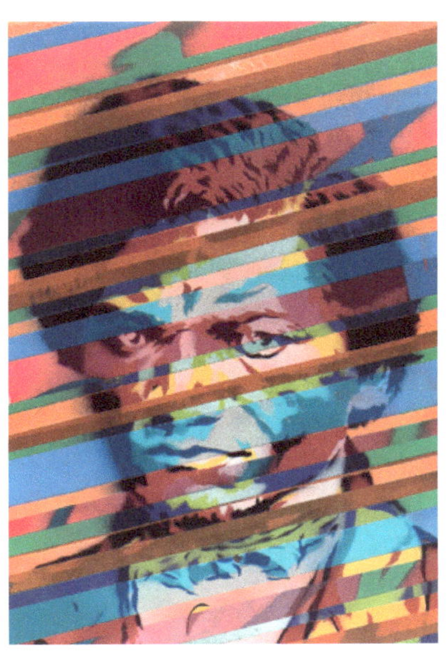

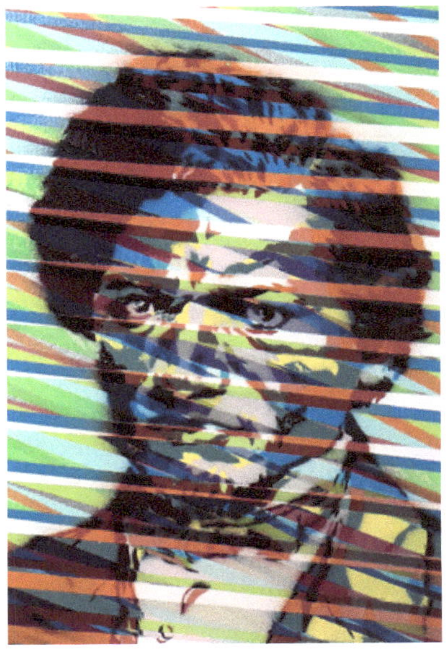

TWENTY TWENTY

It was the summer of 2020. Everyone remembers what that was like.

I remember, but for me there was a feeling of excitement. I felt like I was really doing something with my work. I was able to be part of so many causes and, for the first time since moving to New Orleans, I really felt like I was home and part of the community, despite us being separated by Covid.

First there was "Feed The Front Line," an effort to keep restaurants open and gig workers and musicians employed. The effort in New Orleans was spearheaded by the Mardi Gras krewe, The Krewe of Red Beans. The community donated money if they could. The krewe would buy food from local restaurants and then hire local musicians and gig workers to deliver it to hospitals, the "front line" in the war against Covid. I started out as a delivery driver and then was hired to make artwork for the campaign.

At the time, it was my most widespread and most reproduced image. To see my work being used to do such a good thing in the community filled me with pride. The message, "Nola's Healthcare Workers Won't Bow Down", a Mardi Gras Indian chant (not my idea), also helped spread hope in a very uncertain time.

Then there was a second iteration called "Feed The Second Line." It was basically the same premise, but this time the food was being delivered to elder culture bearers who couldn't leave their homes because they were at higher risk of catching Covid. I was hired again to create artwork. That image was also heavily reproduced and spread across the city, even landing on a beer can, which also helped raise money for the cause.

At the same time, in New Orleans, the hoppers (a local term for garbage men) were on strike. Doing trash pick up during this time seemed like one of the most dangerous jobs on earth, and they were demanding hazard pay and safer working conditions. My friend, Katie Sikora, had covered the story, photographing their strike. She had also taken the photograph of the nurses we used to make artwork for the "Feed The Front Line" campaign. They saw the sticker on her car and asked if we could help them make a poster for their cause as well. Once again, I was in the right place at the right time to help make a difference through my artwork. The Black Lives Matter protests were also in full swing during this period, and people started flying these posters at protests.

Then I got a call about doing Flint's Pride Month activation on account of another artist not being able to make it. At the time, it seemed really risky to fly anywhere... but with the world being shut down, it also felt like I should say yes to any gig that came my way. Again, I was presented with an opportunity to have my work used for a cause that I believed in. It was another chance to use my work for good.

I was greeted warmly in Flint by Joe and Philip. The idea was ambitious: for Flint's Pride celebration, because people couldn't gather, we would go around town stenciling on the ground. Each stencil would have a microchip embedded in it that, when scanned, would direct to a historical video about pride. Participants would tour the city of Flint (and all of its public art) while simultaneously getting a pride history lesson.

I've used hearts in my work quite a bit over the years, so my initial idea was to make a simple pride heart with the classic rainbow making up its shape. Both Joe and Philip stressed to me how important it was to include the colors of the all inclusive pride flag, representing transgender, nonbinary and people of color. The design developed from there and really became its own unique design, with the pink, white, baby blue, black and brown bars framing out the traditional rainbow heart. It seems very simple, but I was astonished at what we did.

Once the design was complete, Joe and I spent an entire day out on the streets, spreading this new symbol around town. In a time of great turmoil it was incredible to be part of this project, literally spreading an image of love and equality across the city. After the fact, I was able to continue spreading this symbol, spraying it again around New Orleans, putting it up as stickers, and even having a giant heart installed on the side of the Contemporary Arts Center.

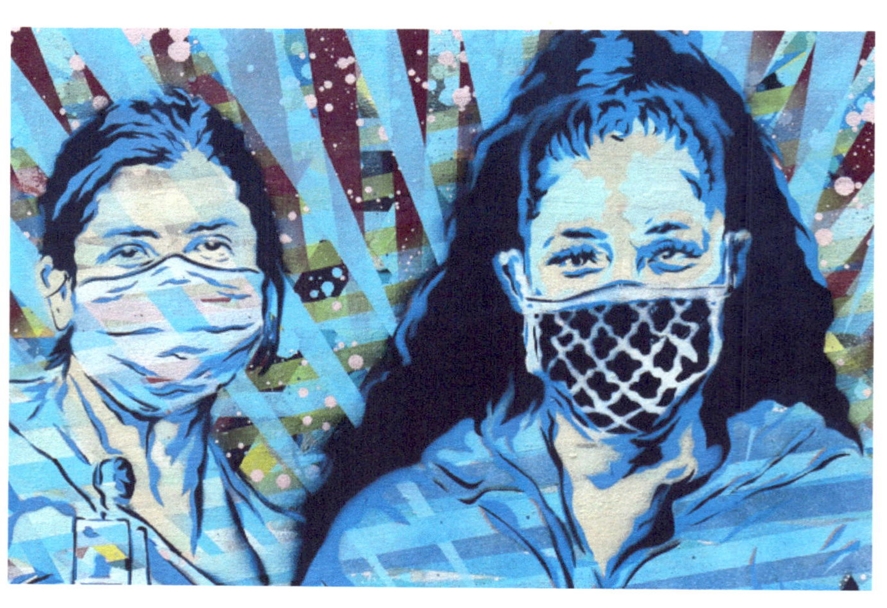

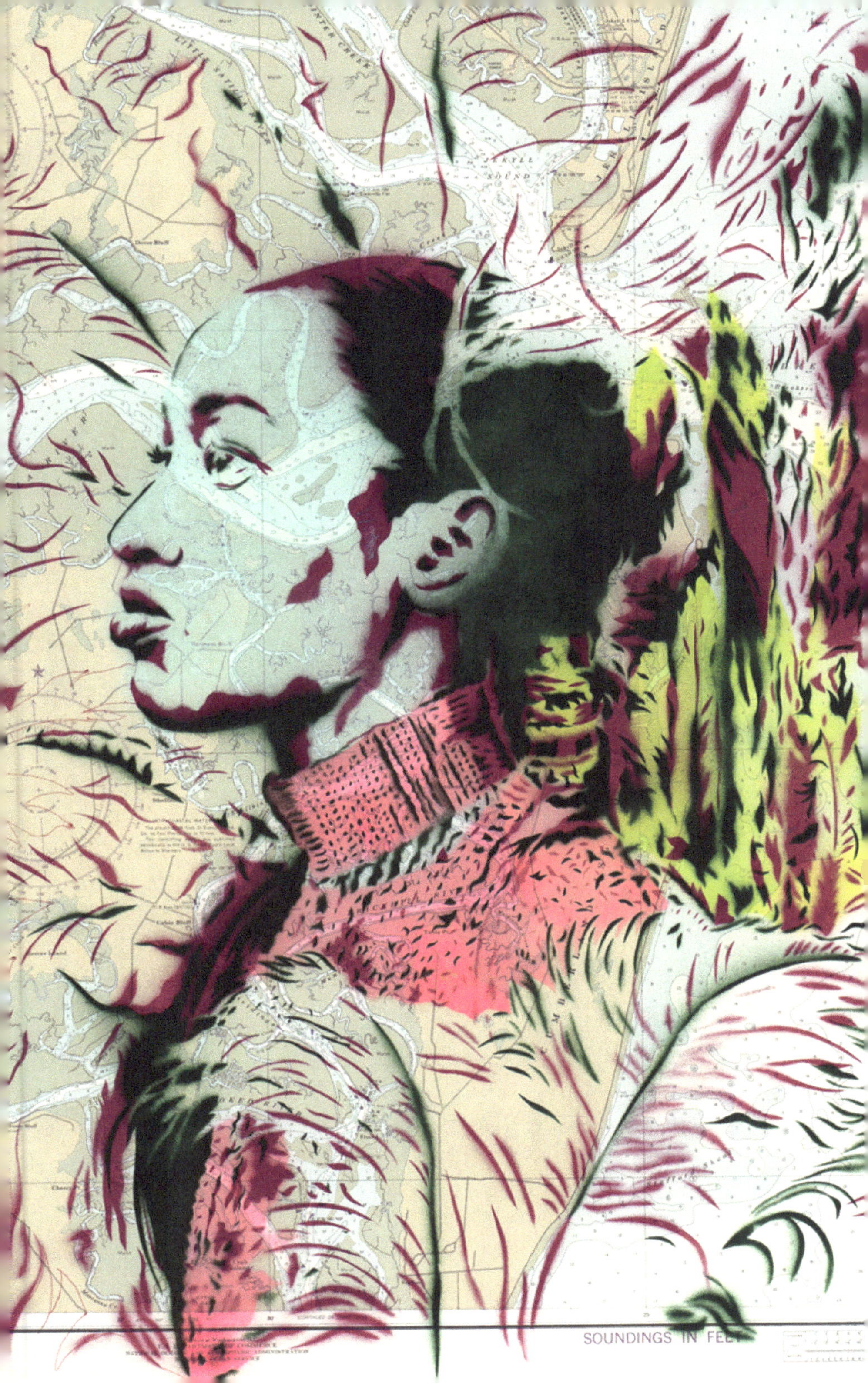

SOUNDINGS IN FEET

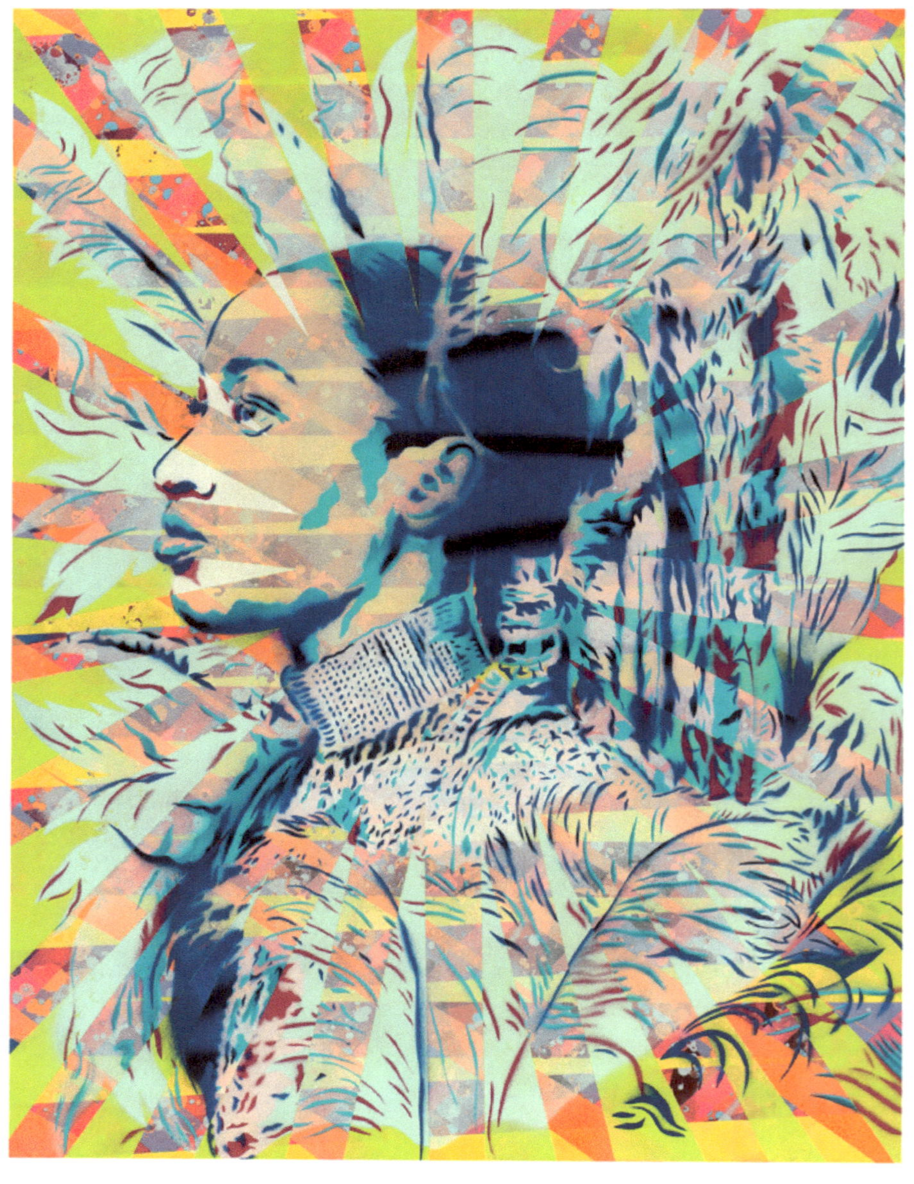

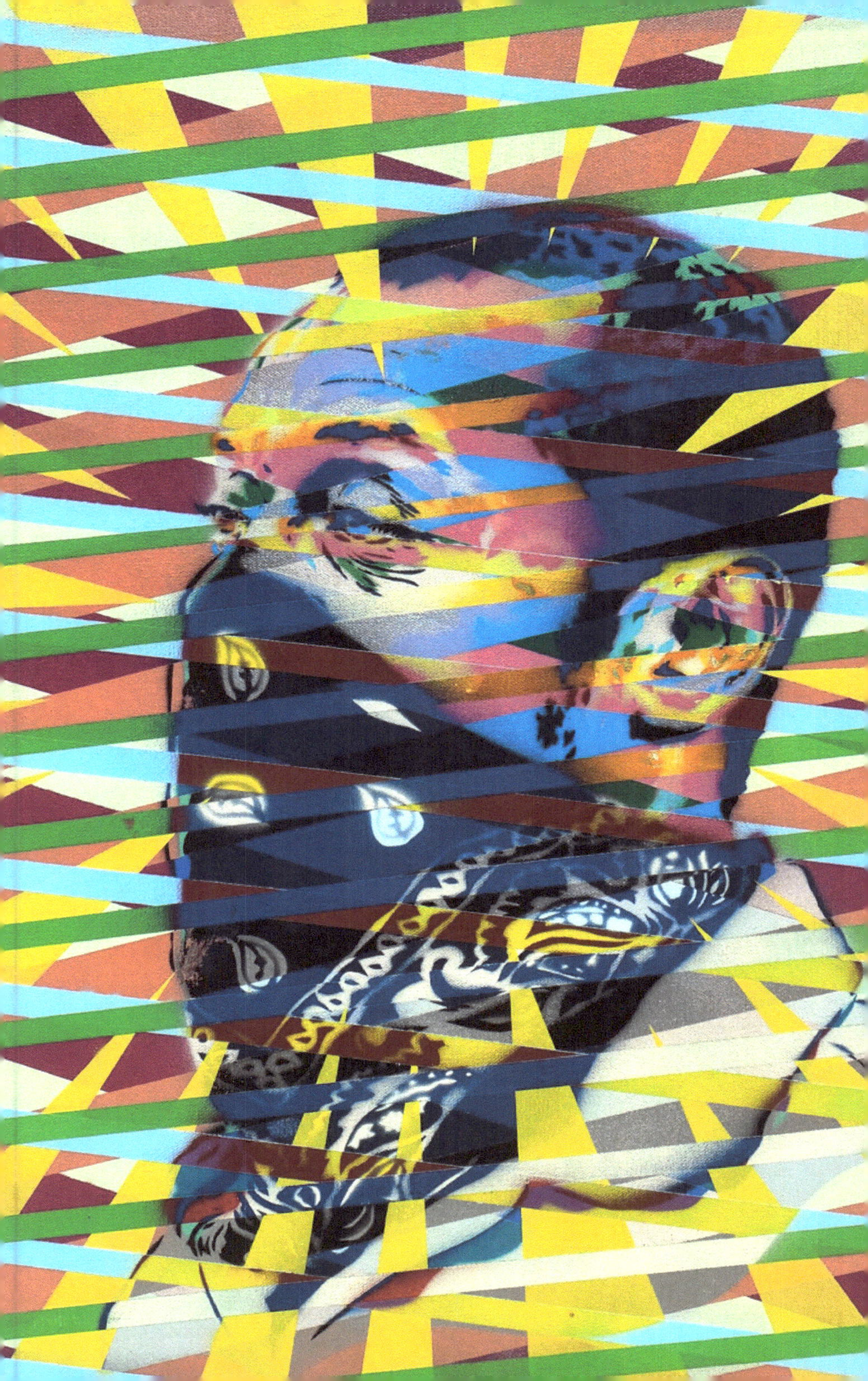

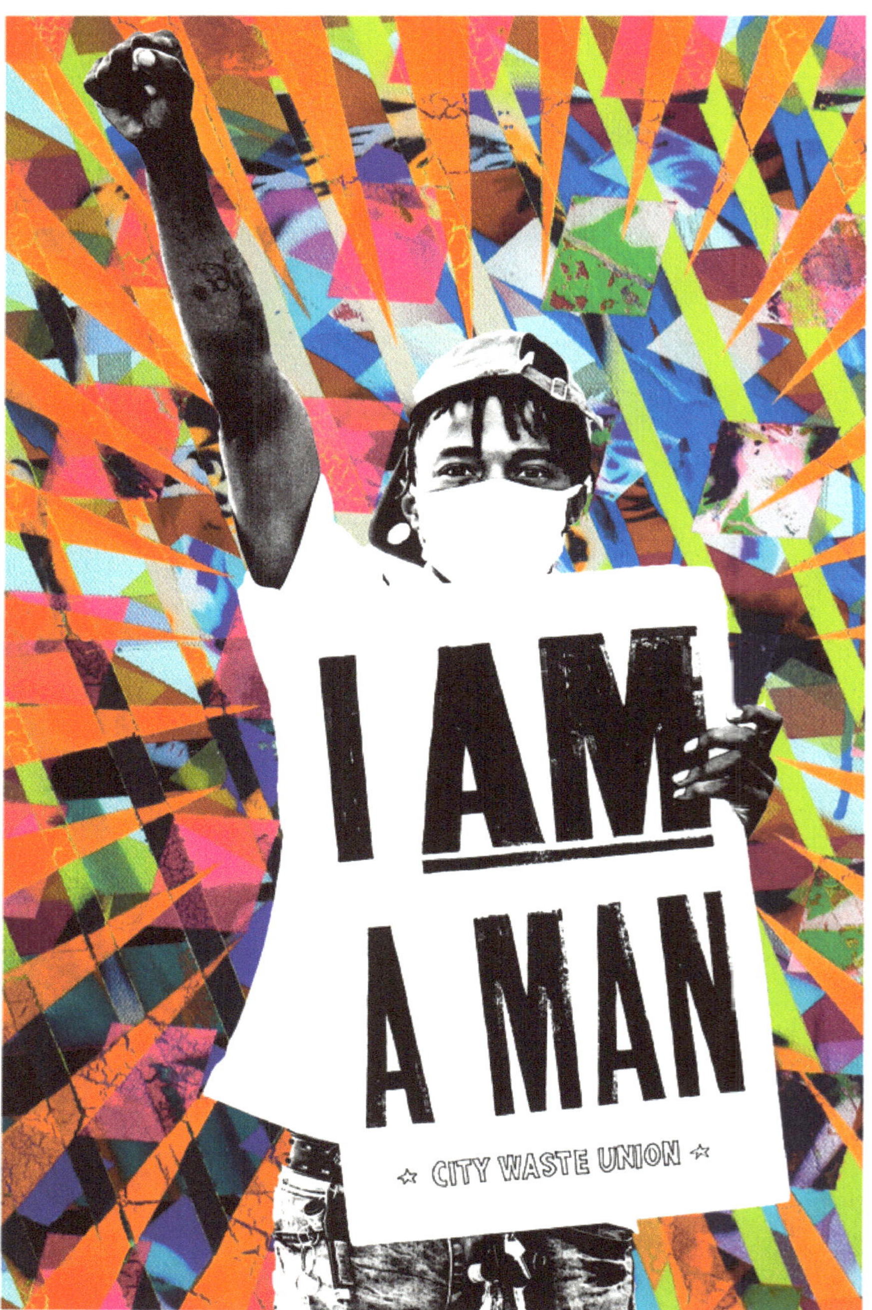

I AM
A MAN
CITY WASTE UNION

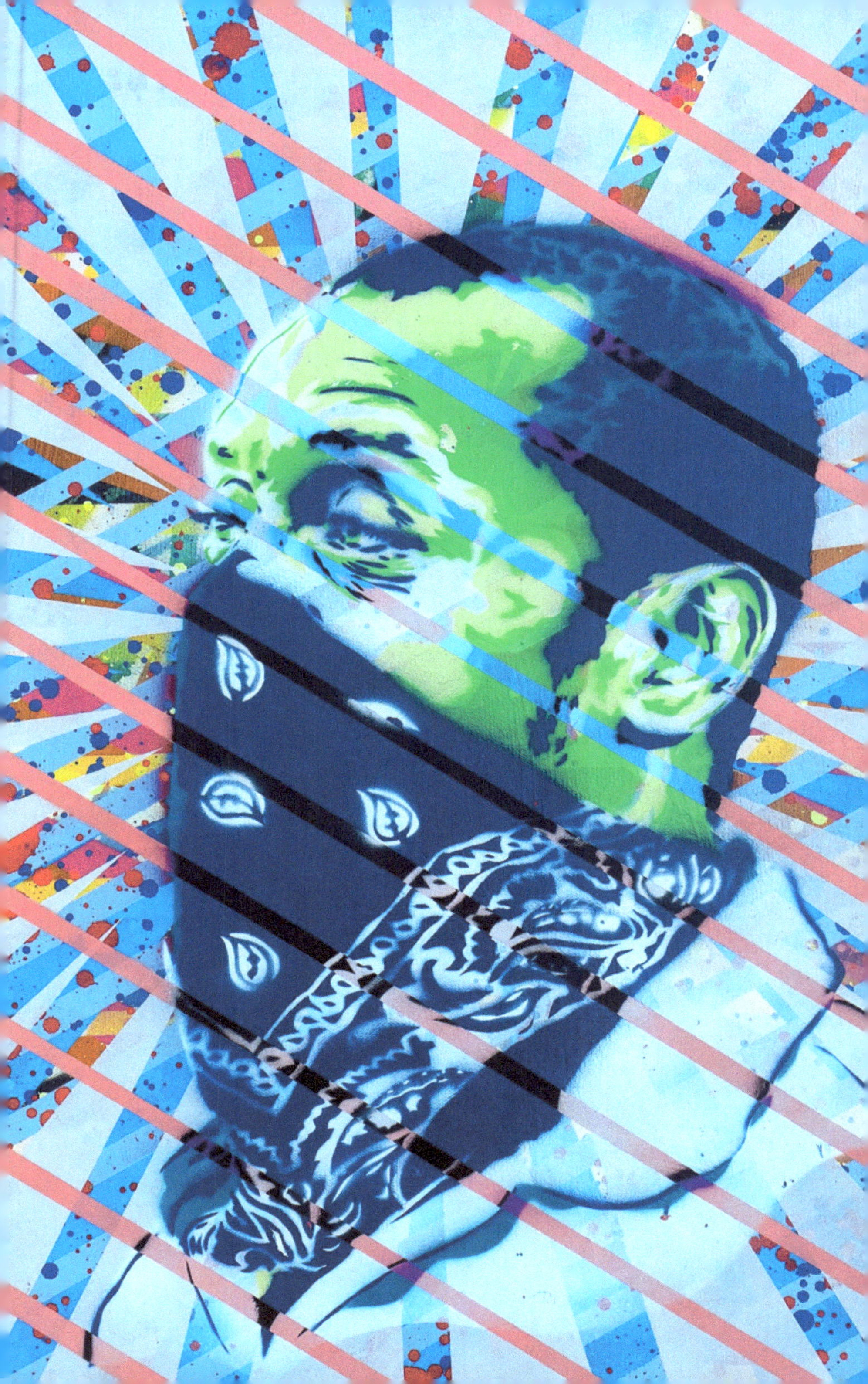

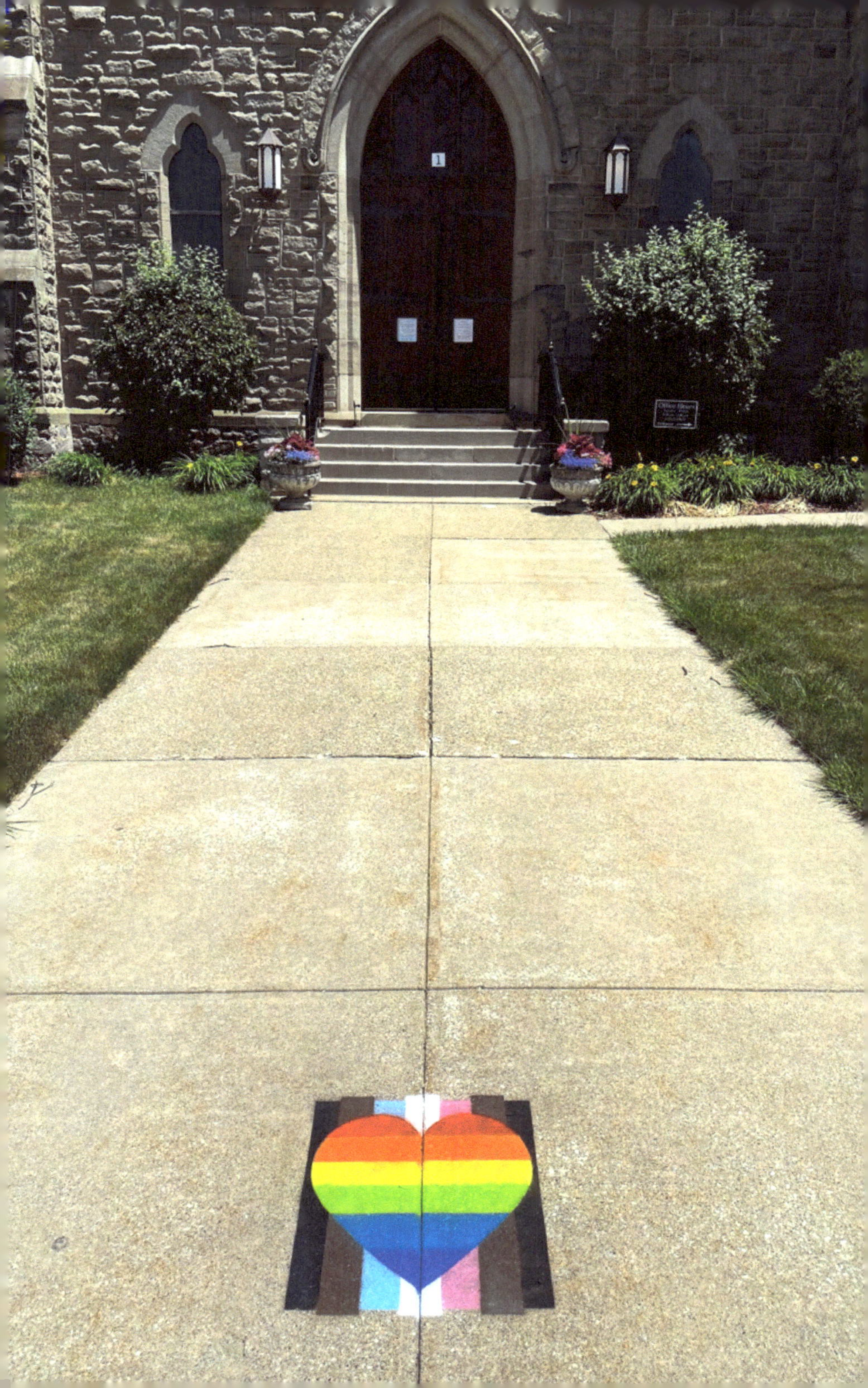

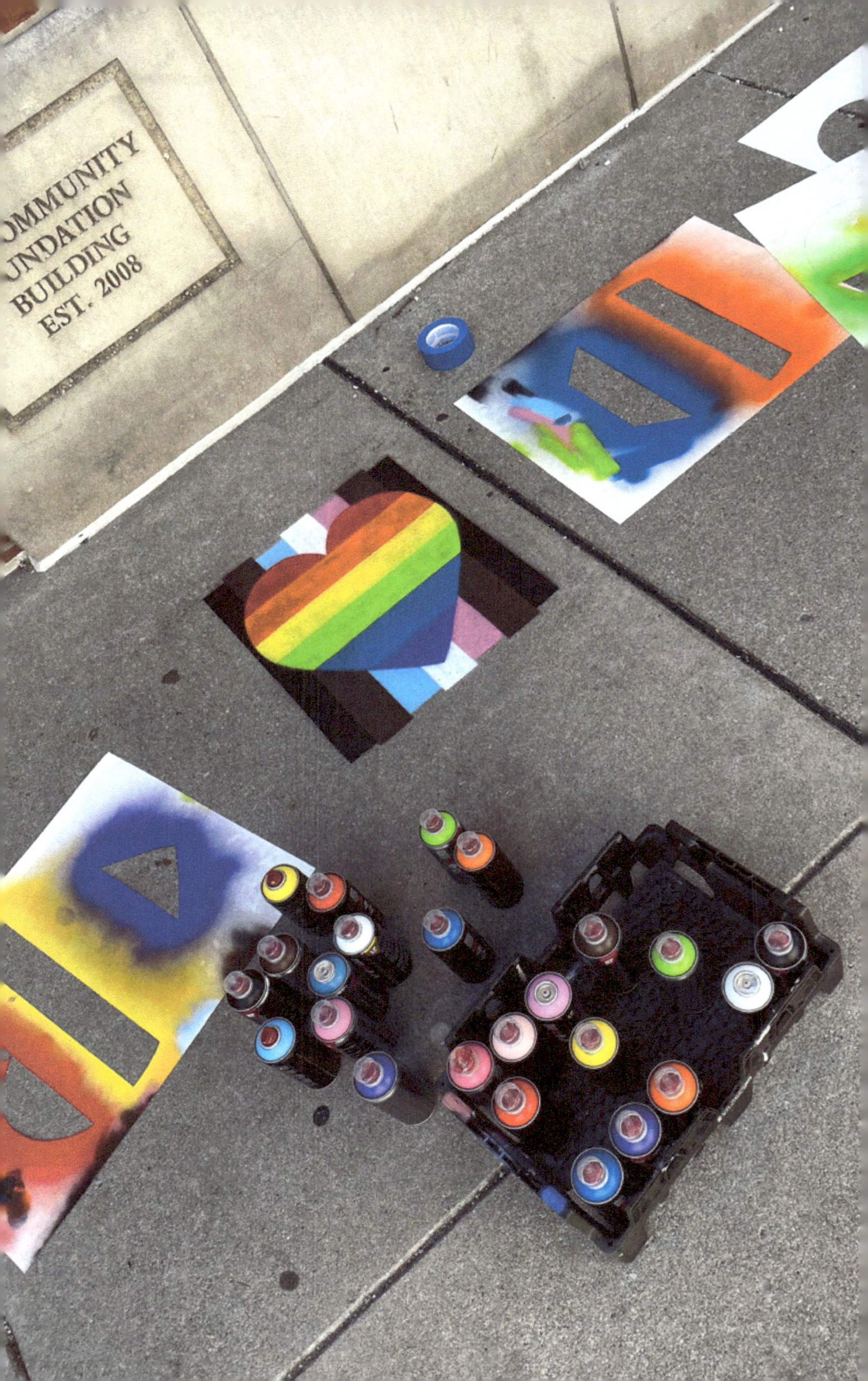
COMMUNITY
FOUNDATION
BUILDING
EST. 2008

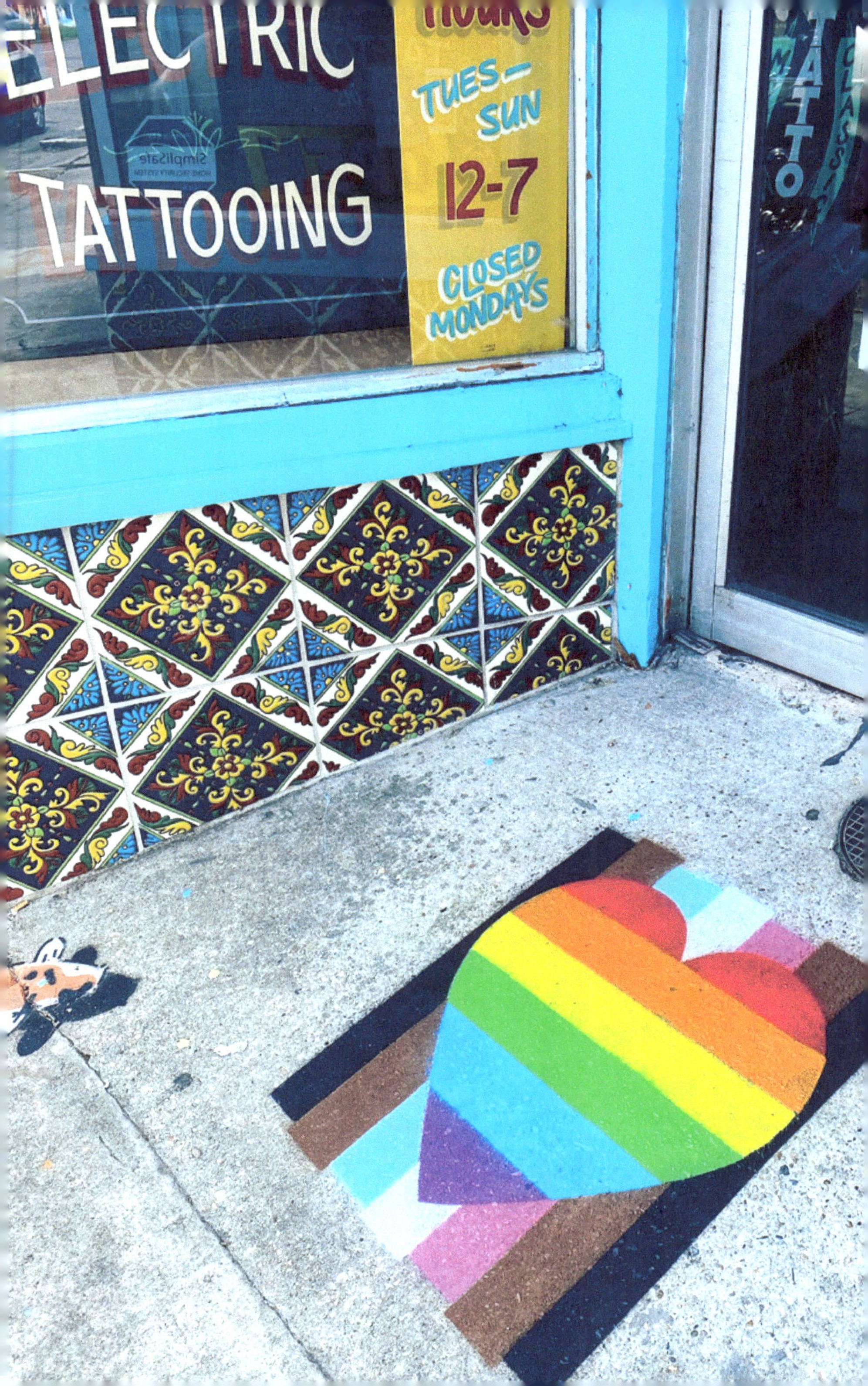

ELECTRIC
TATTOOING
HOURS
TUES — SUN
12-7
CLOSED
MONDAYS

EMMELINE PANKHURST

During the BLM Protests in 2020, there was some news circulating about a window getting smashed at a certain major retail store. It was at the top of the headlines and all the talking heads couldn't stop babbling on about it.

A small group of us were hanging out one night talking about this. At the time, I wouldn't say that I was in any way well versed in the history of liberation, but somehow I already understood that protests alone don't do anything. No one takes you seriously unless you're fucking with their money or their personal lives, and I said something to that effect, to which my friend Susan replied: "You should look at the suffragettes. They did a bunch of crazy shit."

Odd that such a flippant conversation should lead to such an academic outcome, but that was where my real fascination began. I got to reading the next day and, indeed, the suffragettes pulled a lot of crazy stunts in the fight for women's rights. Obviously, when you're talking about a movement, it's hard to pick just one person… but Emmeline Pankhurst came up and I loved this image of her.

The other part of her story that really grabbed me is that in her own time she was called a troublemaker and considered dangerous. Now, there is a statue of her outside of Parliament. It made me understand that drastic measures are often needed to get your point across, especially when it comes to the issue of human rights. Somehow there is always this opposing, oppressive side that wants to hold on to its power. Some of these movements throughout history may seem extreme, but it is indeed the only way that the oppressor will listen. Many times, it is only in hindsight that these movements get the recognition they deserve for pushing the needle forward on human rights. And it's a story that repeats itself, time and again.

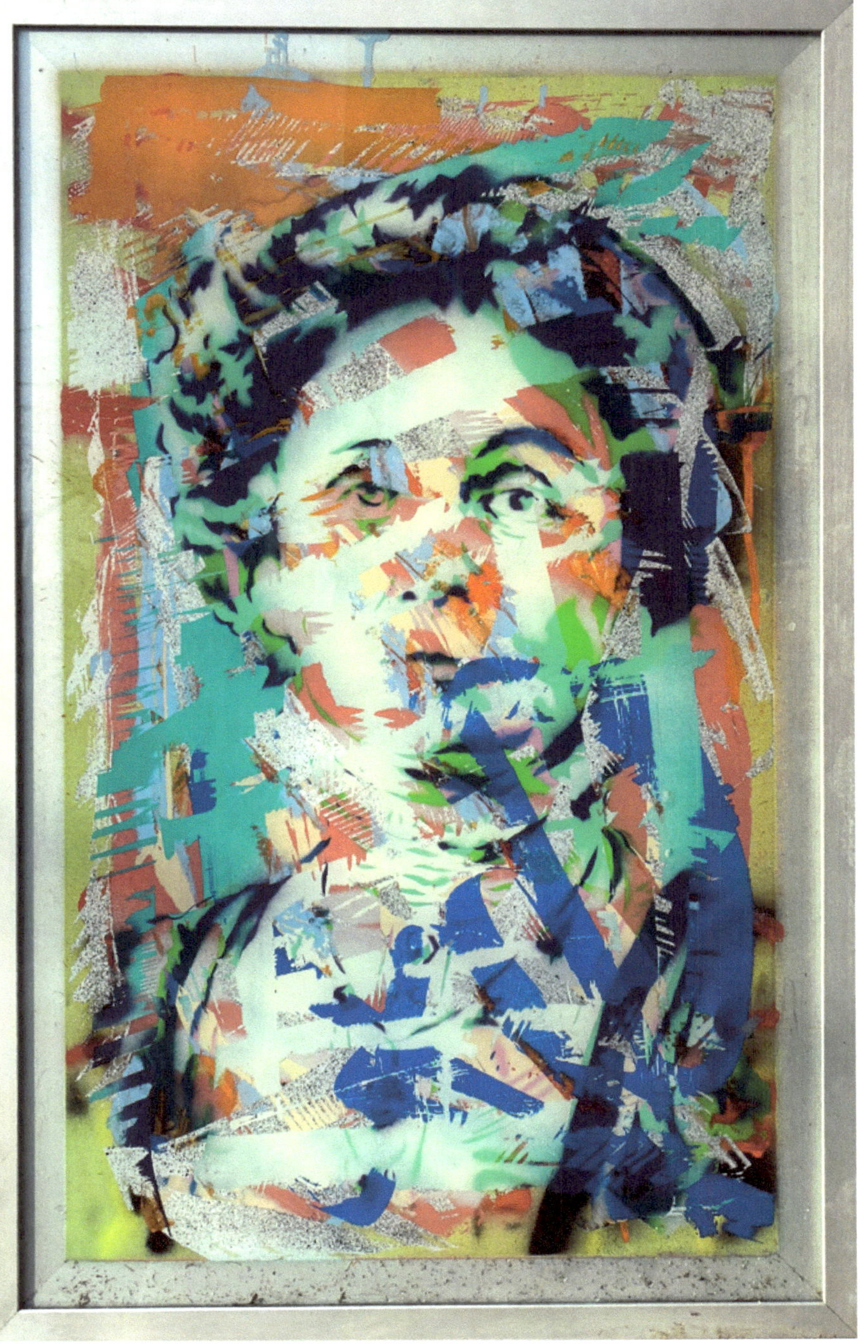

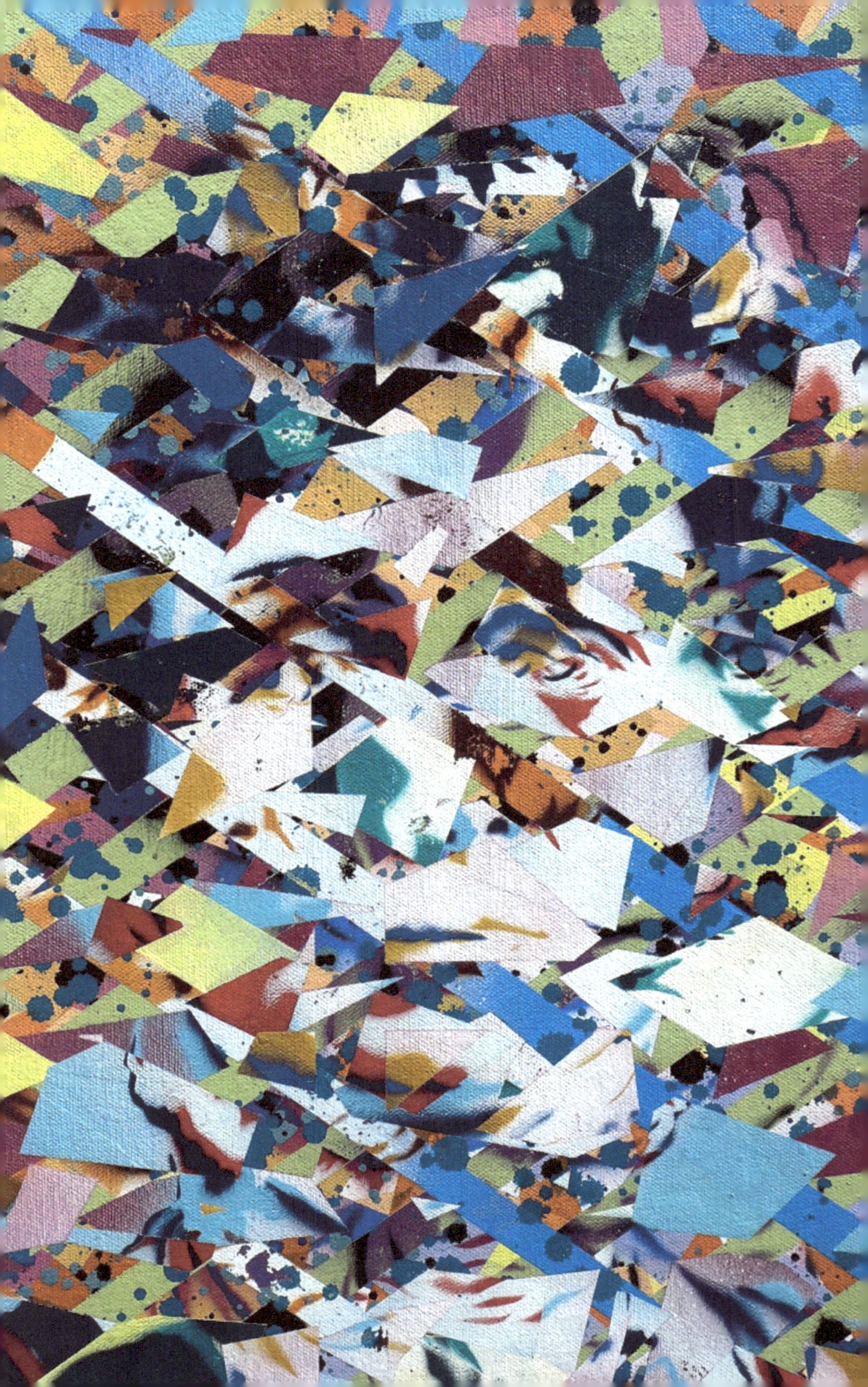

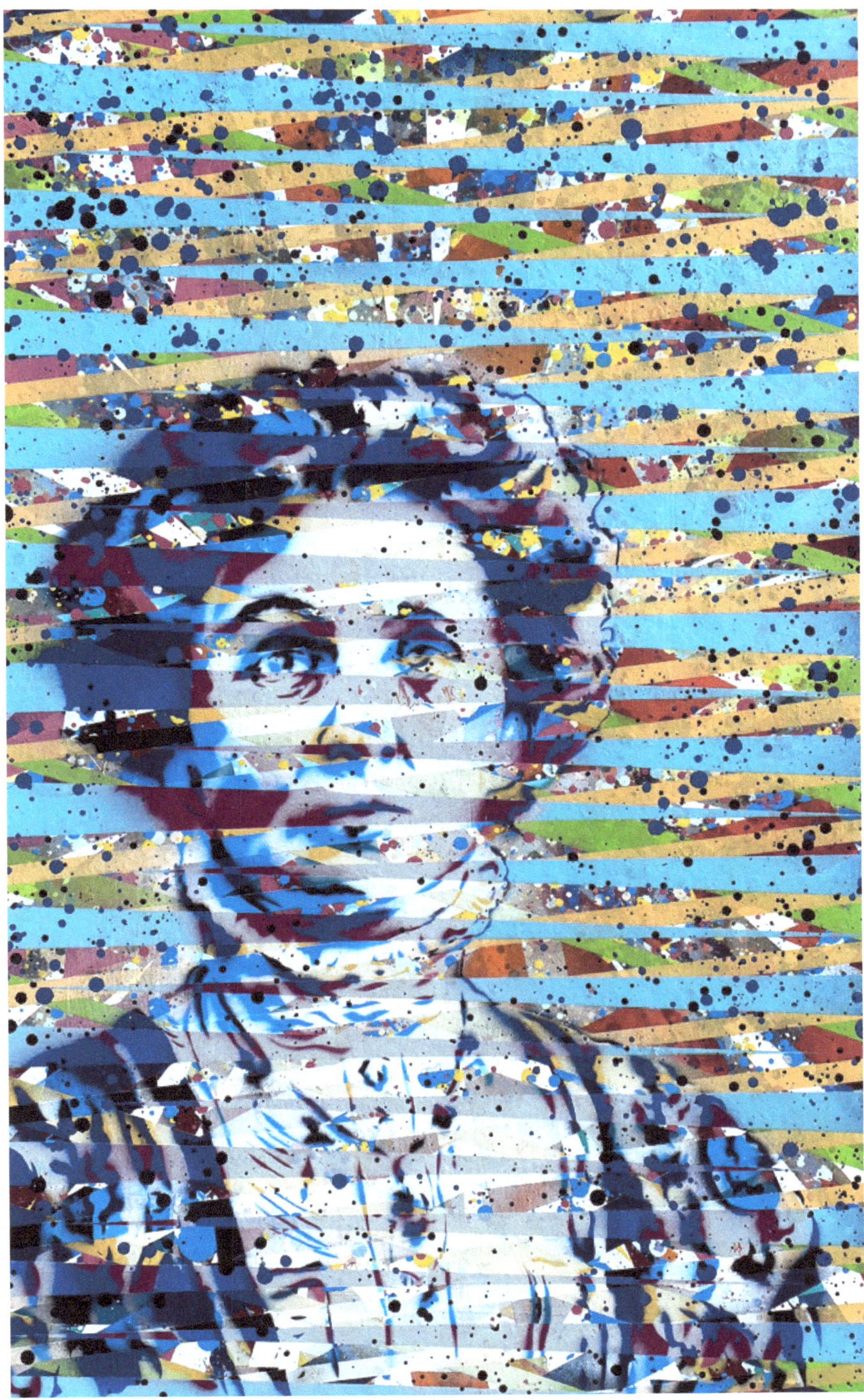

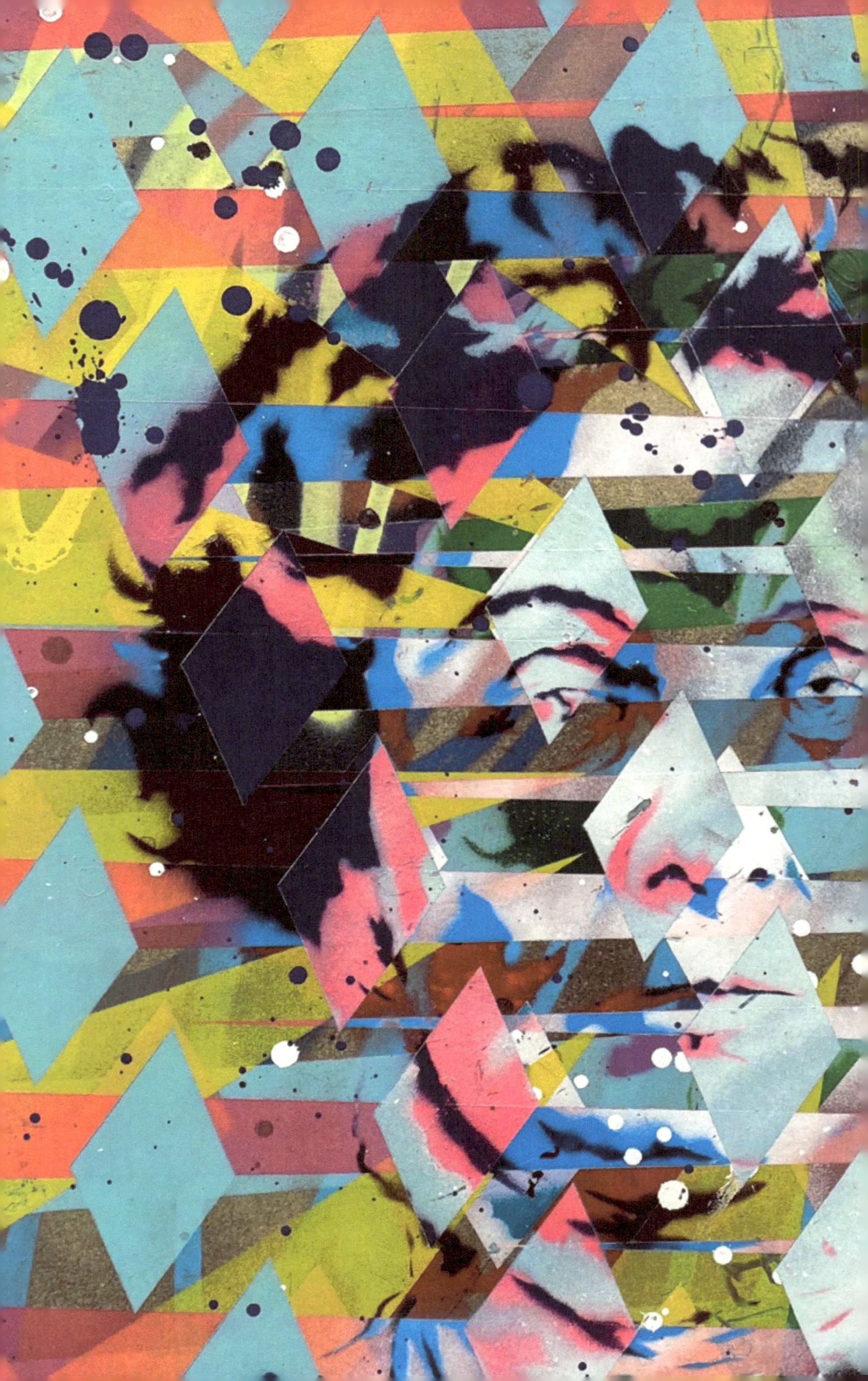

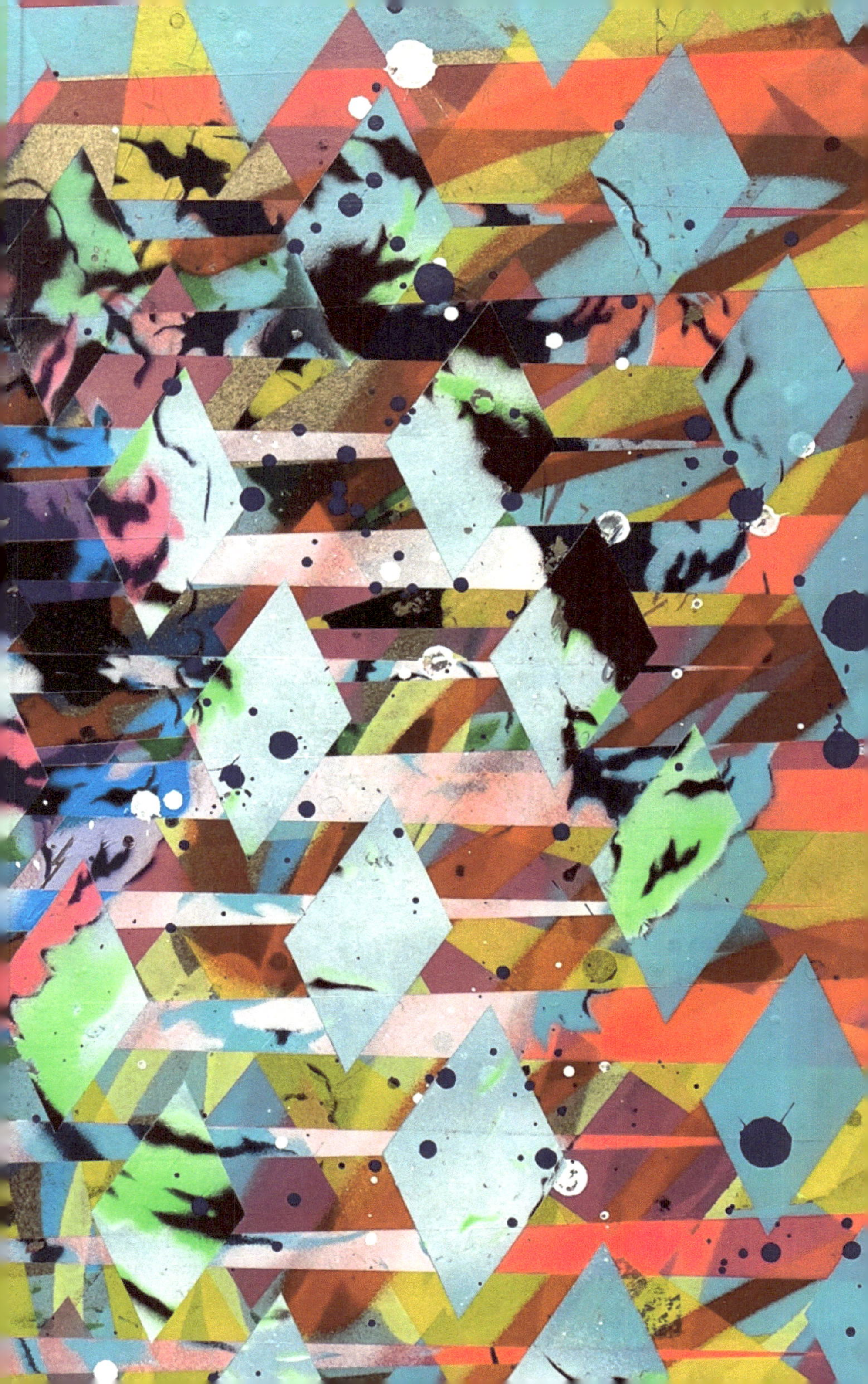

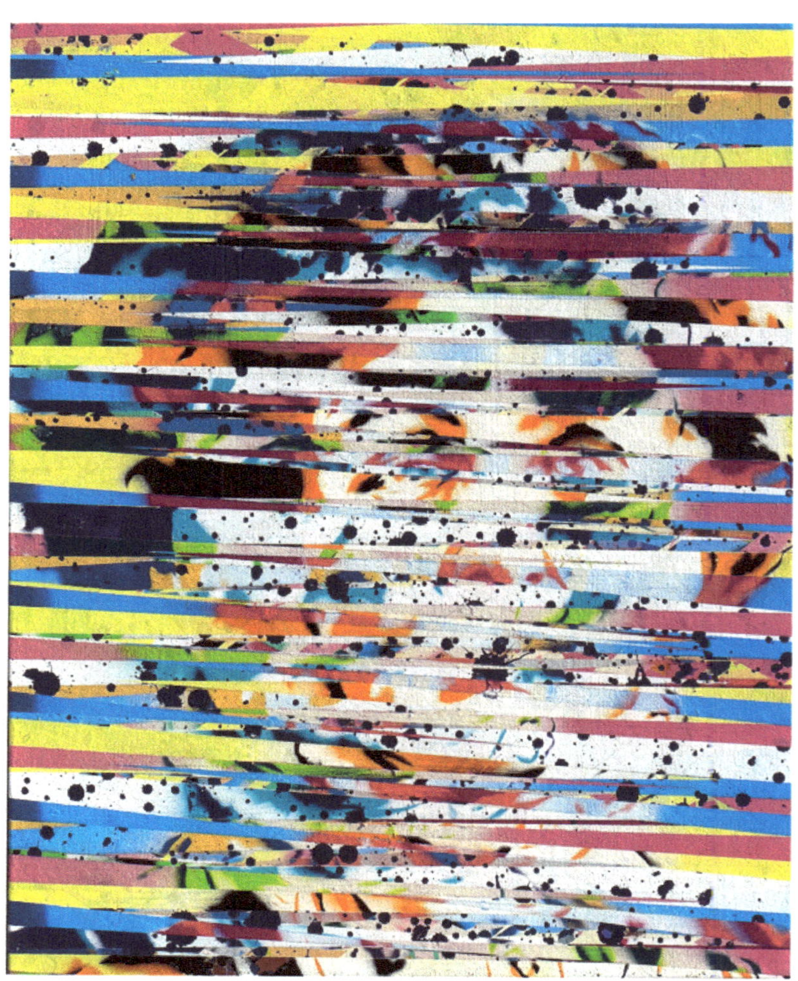

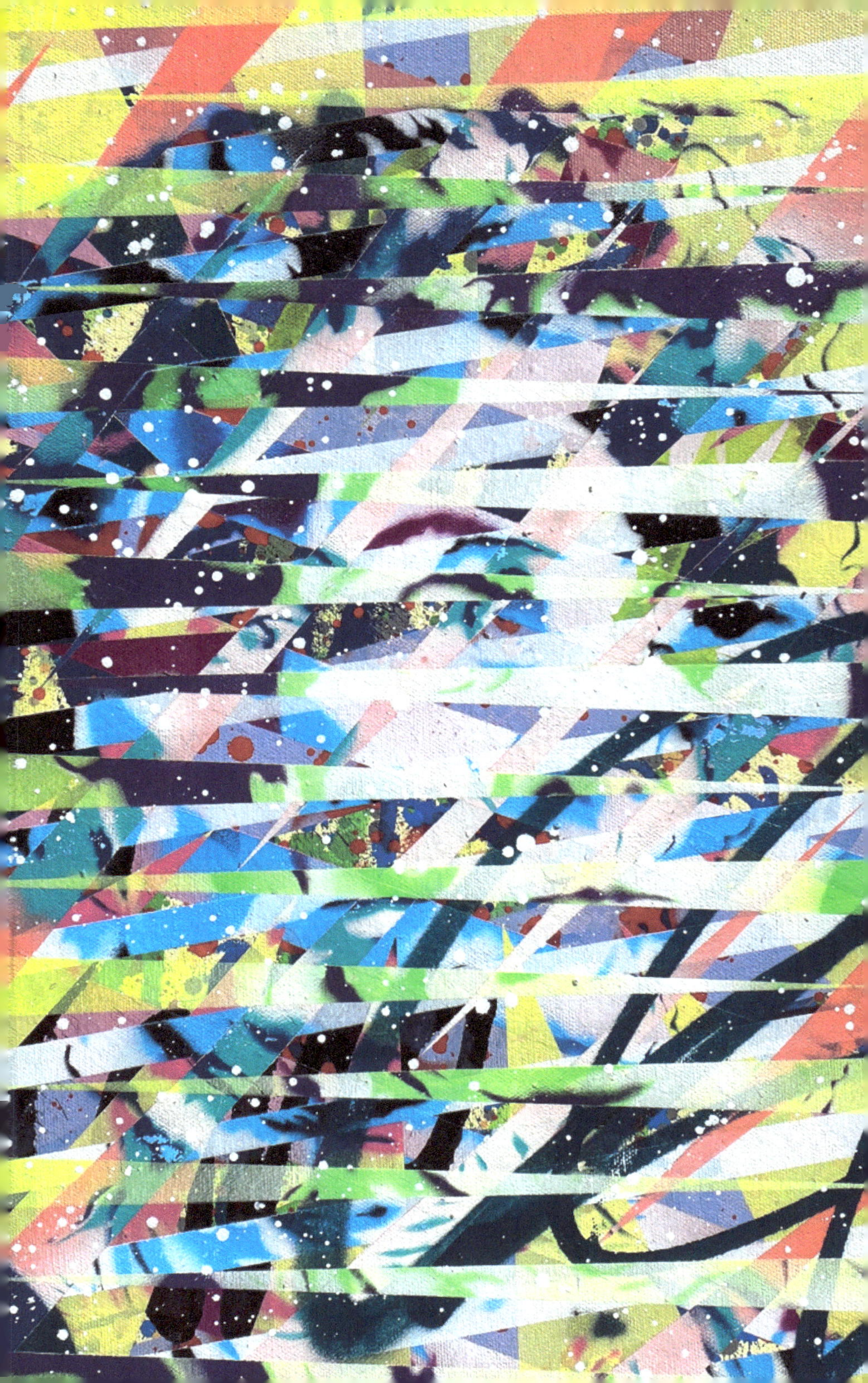

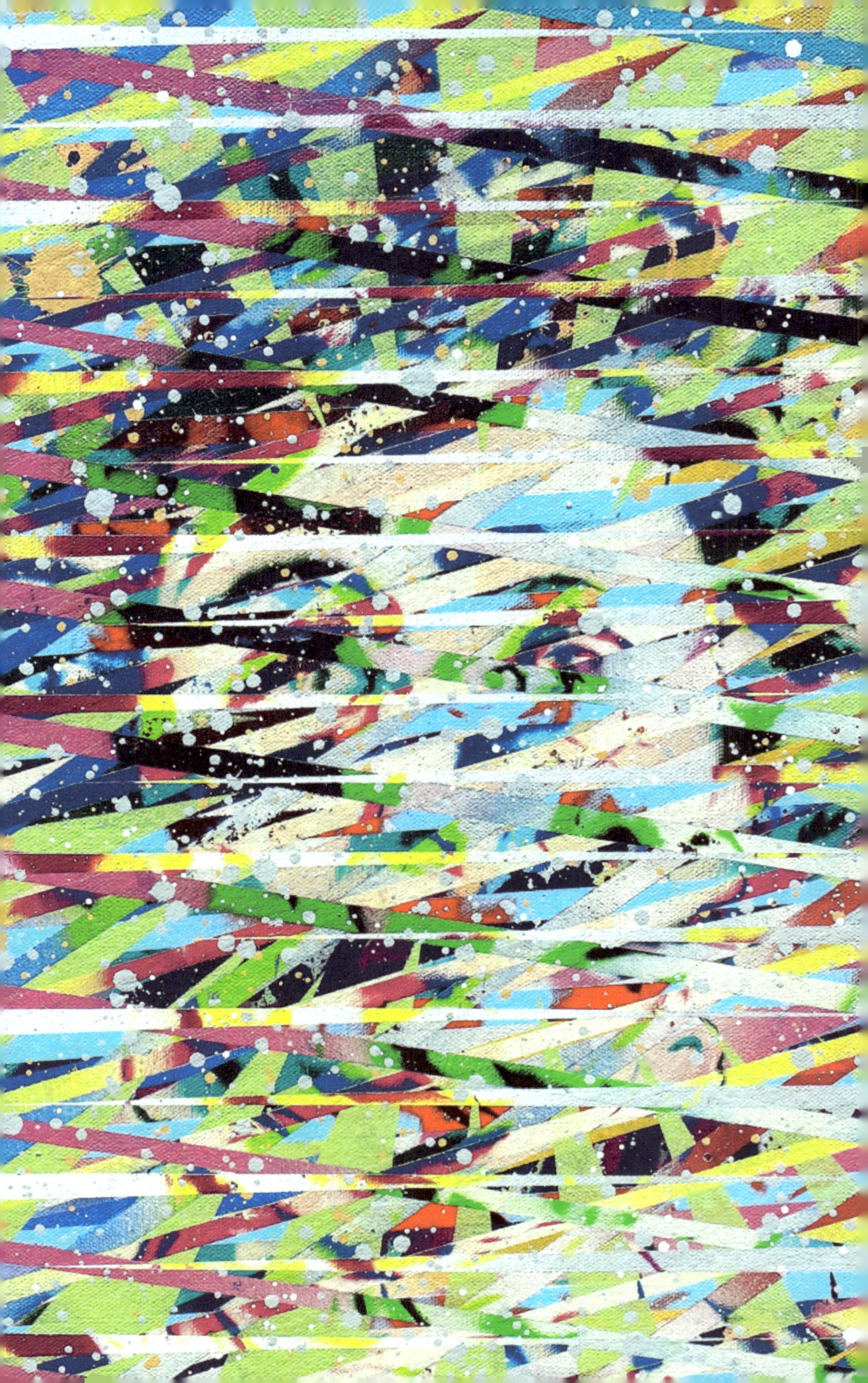

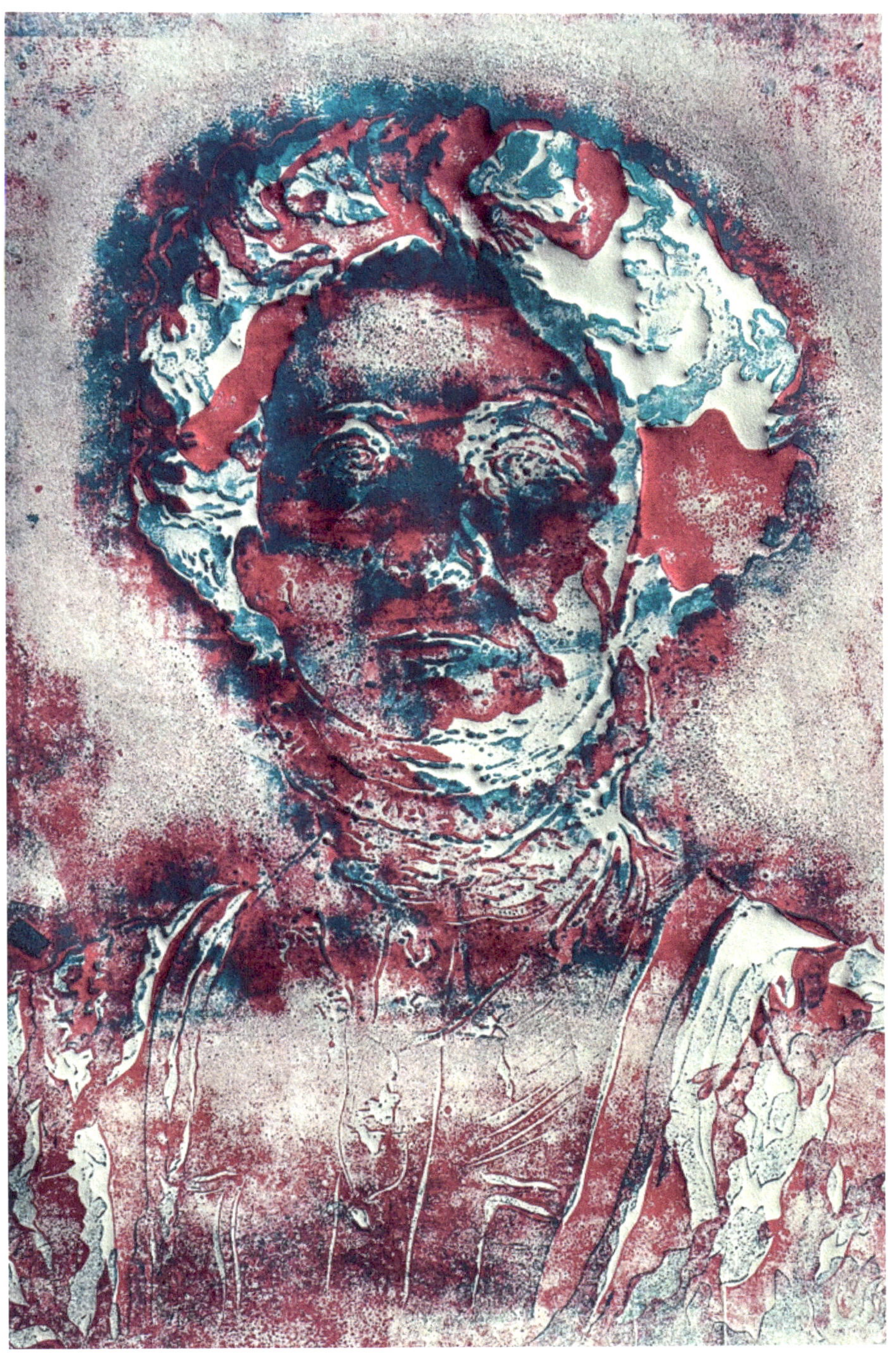

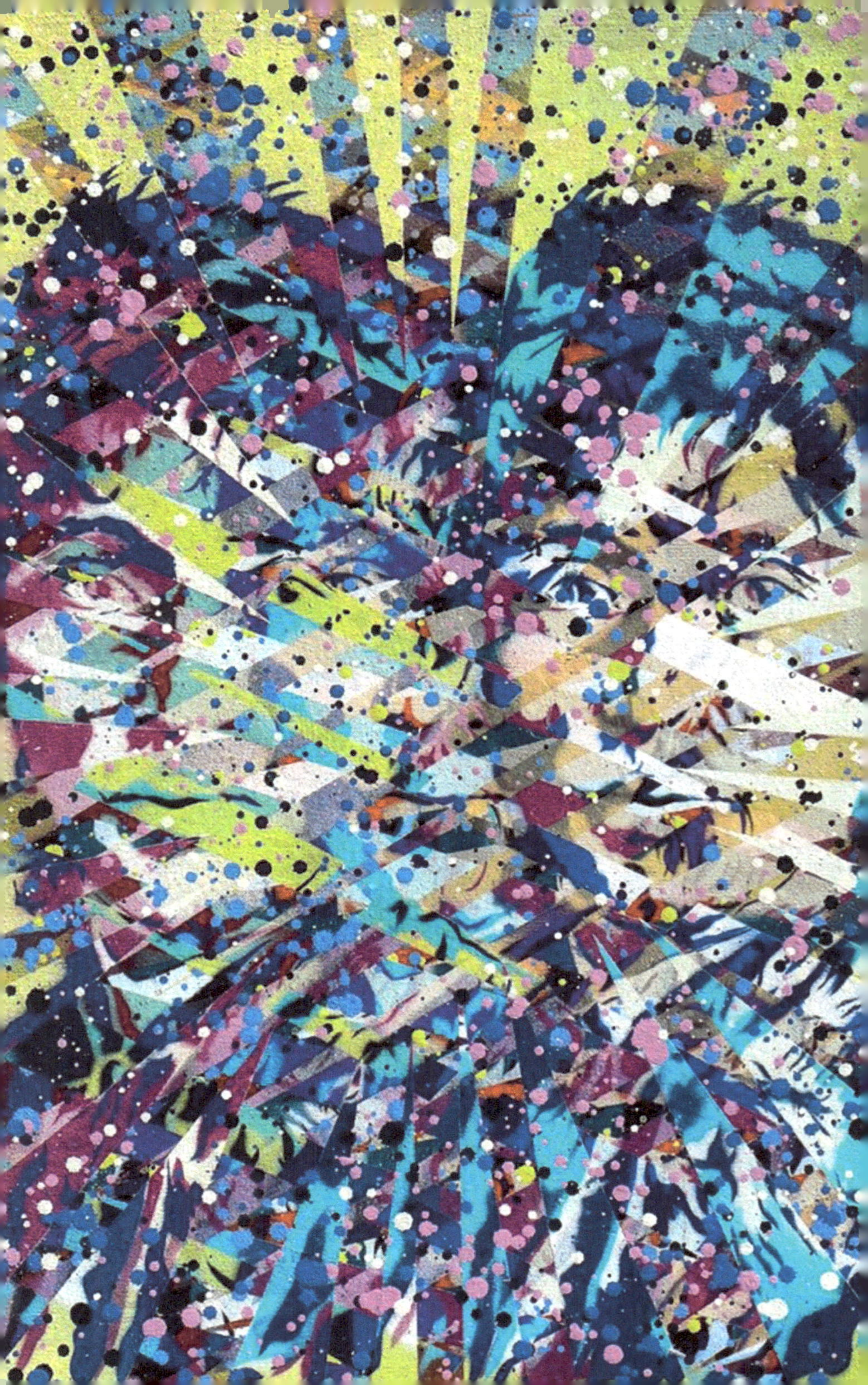

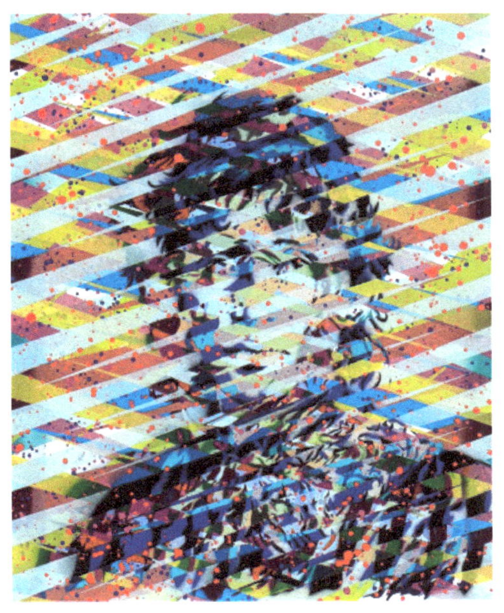

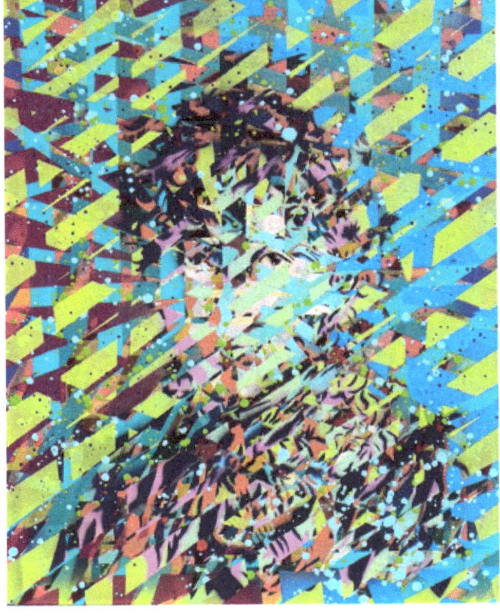

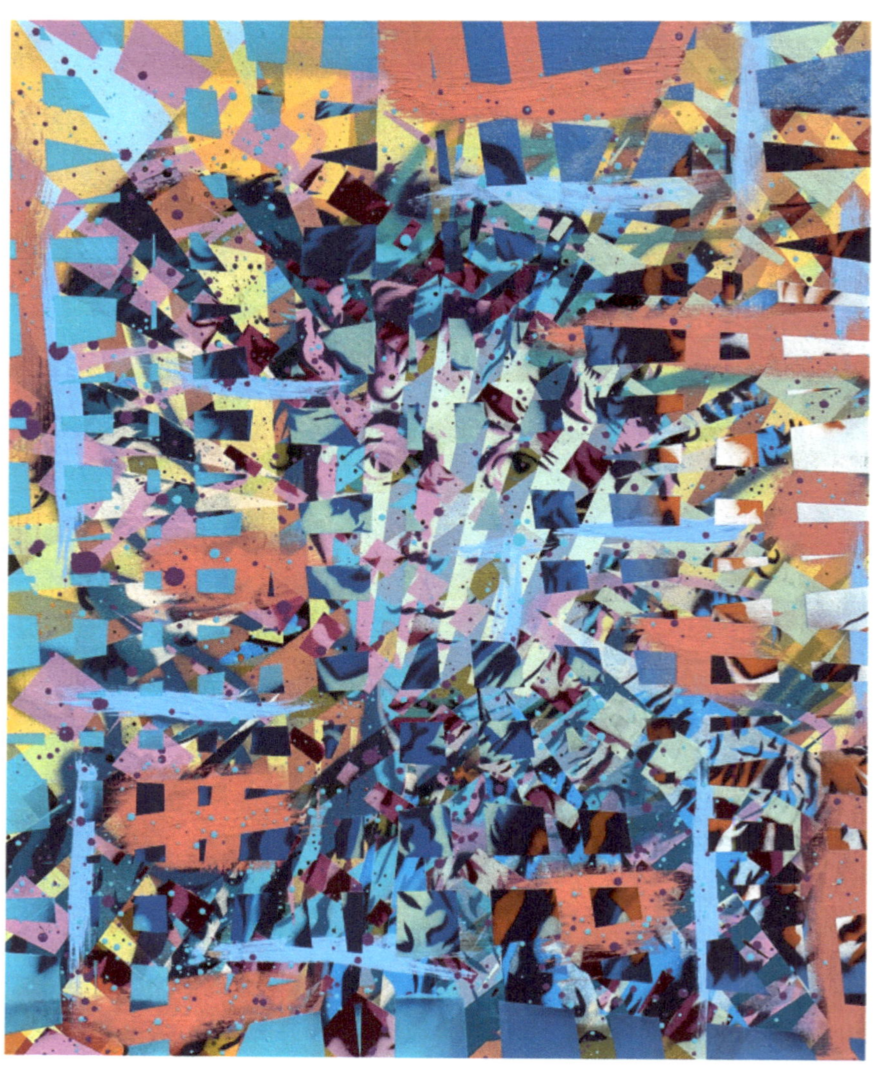

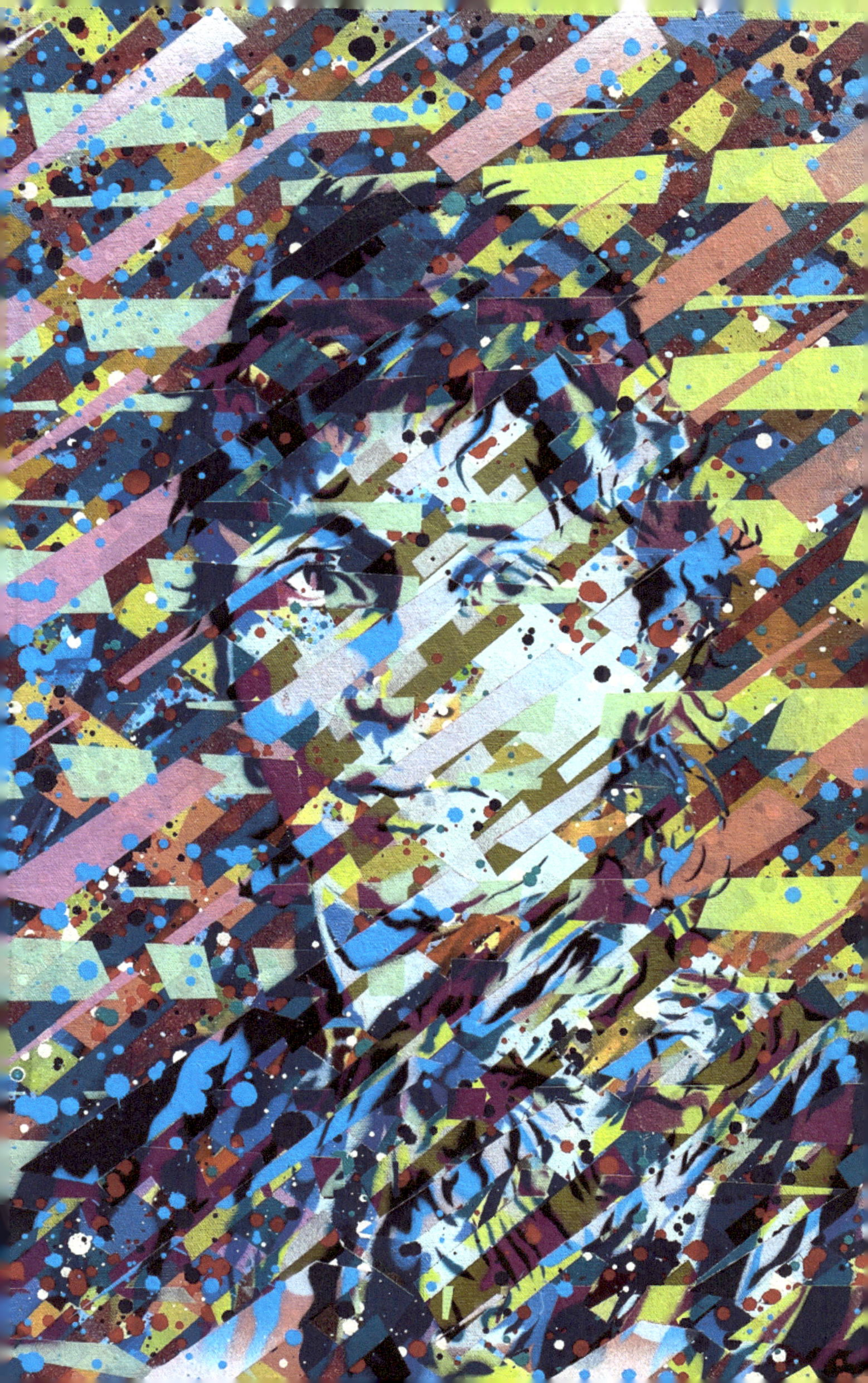

Half of what I've read I have sought out. Half of it has sought me.

Somewhere in the middle of doing the aforementioned work, I got an email. A patron, local to New Orleans, wanted me to paint a portrait of Thomas Garret, the famed abolitionist. Their family has direct lineage to Garret and, seeing what I had been up to, thought I would be the perfect artist to make this portrait. Although I had heard his name, I wasn't super familiar with his story. Reading about him and the other people surrounding that movement was an eye opener. So many connected threads. So many courageous acts.

A strong synchronicity; this is what I'm talking about. Your antenna starts to become tuned and you begin picking up multiple signals, in many instances without even trying. Somewhere in this line of reading there was mention of Thoreau's letter: *A Plea For Captain John Brown*. John Brown was a radical abolitionist who led the capture of the armory at Harpers Ferry. He and his comrades' aim was to use that weapon stockpile to arm the slaves and create a violent rebellion against the South. He was captured and hung, but this event and its aftermath helped fuel the Civil War.

Again, another story I didn't know. Thoreau? I knew he was an author. I knew his name from English class… Why didn't I know this story? Why didn't I know this part of the story?

As history would have it, Thoreau and his family were abolitionists. As I delved deeper into his life and work, so many clear instances of his rebellious nature came up, over and over. He is known as a naturalist, an essayist, a poet, a philosopher… But what stood out to me was that he was a punk, well before that word meant anything.

While his most famous piece of writing, *Walden*, is often seen as a guide on living simply and observing nature, it was really a refusal to go along with capitalism and what society had deemed was the right way to live. He believed it was a human right to simply be. How else would he have had the time to observe all of these natural occurrences?

Thoreau's *A Plea For Captain John Brown* highlighted the fact that this man did what he thought was right, even if everyone thought he was a fool. His essay *Civil Disobedience* was all about standing up to an unjust state. These themes persist throughout his life and writing, and, in reading his biography, I was stunned time and time again by how much I related to his outlook.

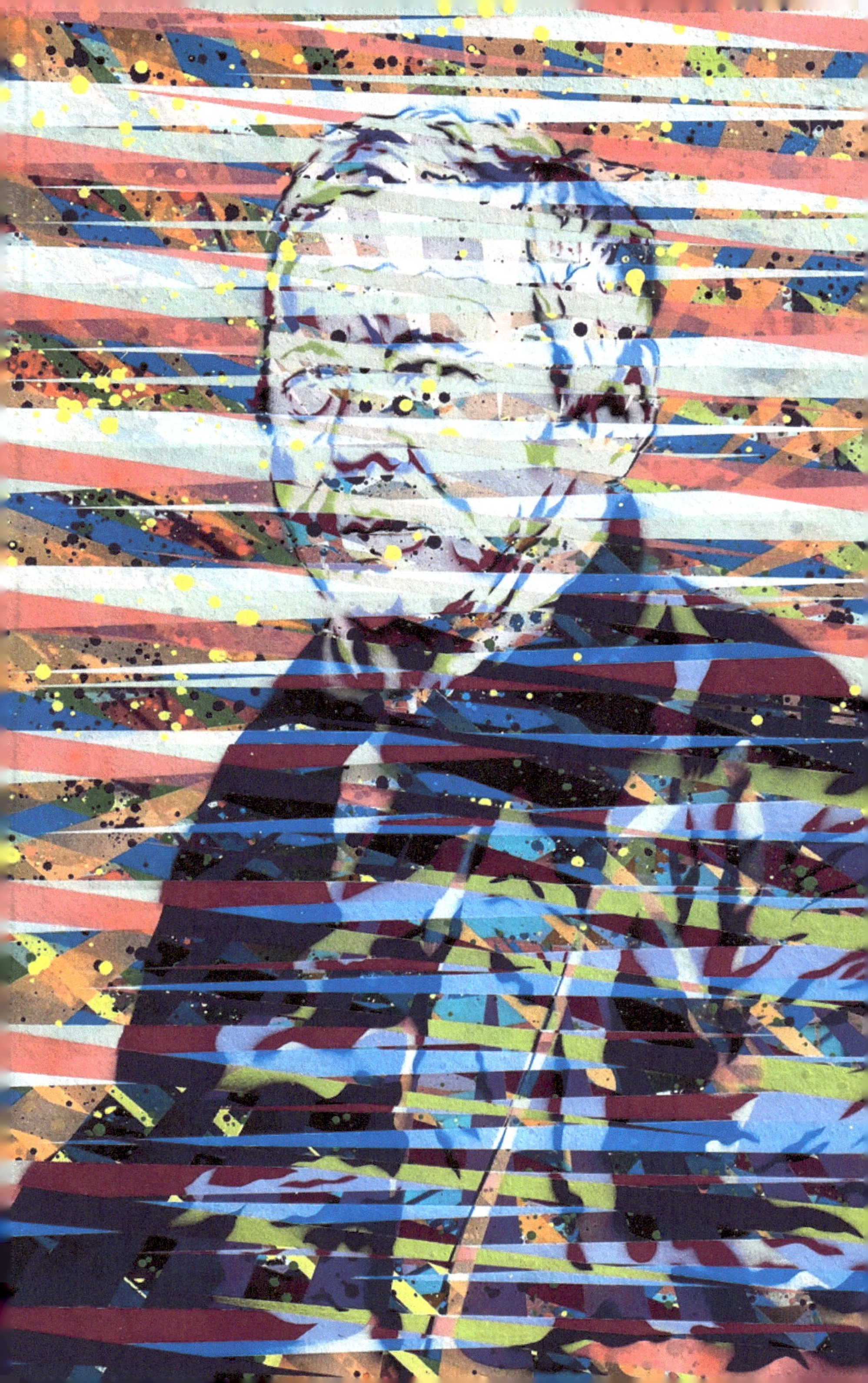

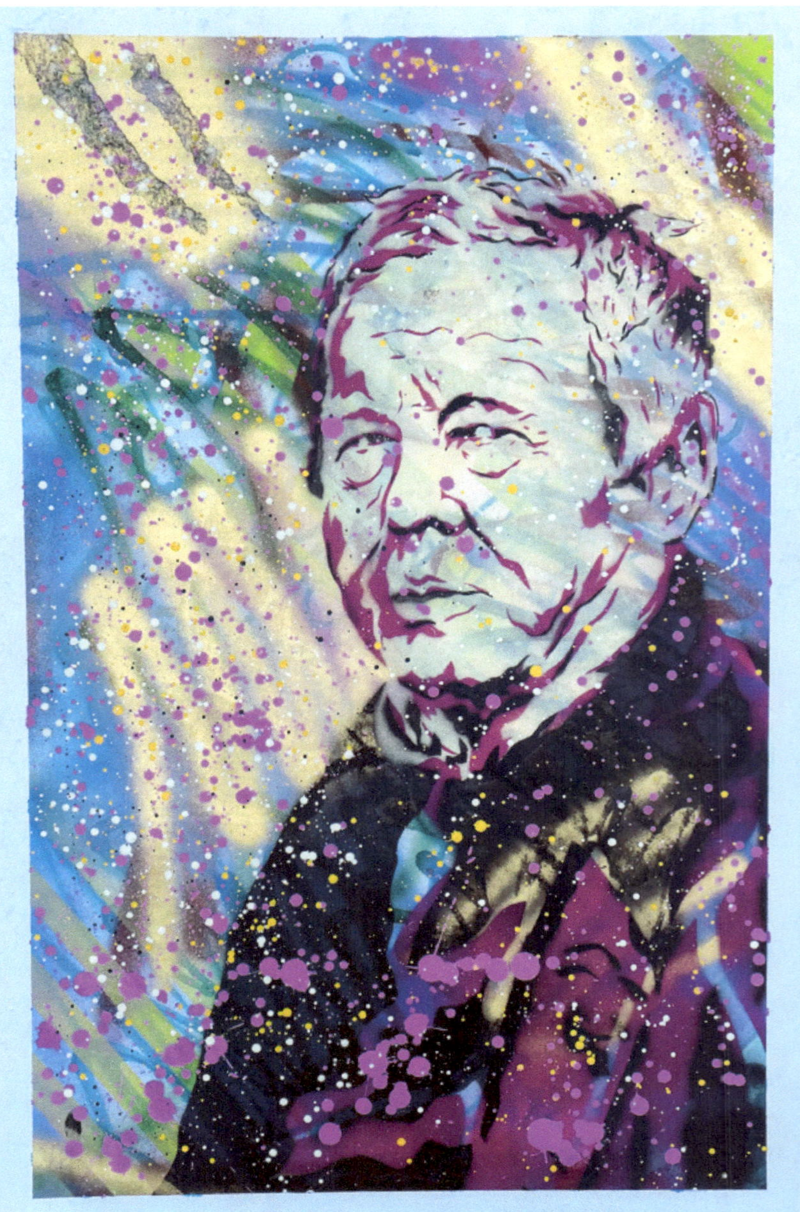

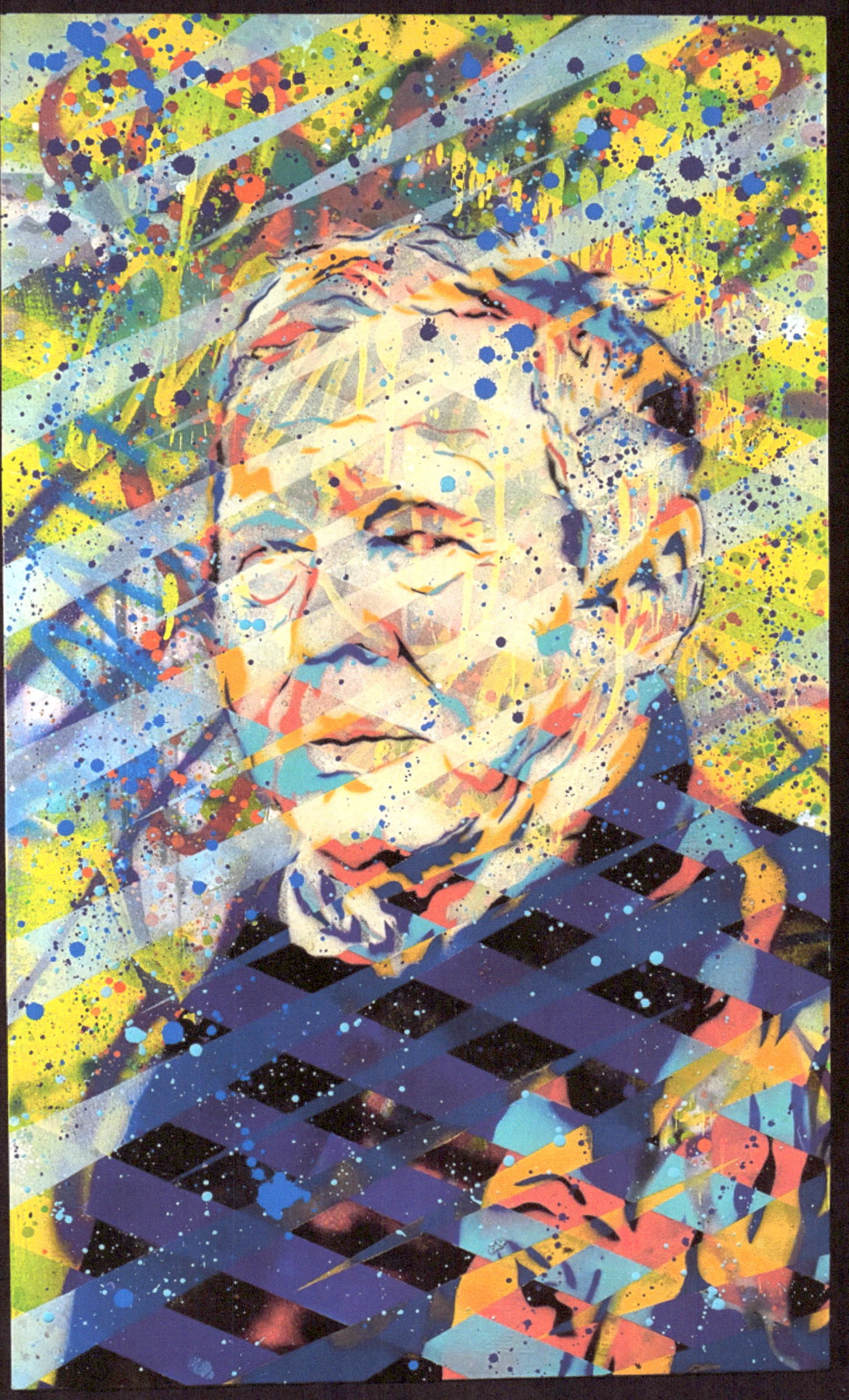

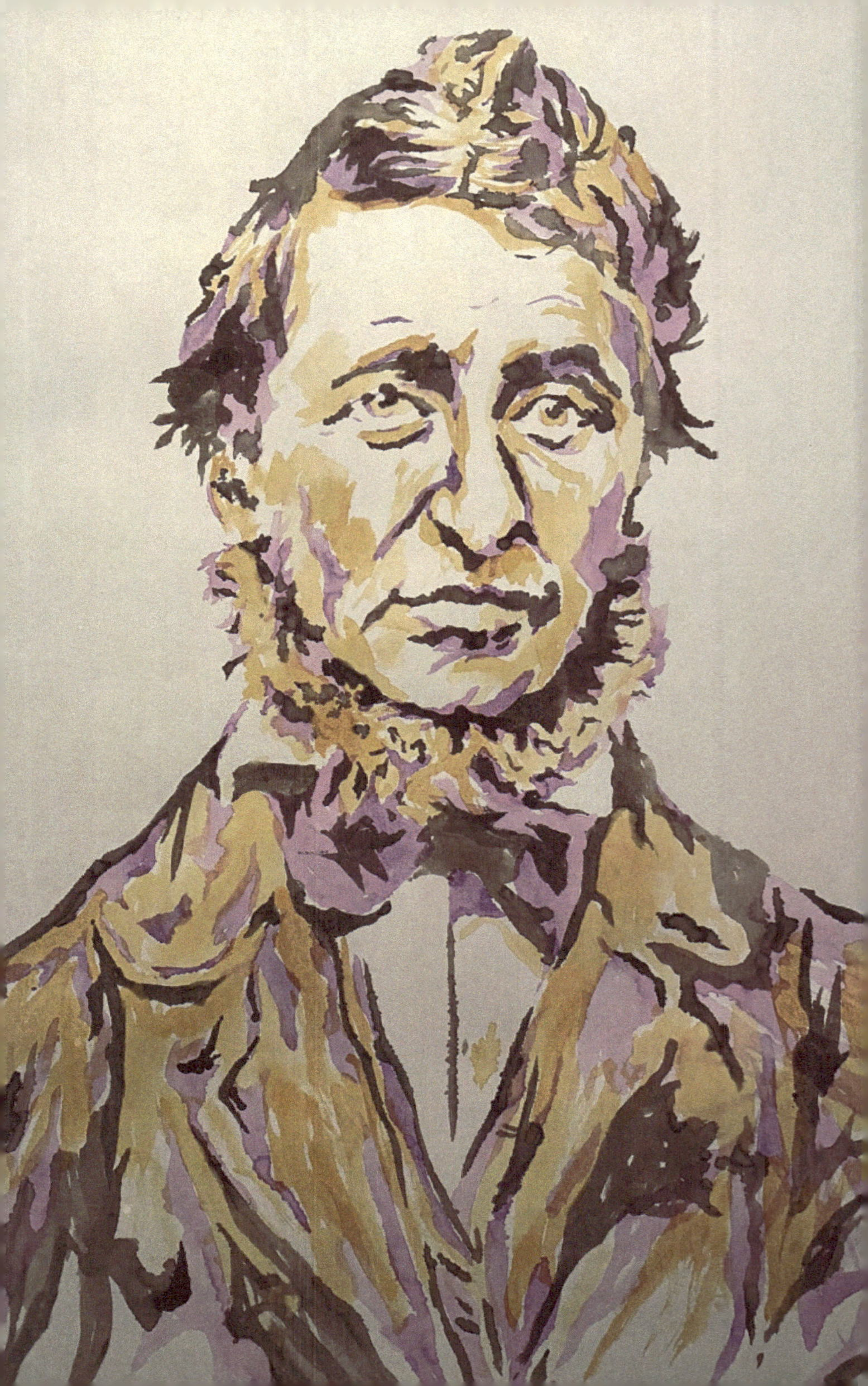

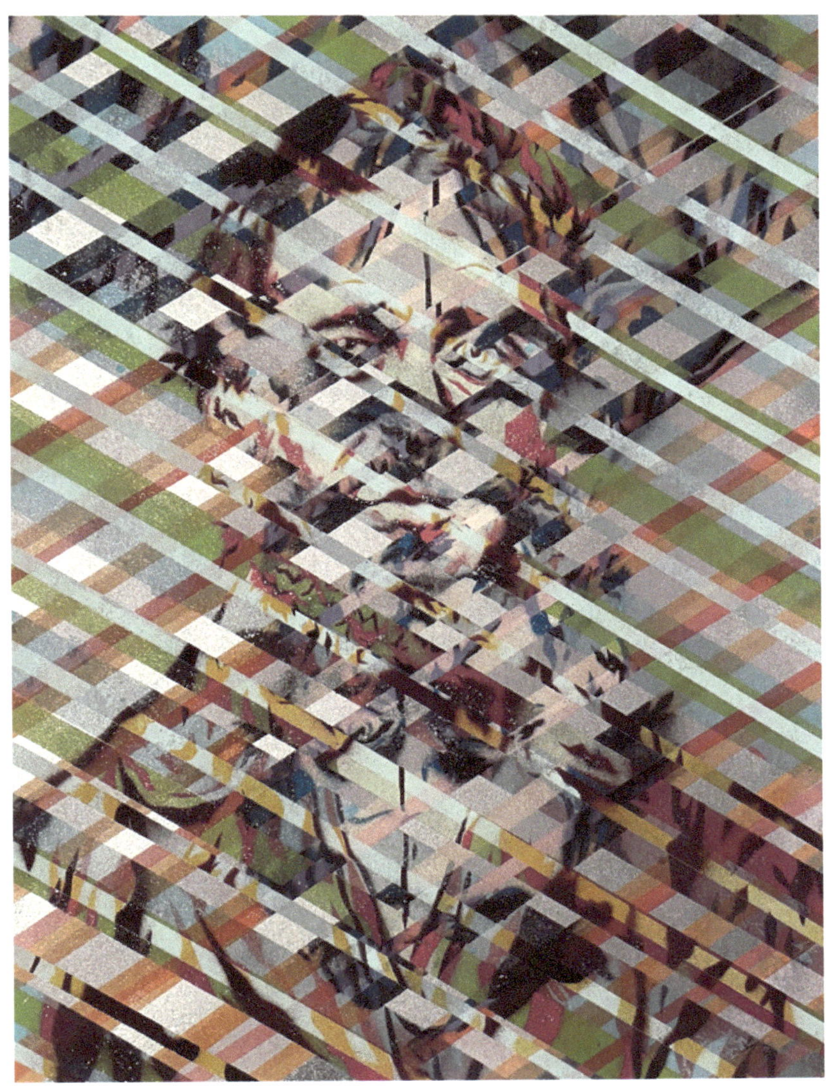

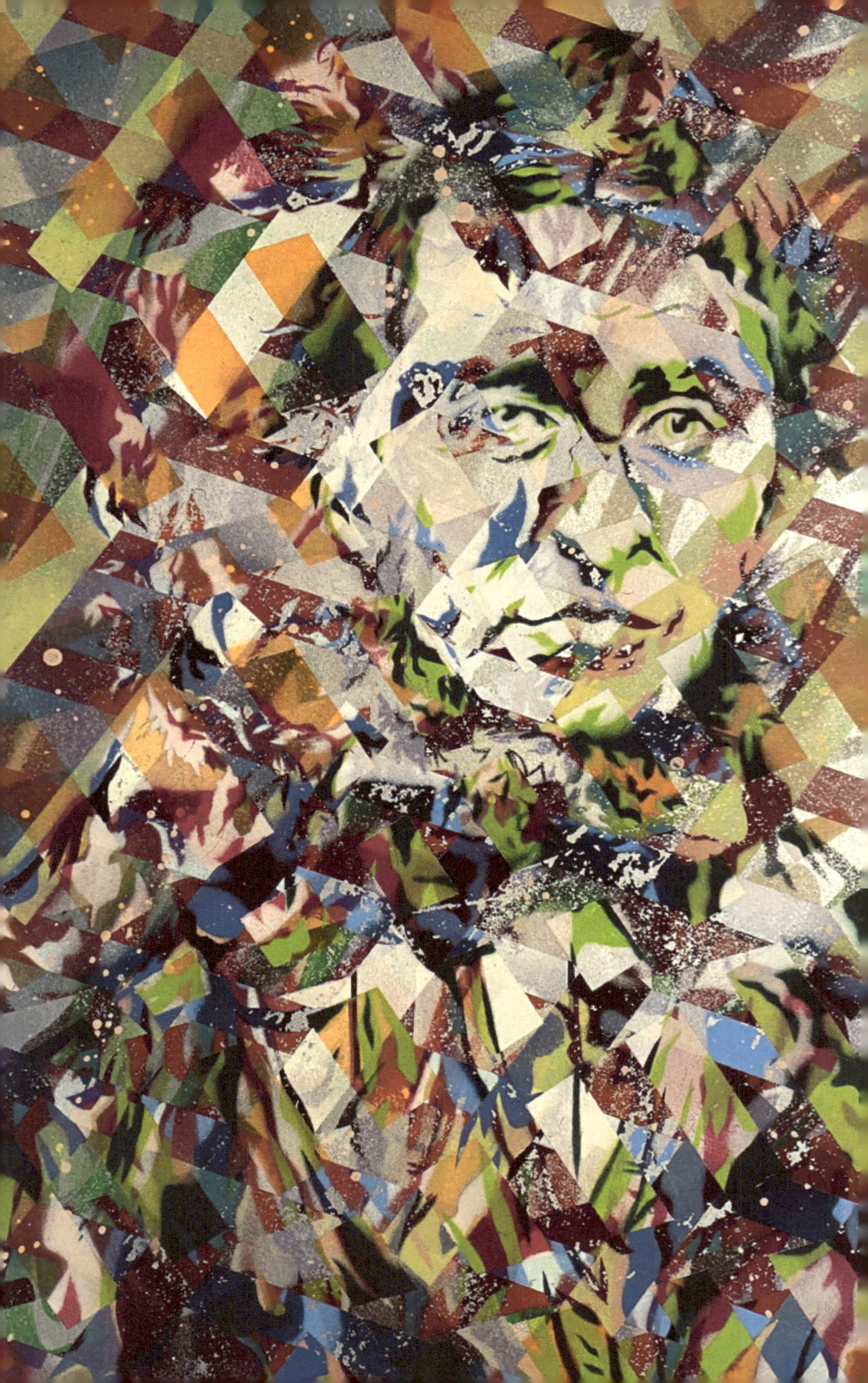

JOHNSON CITY - GEORGE F. JOHNSON

Talk about stories finding me.

Early in 2020, before I knew anything about Covid, I applied to a mural program in Upstate New York. I got an email saying that I was accepted into the program. From here, they would try to match me up with a property owner. I was stoked… but then… the world shut down and I forgot about it completely.

So much happened between 2020 and 2023, that I hadn't thought about my application since receiving the acceptance email. Then, in early winter of 2023, I got an unexpected phone call: the program was back in business and they had found a property owner who liked my work. Immediately I remembered the project, but I was blown away by this news. Any thoughts of this project had been absent, and now here it was again. A big project, 1,500 miles away, seemingly popping up out of nowhere. This was exciting news.

Within a few days I was introduced over the phone to the owners of the building. We immediately connected over music and punk rock and various life experiences. They had seen my work and liked it, and it was at their suggestion that I paint George F. Johnson, the founder of the city where the building was located. They gave me a brief synopsis of who he was and what he did, and after getting off the call, I got to work reading up about him. Another incredible story found me.

George F. Johnson was not a revolutionary, nor was he an anarchist. He was, in fact, a businessman… but not just any businessman. Johnson was quite possibly one of the most equitable businessmen of his time, if not of all time. He had a shoe enterprise that employed over 10,000 people across eight factories. They manufactured every American boot for The First World War. They were one of the first companies to implement the 8-hour work day and the 40-hour work week. To this day, Johnson City is still known as the "Home of The Square Deal," as employee pay was based on unit production and not on an hourly wage. Workers were paid for how much work they completed, and Johnson's Square Deal would go on to influence Roosevelt's New Deal.

In many ways, Johnson City was a standard company town, except that Johnson and his company were much more equitable in sharing their wealth to help locals purchase their own homes (versus other company towns where the corporation owned everything) and provide benefits to the citizens who lived and worked there. To these people, George F. Johnson was a hero, and he still is to many of the current day locals, although the town has shrunk in size since its heyday and after his passing.

It was such a strange thing to see that capitalism actually could be fair and work for all the people while still remaining fully profitable. The story of this man and this town was hopeful, and I was seemingly introduced to Johnson by no impetus of my own. Over the years, I have begun to wonder if these people are seeking me out from the other side… especially in this case.

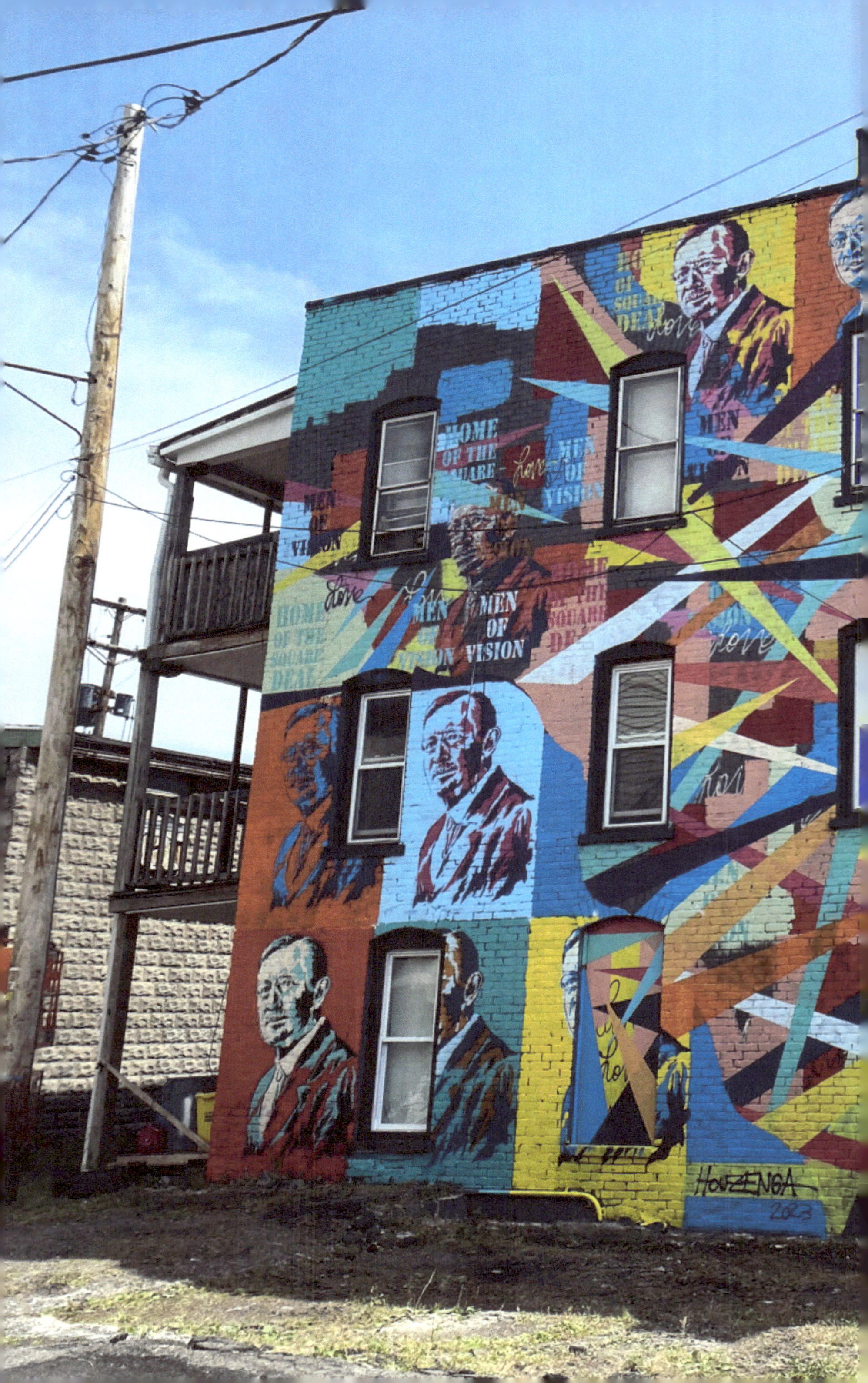

HOME
OF THE
SQUARE - DEAL
MEN
OF
VISION
MEN
OF
VISION
Love
MEN AND WOMEN
OF
VISION VISION
HOME
OF THE
SQUARE
DEAL
HOUZENGA

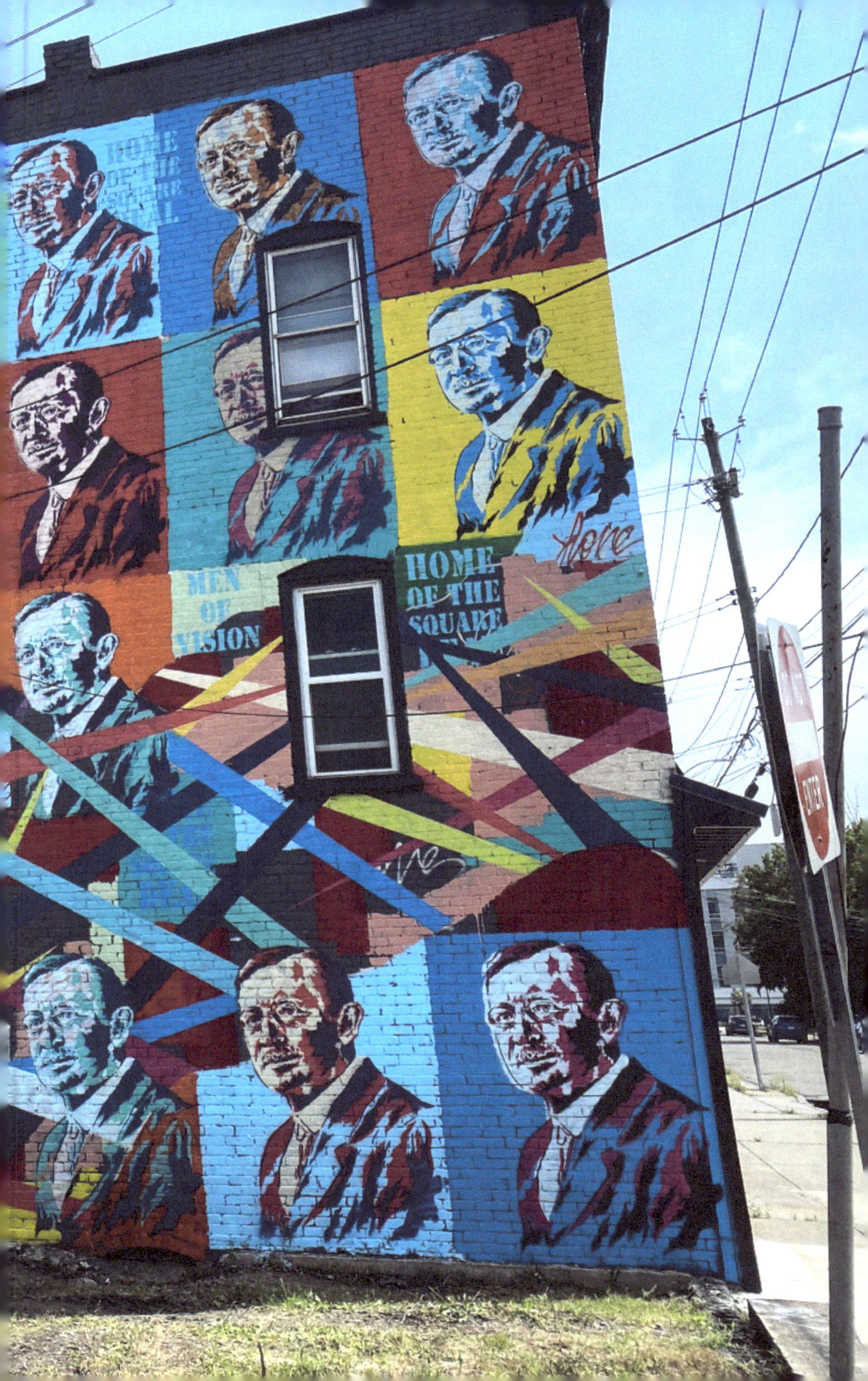

HOME OF THE SQUARE DEAL
MEN OF VISION
HOME OF THE SQUARE

LOUISE MICHEL

In the summer of 2024, the genocide in Palestine was already in full swing, and there we were, watching the whole thing unfold on our screens. My friend sent me a video of a rescue ship in the Mediterranean. The video attributed the ship to the anonymous British artist known as Banksy and made mention that the boat was named after French anarchist Louise Michel. Who was that?

In my initial readings about her, I could tell right off the bat that she was an incredible person. She was a prominent figure during the Paris Commune in 1871, which helped lead to her being deported. During her expulsion, she began to embrace anarchy and, upon her return to France, she emerged as an important French anarchist and went on several speaking tours. She became a hero to the oppressed. At a demonstration in 1883, she flew what would become known as the anarchy black flag for the first time. When I came to the part in my reading where she hung out with and influenced Emmeline Pankhurst and Lucy Parsons, chills ran down my spine. I had already painted them. Something was synching.

I always work in series. I always make more than one painting with each person I do, which gives me a lot of freedom. When I feel like something is done, I am free to move on and start a new piece. In the case of Louise Michel, I had just come into a lot of paper. More materials mean more freedom. I also had an idea to make an animation with all of these paintings, which prompted me to paint many more than I normally would. The animation never came to light, but these paintings became precious to me. Michel had a powerful voice, a powerful image and a powerful spirit. Looking back, I think this may be why I painted her portrait so many times.

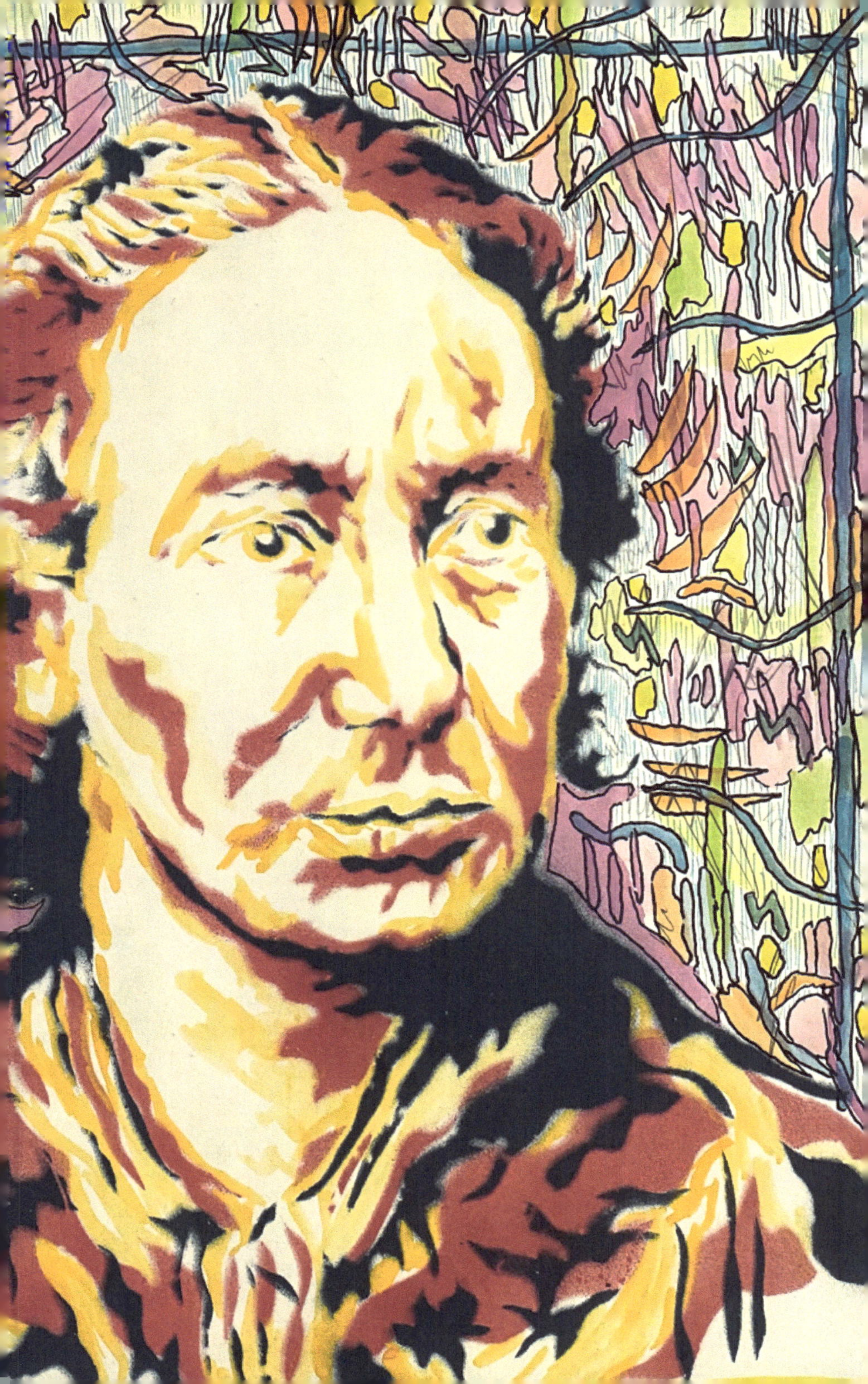

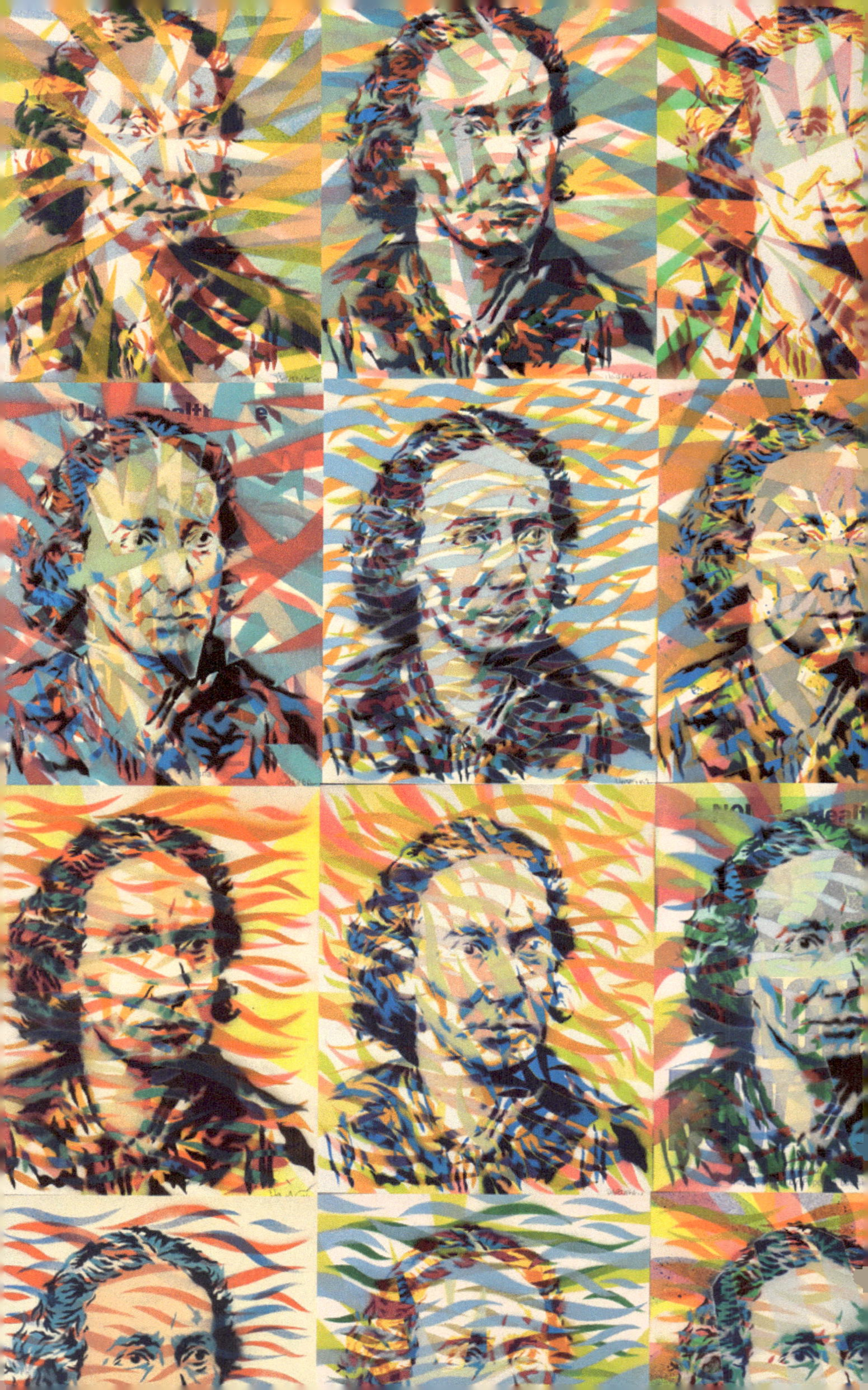

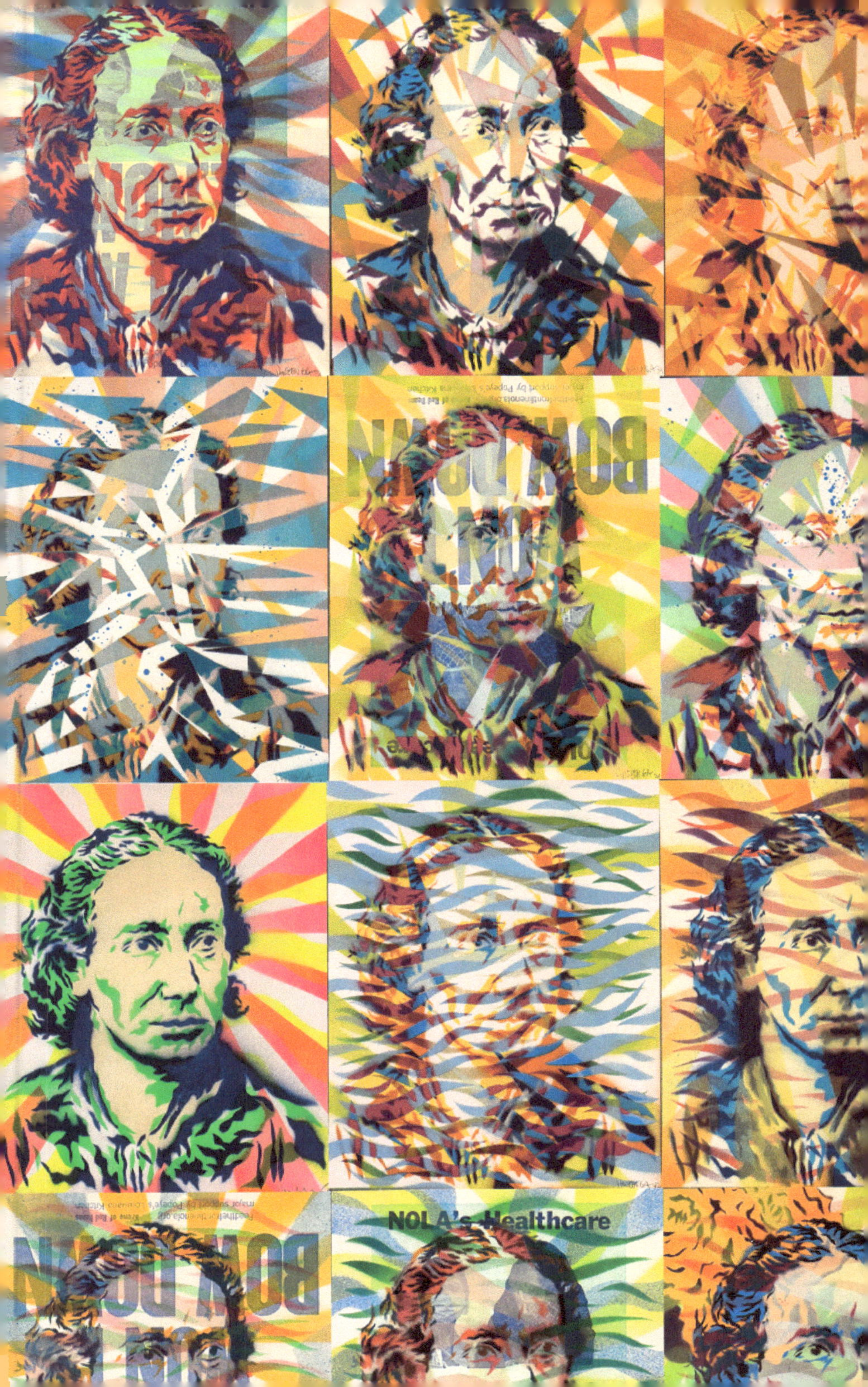

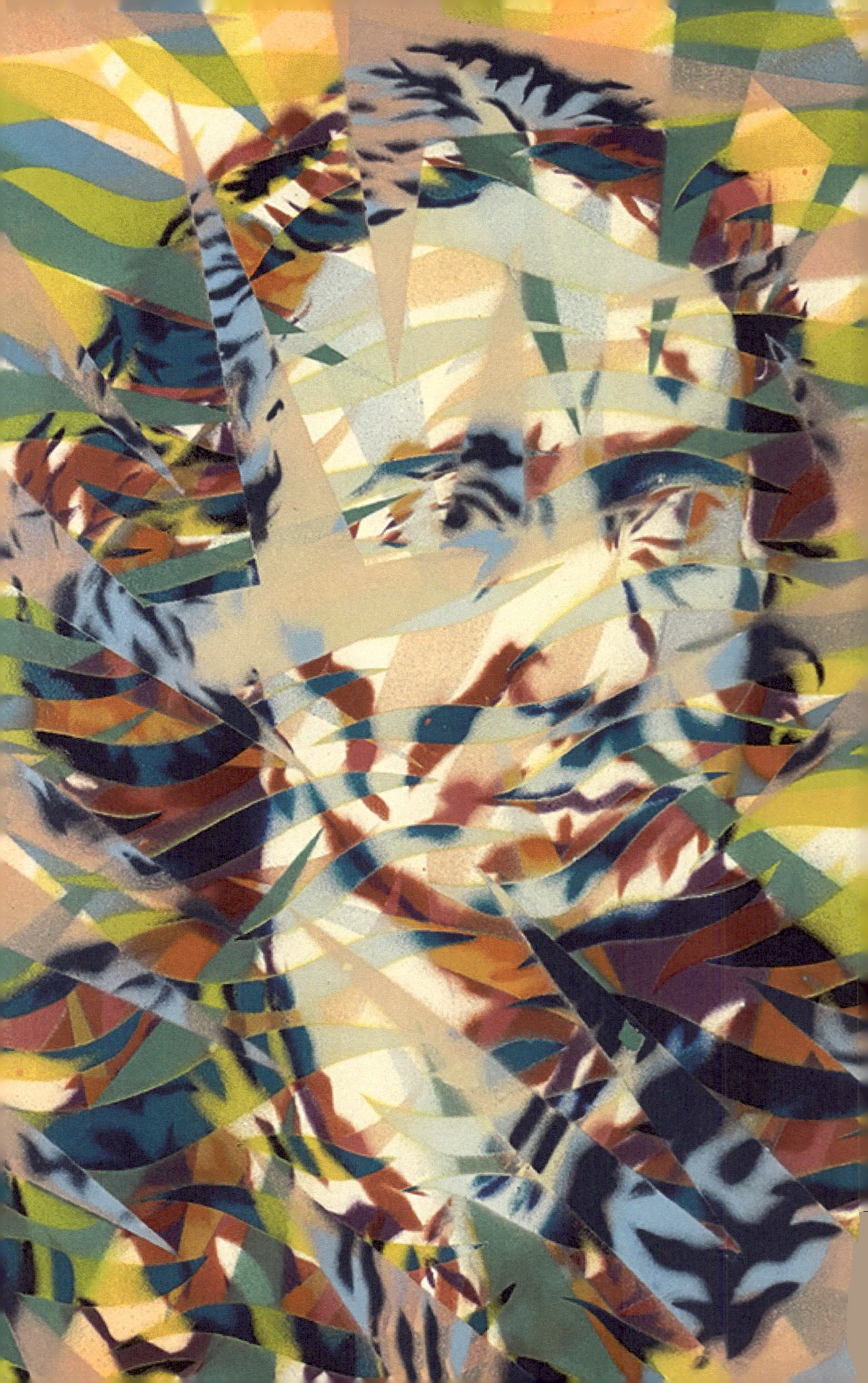

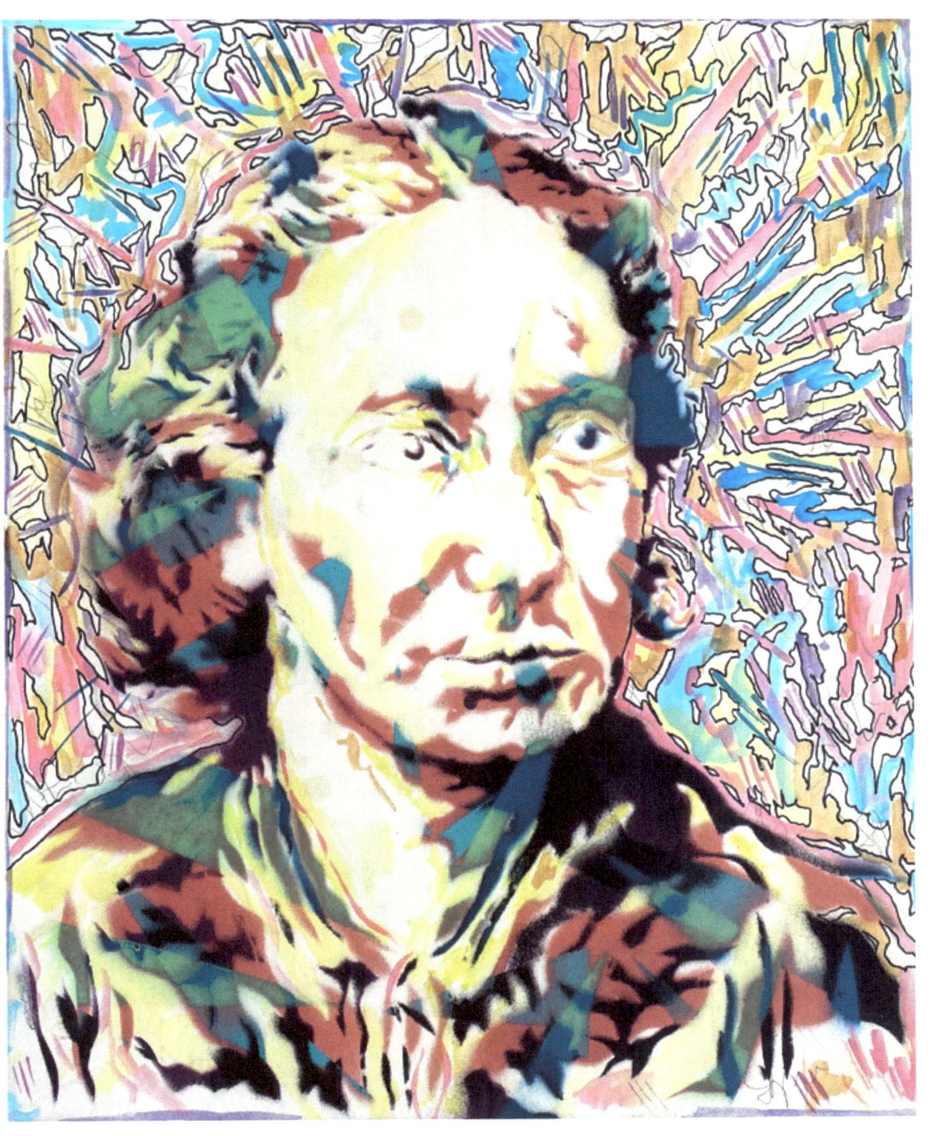

EDWARD BELLAMY

Throughout history, there have been many influential people who have also said, "Fuck This Shit," because "that's just the way it is" has never been and will never be true. Without many of these people, life as we know it would not exist.

I often zig-zag around in my reading. It's hard to read about some of these figures without another being mentioned. Then I have more reading to do, and, when moved, more painting to do. We're at a moment in history where so much is happening and many of us are left wondering what we can even do about it. While I, too, am in that number, at the very least I can point to these people. If nothing else, I can look backwards and see what they did.

These pieces are based on a photo of Edward Bellamy. Bellamy wrote a novel called *Looking Backward*, which was published in 1888. The work is considered an early example of science fiction, as the main character time travels to the year 2000 and finds himself in a utopian society. At the time of its release, the novel was a smash hit, as it spoke to much of the country's ongoing civil unrest and outlined remedies for many of man's ills. Though there was much uncertainty at the time of its writing, Bellamy believed we could have utopia.

Unfortunately, many of the topics discussed in the book remain just as relevant today.

While researching Louise Michel, I came across a graphic novel biography. In one scene, a group of people are talking after Michel's funeral and there is mention of how other people are carrying on the torch. I think this is where I first caught wind of Edward Bellamy and Charlotte Perkins Gilman.

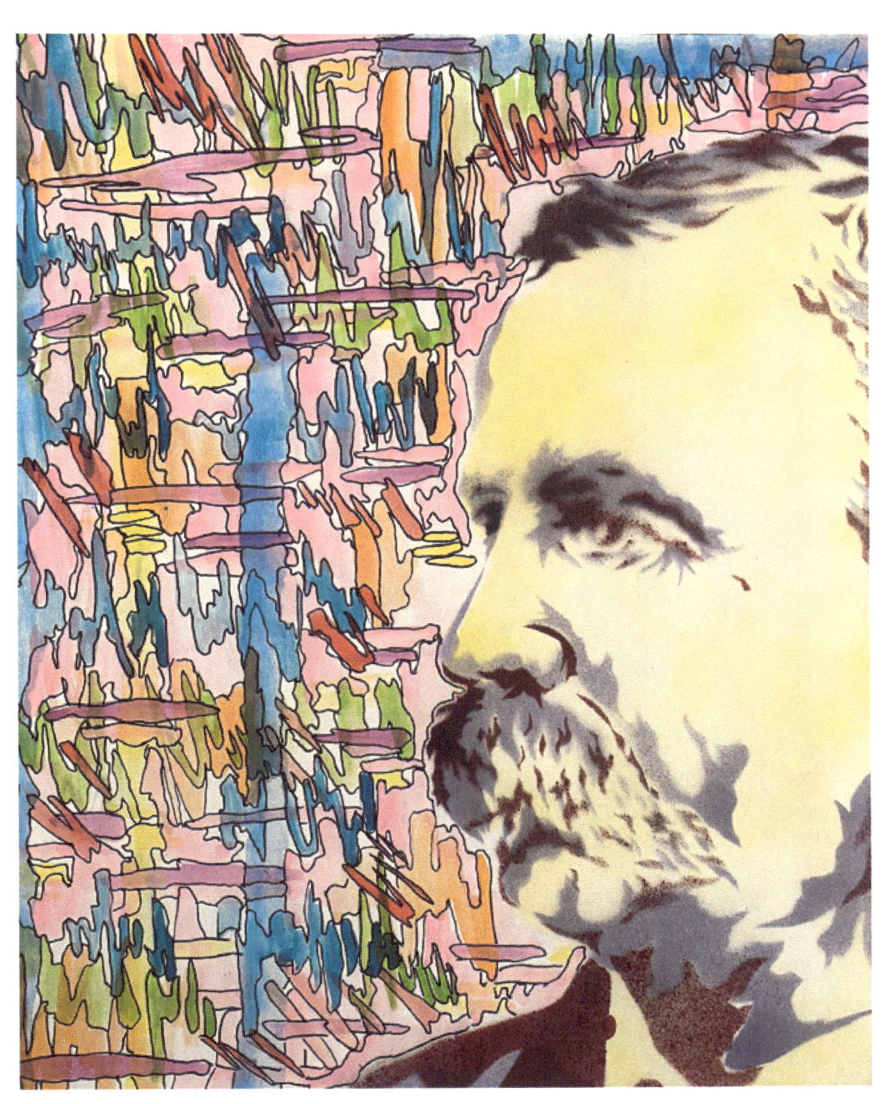

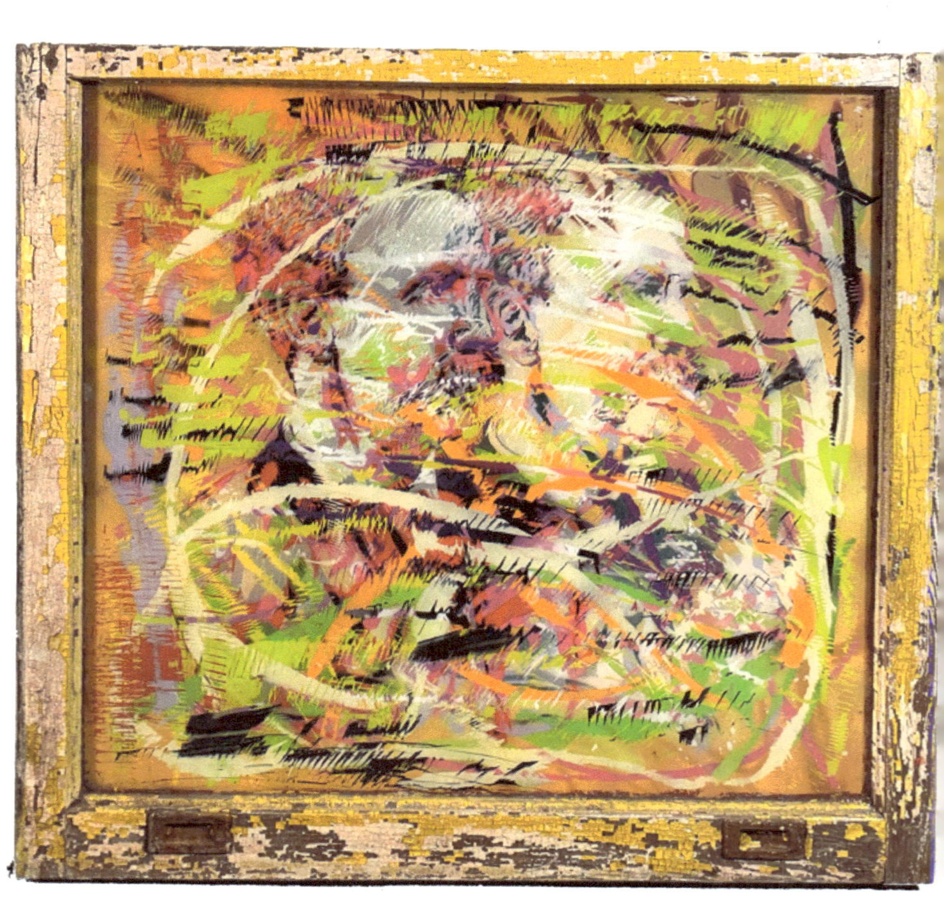

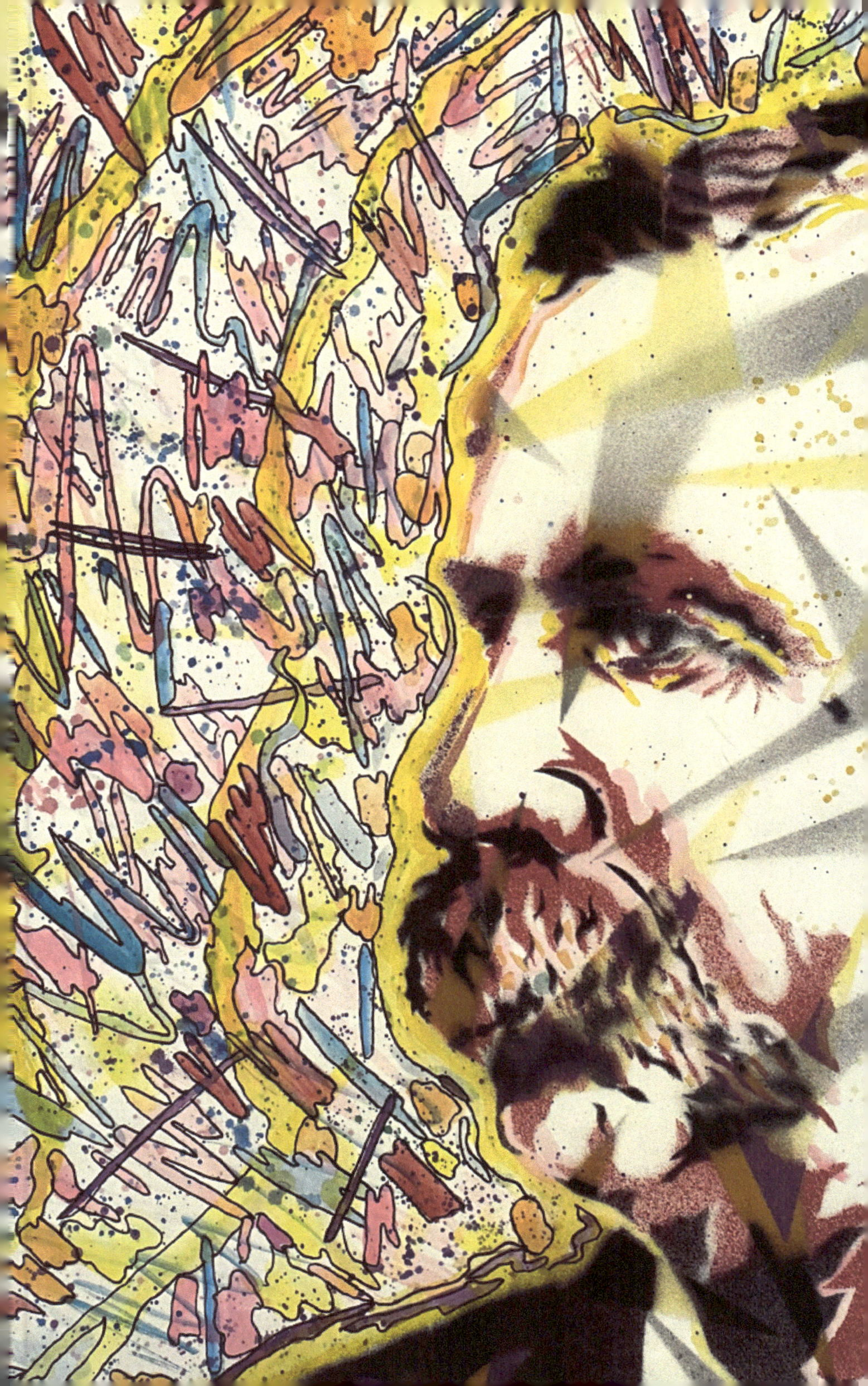

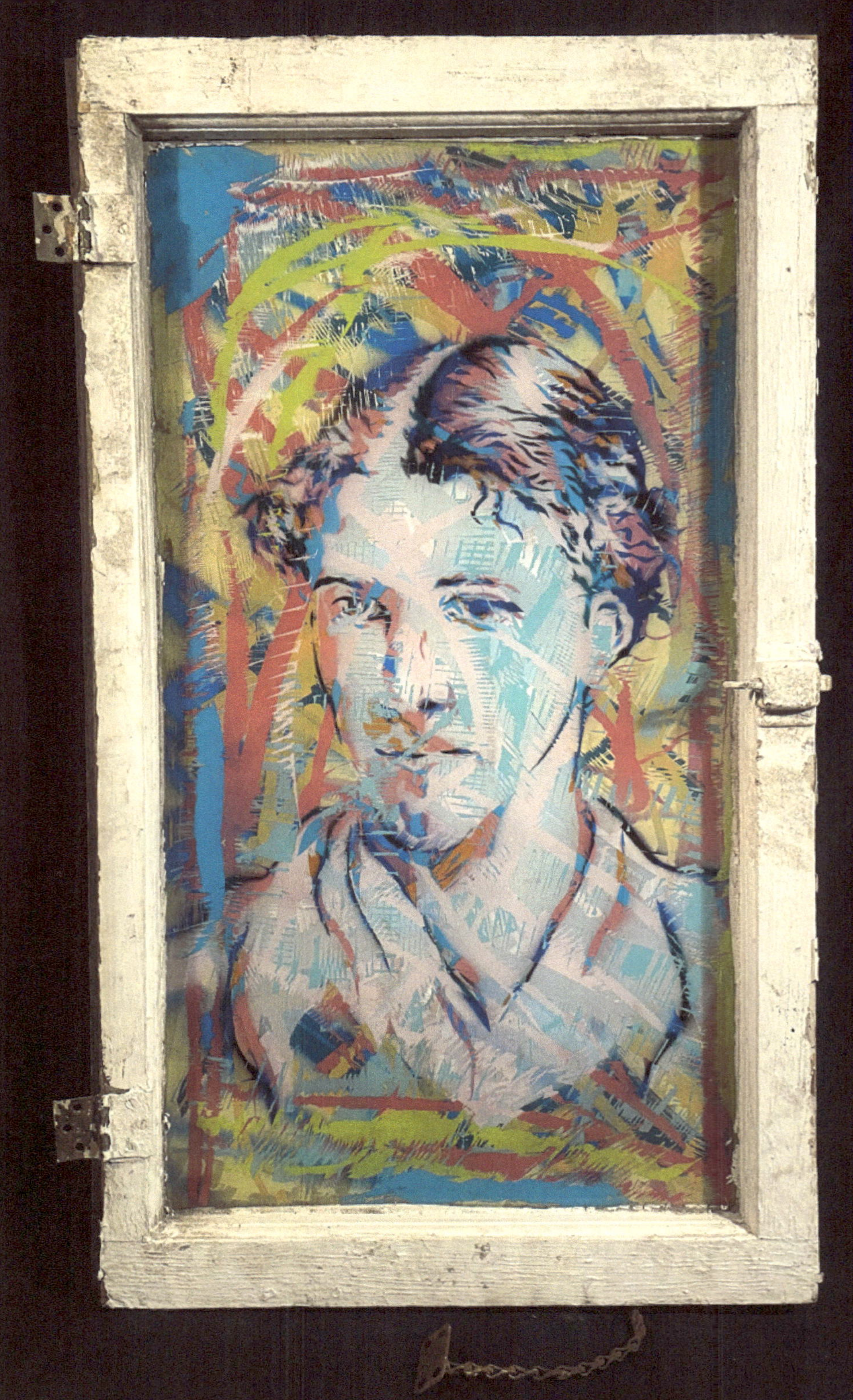

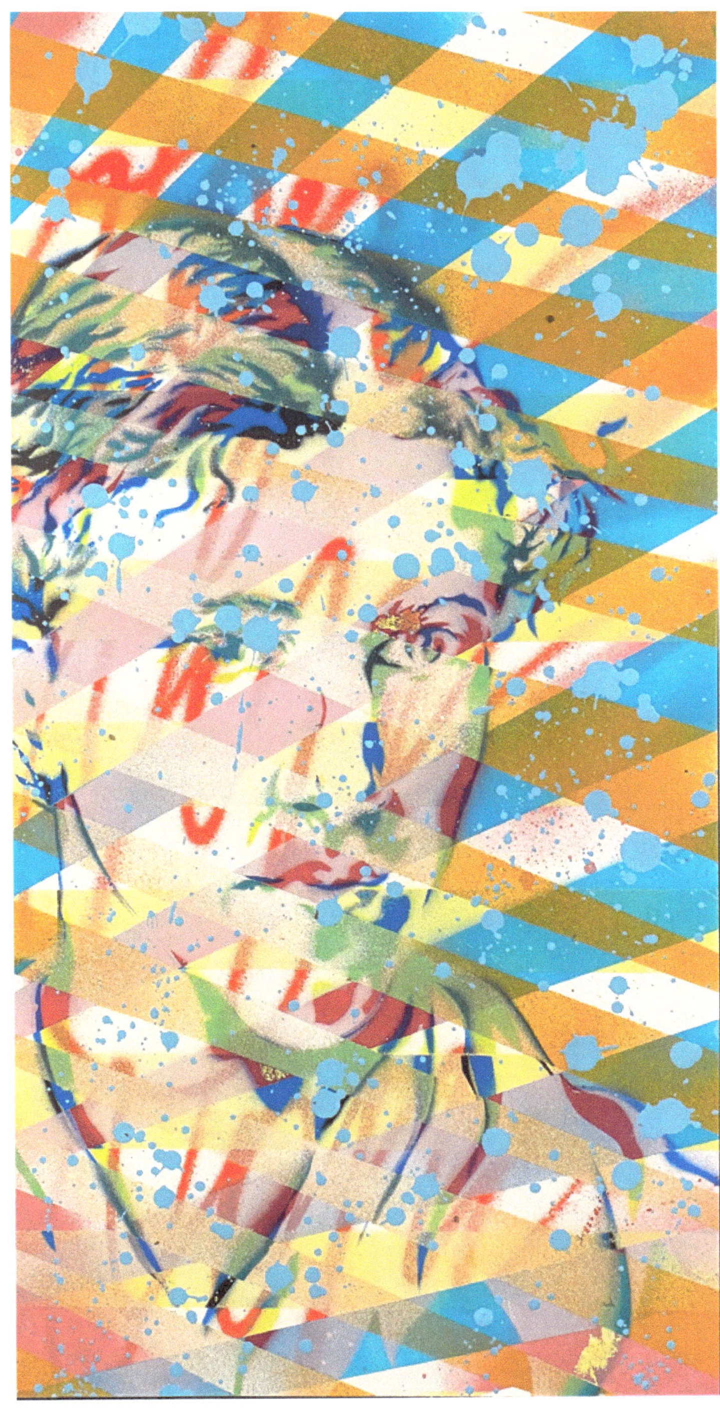

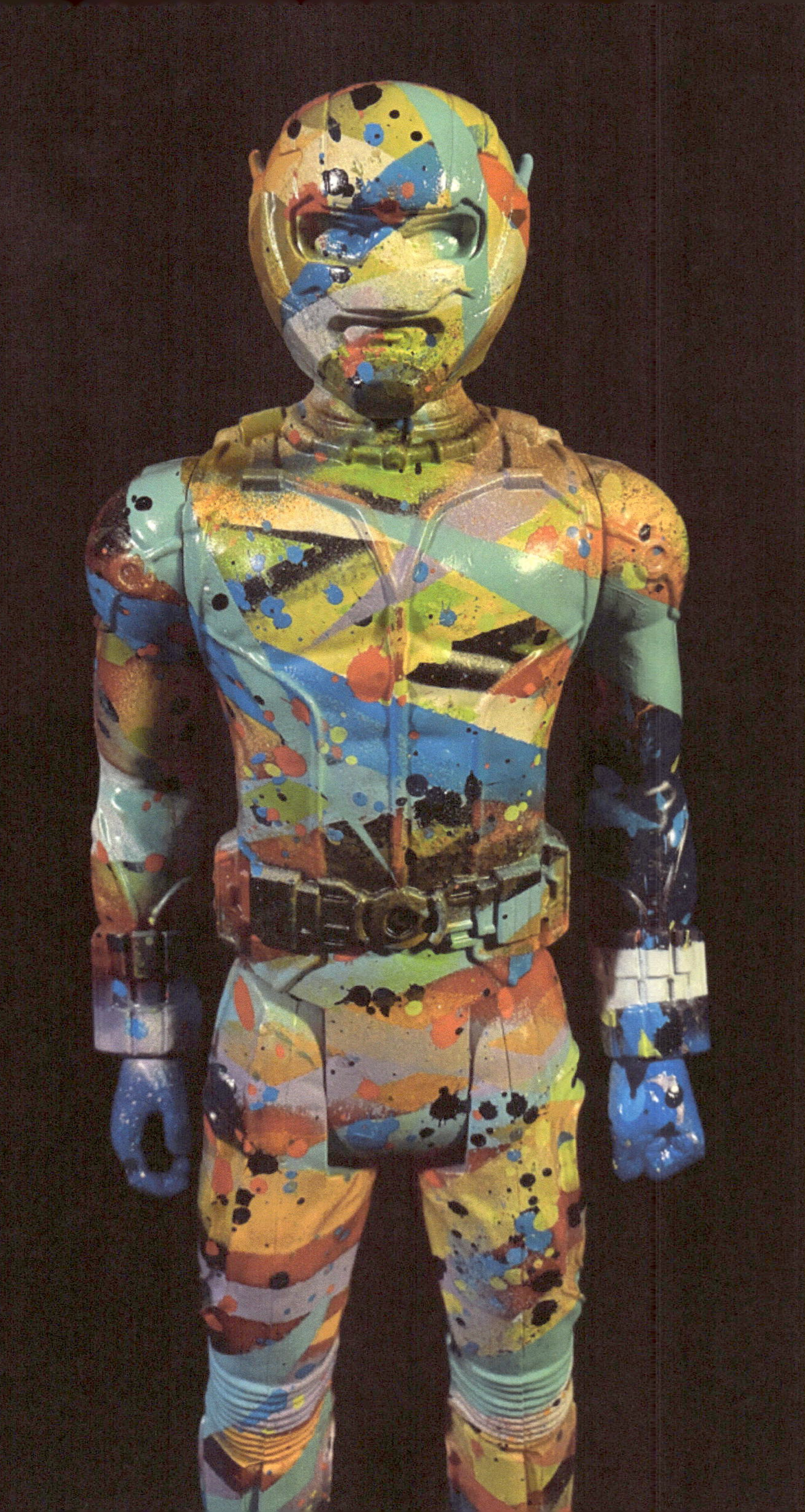

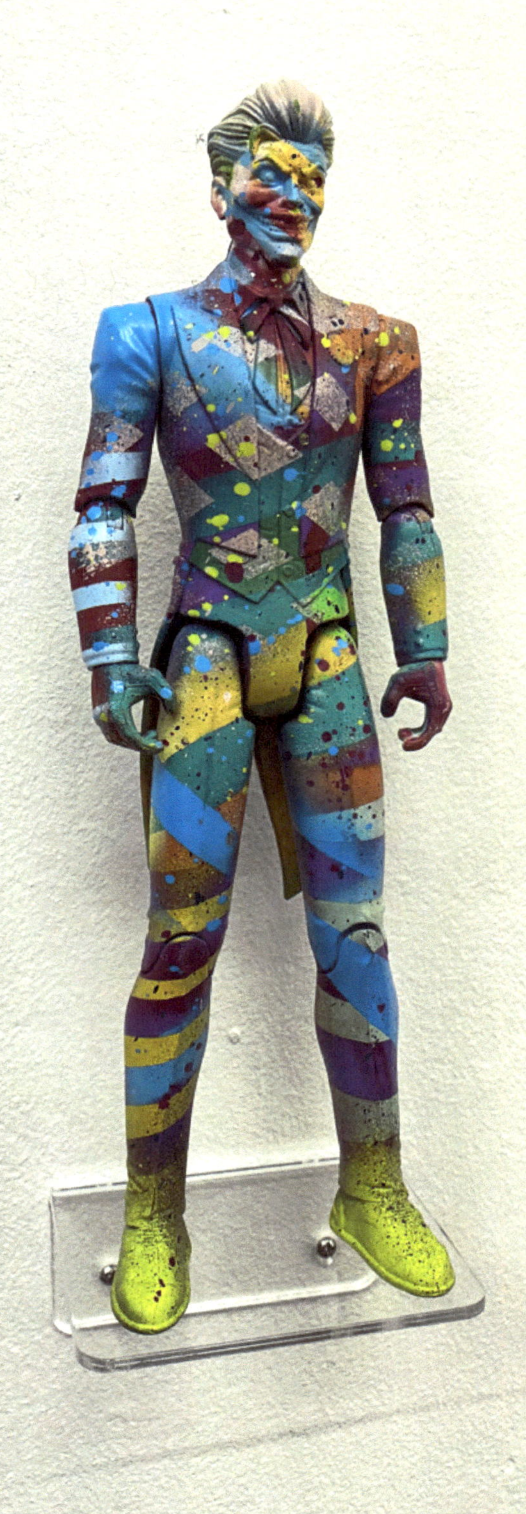

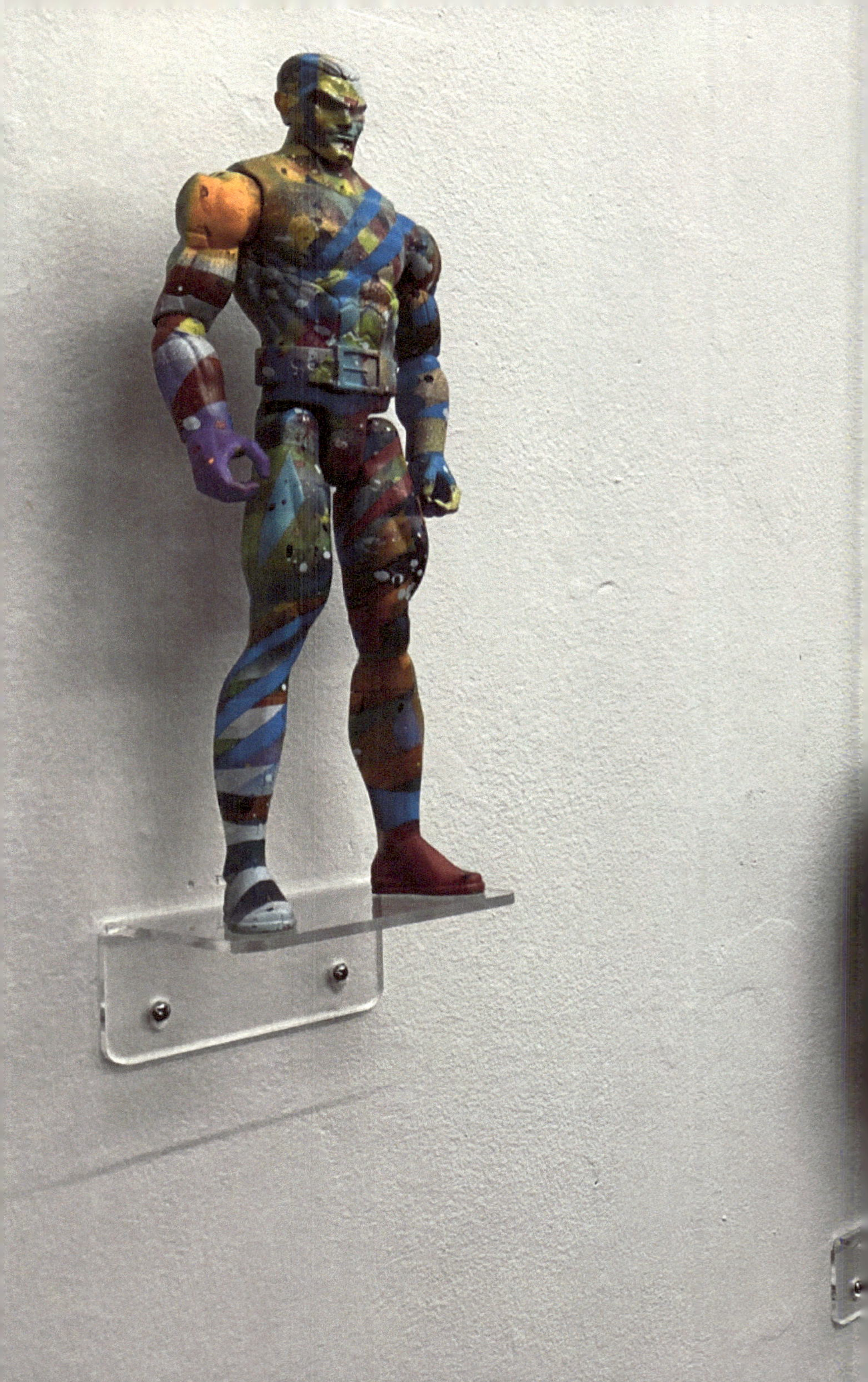

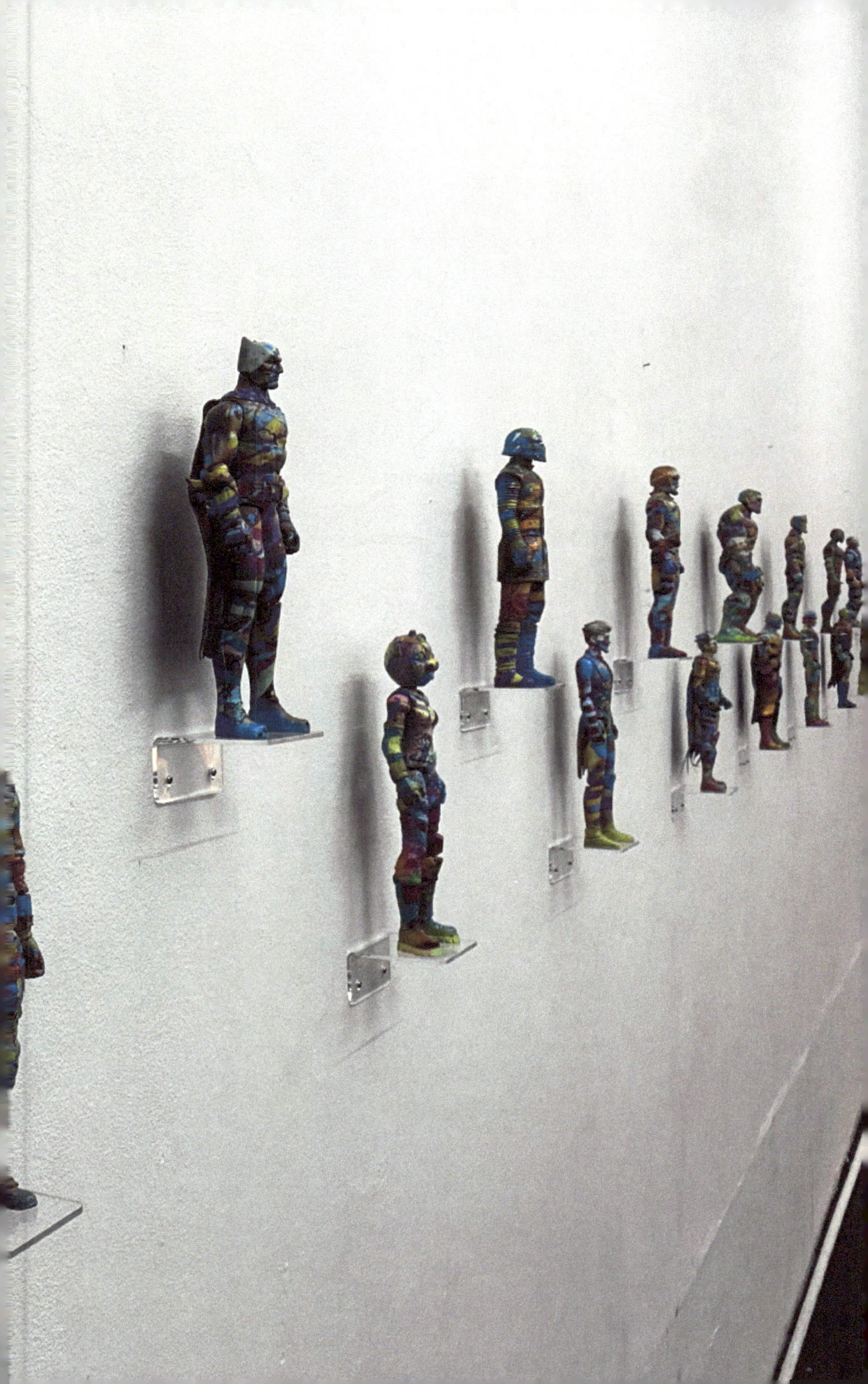

ACTION FIGURES

The body of work for *Time Again* was already well on its way as 2025 approached. After hearing the election results in the United States, at least half of the world was in mourning: how could this be happening again?

Almost immediately, the new administration started putting plans in motion to dismantle and disrupt. These actions are meant to do real damage to our system and take the wind out of our sails. They are designed to make us feel hopeless and I am in no way immune from this.

But as all this chaos was being rolled out for us to consume on our screens, I made a commitment to my own education. I'm going to keep reading and I'm going to keep painting. After all, this is what I do. When I don't know what else to do, I can keep doing what I'm already doing, and perhaps embrace a more pointed focus and a stronger sense of conviction in what I'm saying with my work. Look at what these people did in times of struggle. We should be taking notes.

The idea of *Time Again* as a show and a book came about while planning my second ever museum show at the Waterloo Center for the Arts in Waterloo, Iowa. The timing was right and I realized I was amassing quite a few of these pieces. During my first phone conversation with the curator, he mentioned there was a glass display case. I had put on a gallery show in September 2024 called *Imaginary Friends*, which had featured painted 12" action figures. Comics, toys and superheroes had and still have a huge influence on me. I like to experiment with the size of the pieces I'm making and the objects that I'm painting on, and this body of work had been a test for how to shrink my process down.

While I initially told him that these pieces didn't quite fit the theme—I wanted *Time Again* to be about real people, real heroes—I got a text from my friend Paul Garner just a few hours after that conversation: "What if I made some of my 3D-printed figures bigger so that you could do your thing on them?" Almost all of Paul's work is political, so I was already familiar with the figures he was talking about. We had already worked with some of the same people, but some of Paul's figures were also new to me.

The timing of that conversation could not have been more synchronistic. Another part of the show was being created, seemingly out of the ether. As it turns out, I didn't realize how powerful *Time Again* would be until I started putting all of the pieces together.

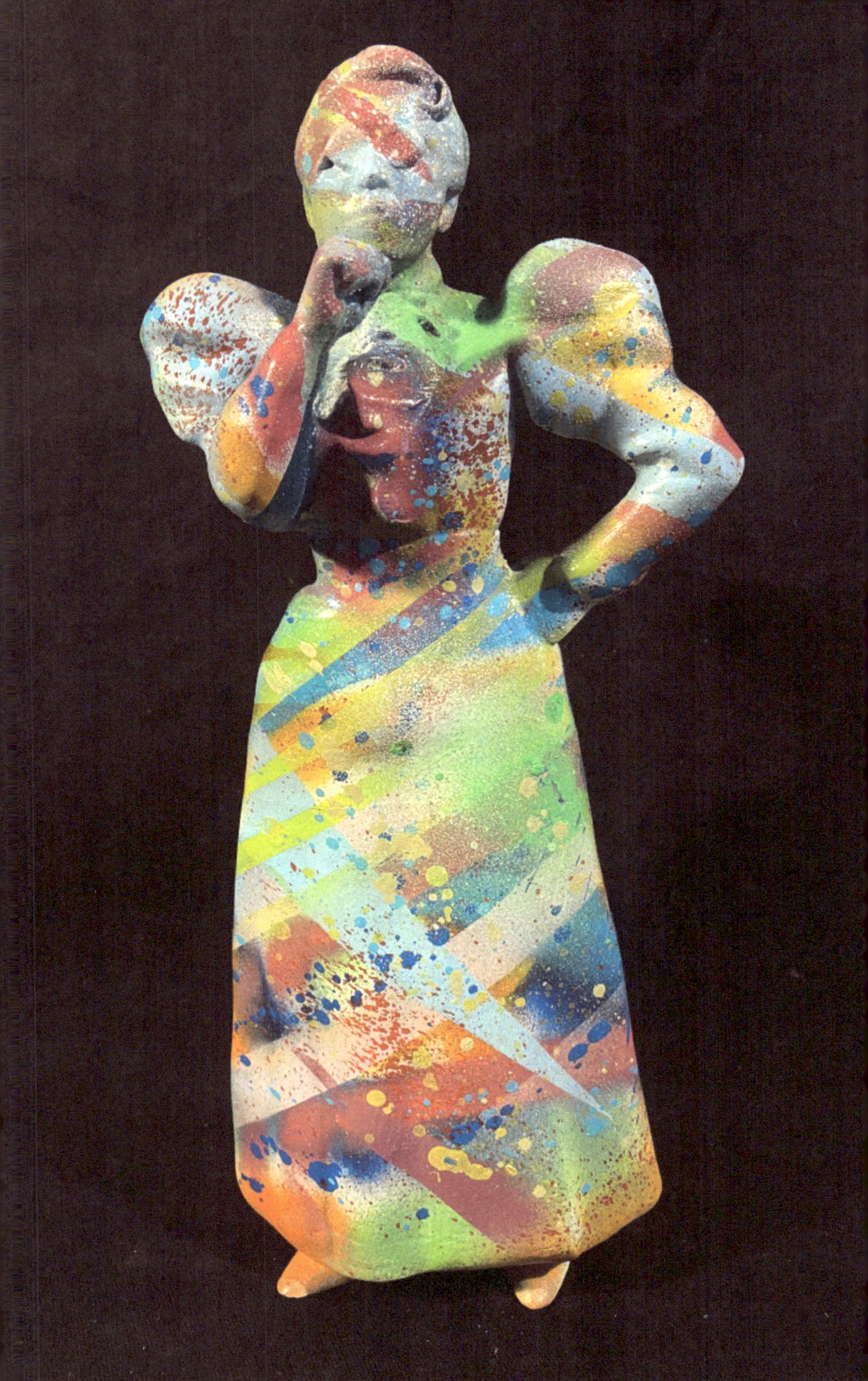

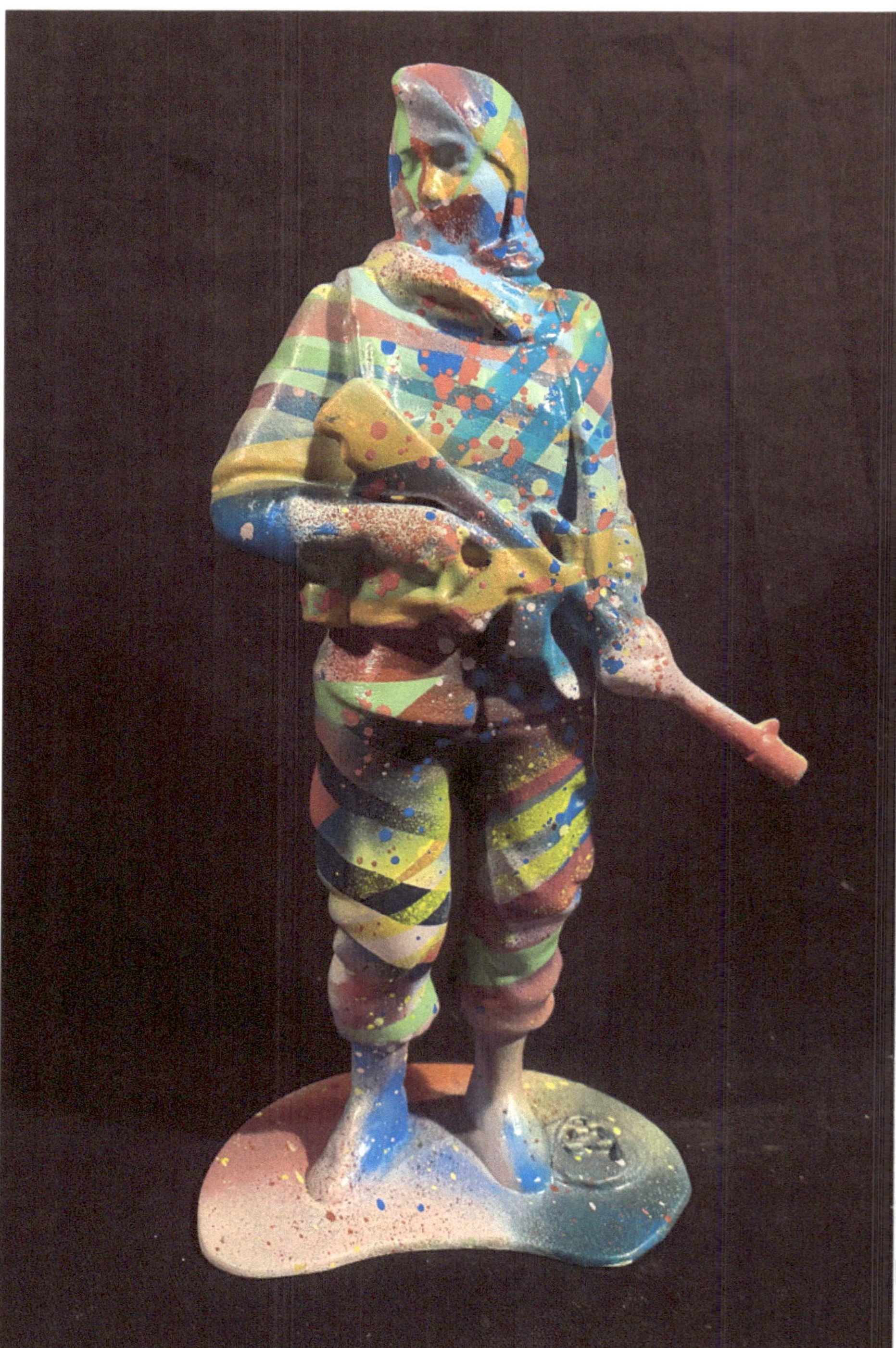

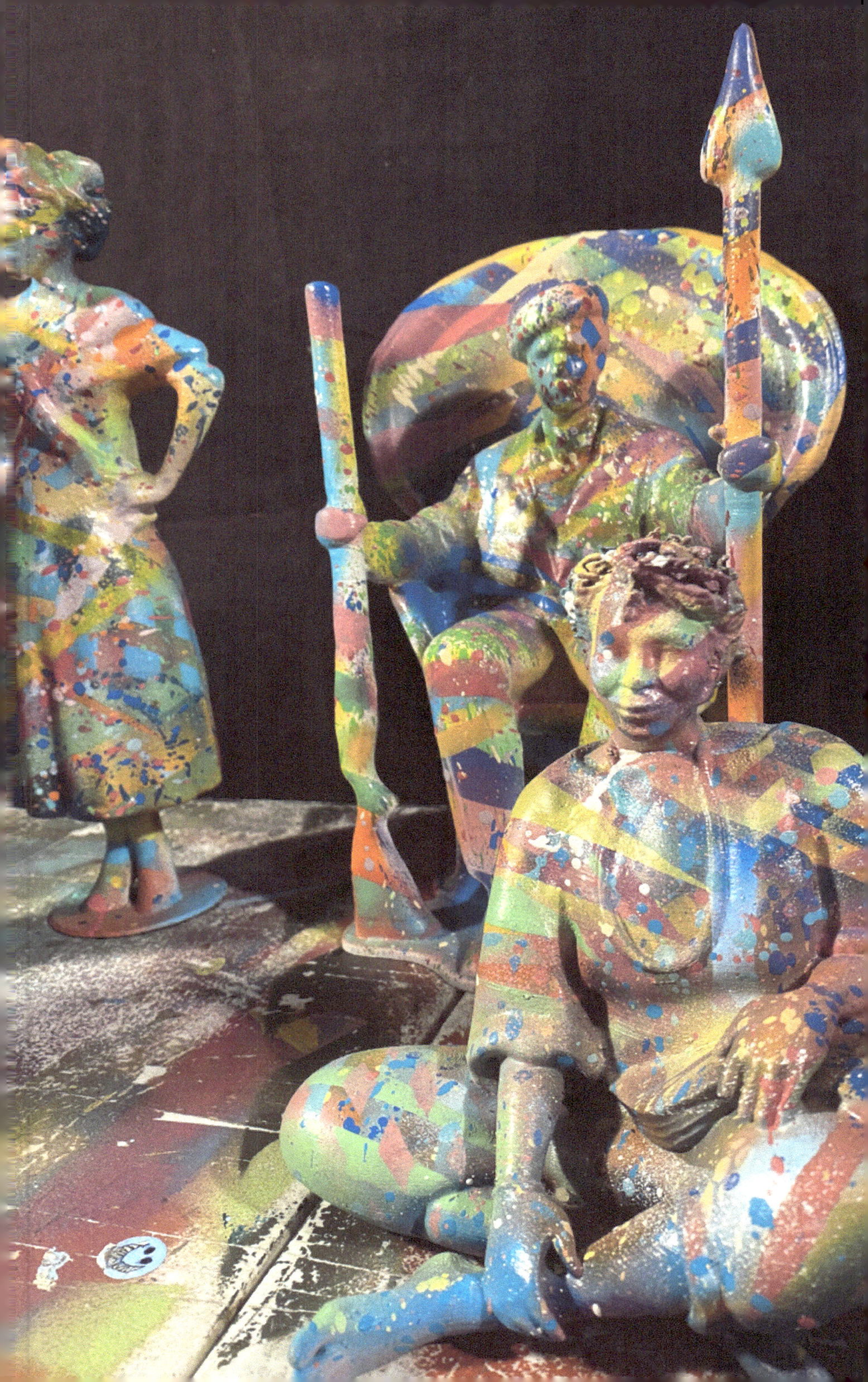

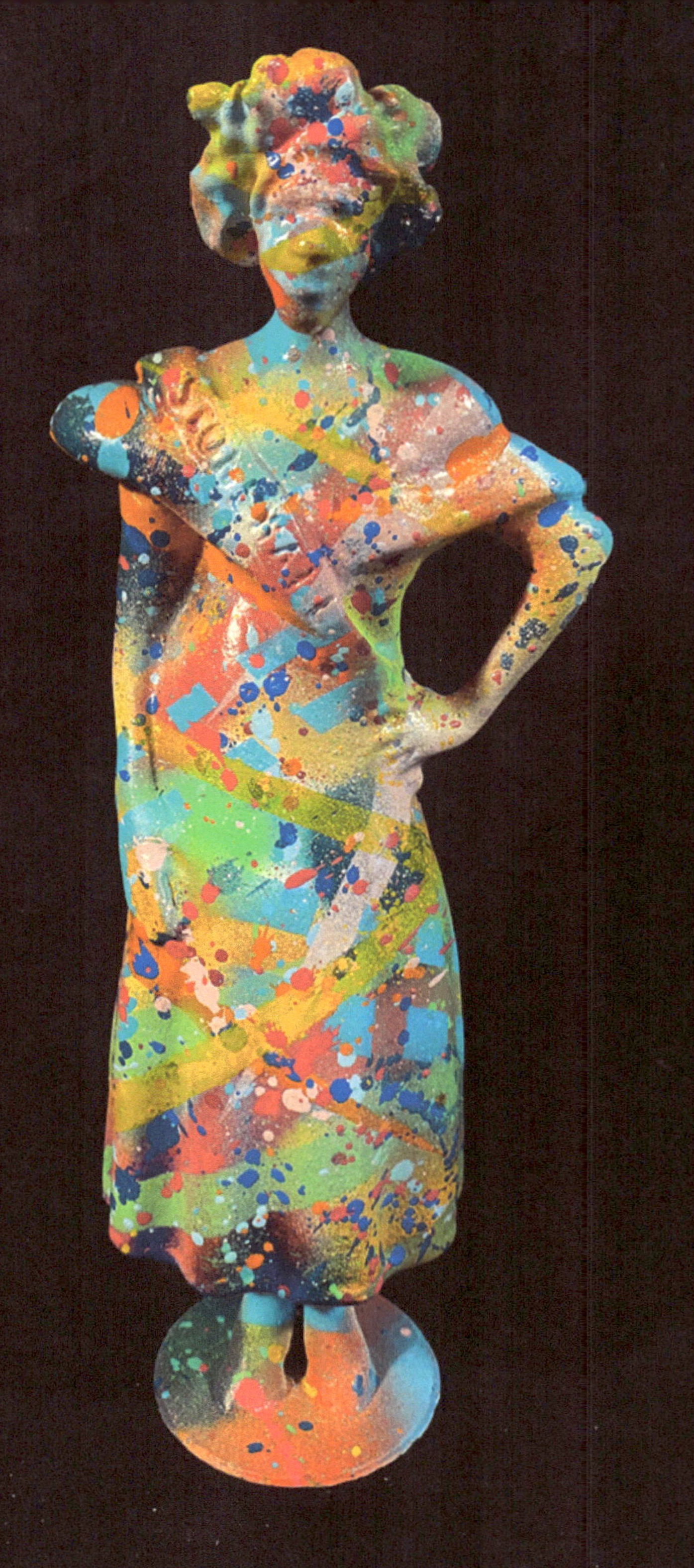

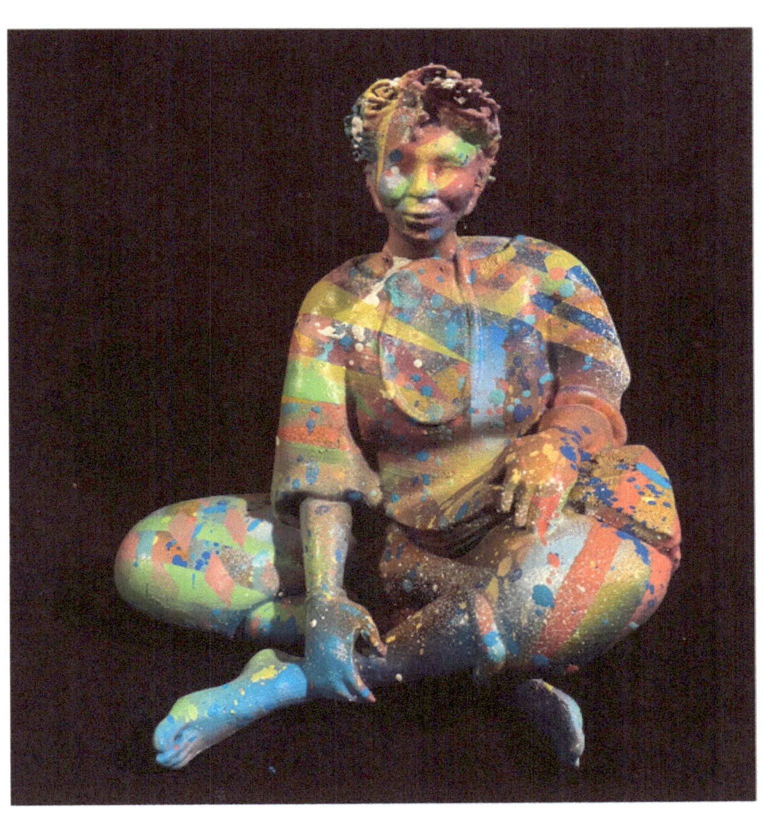

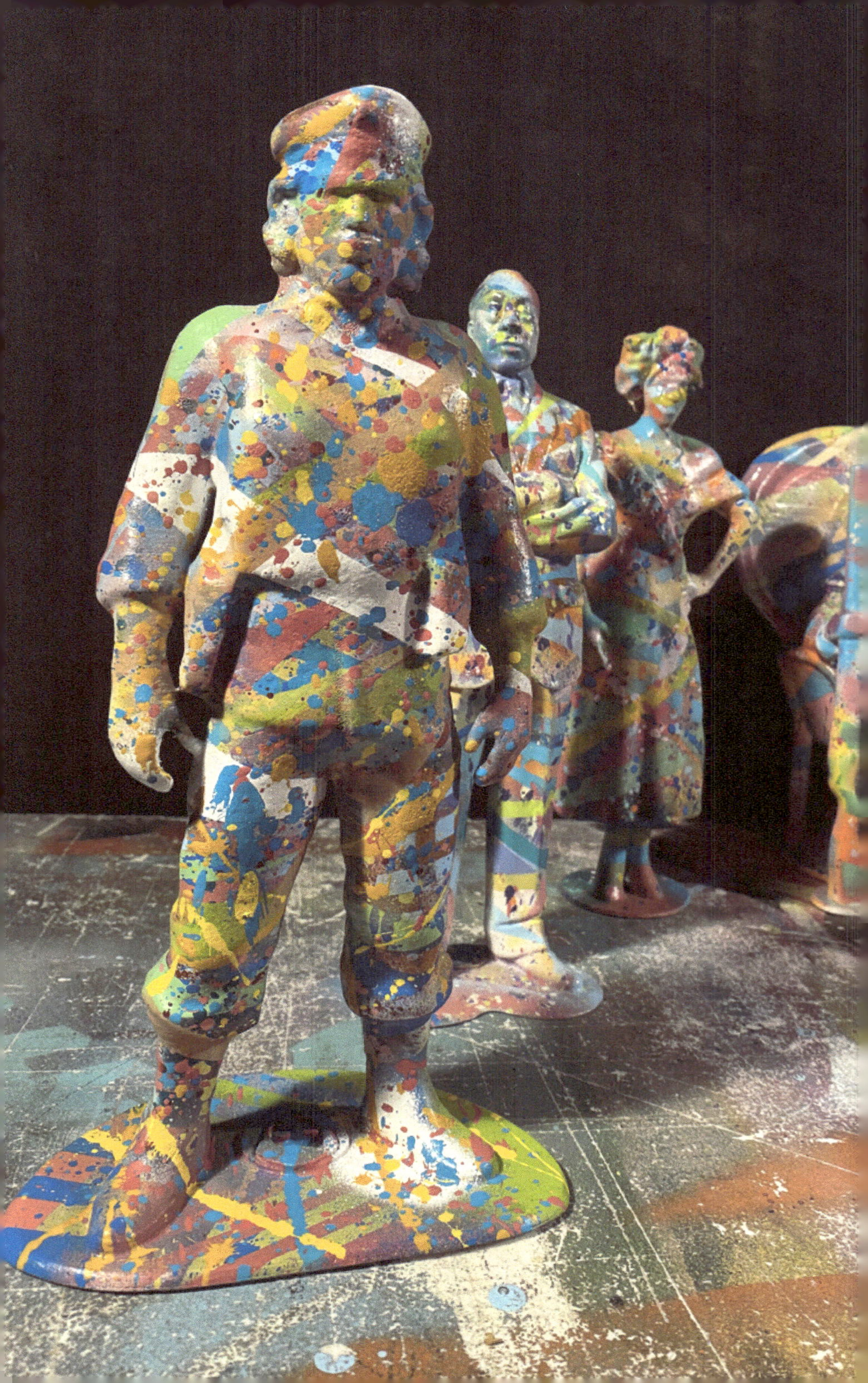

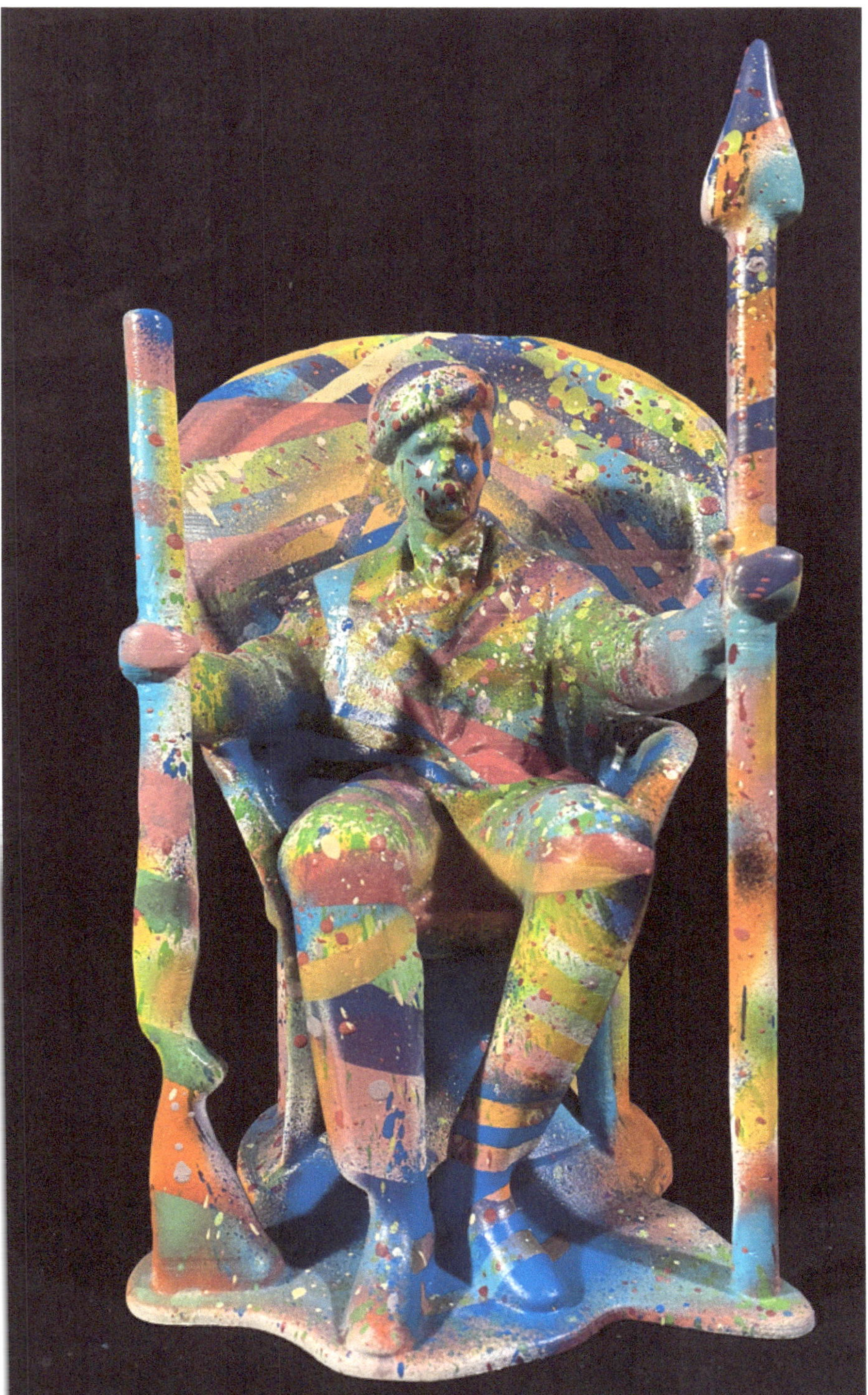

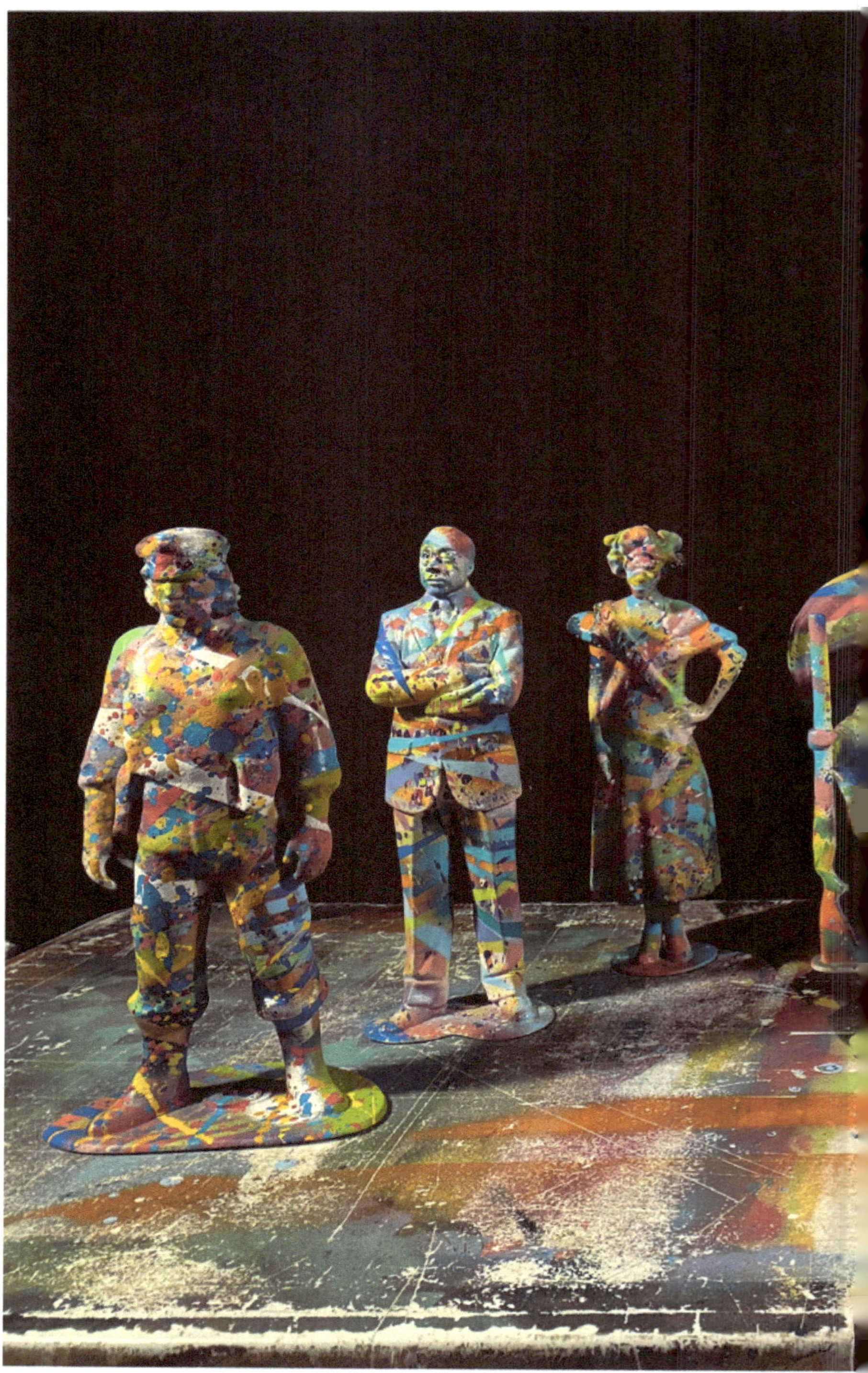

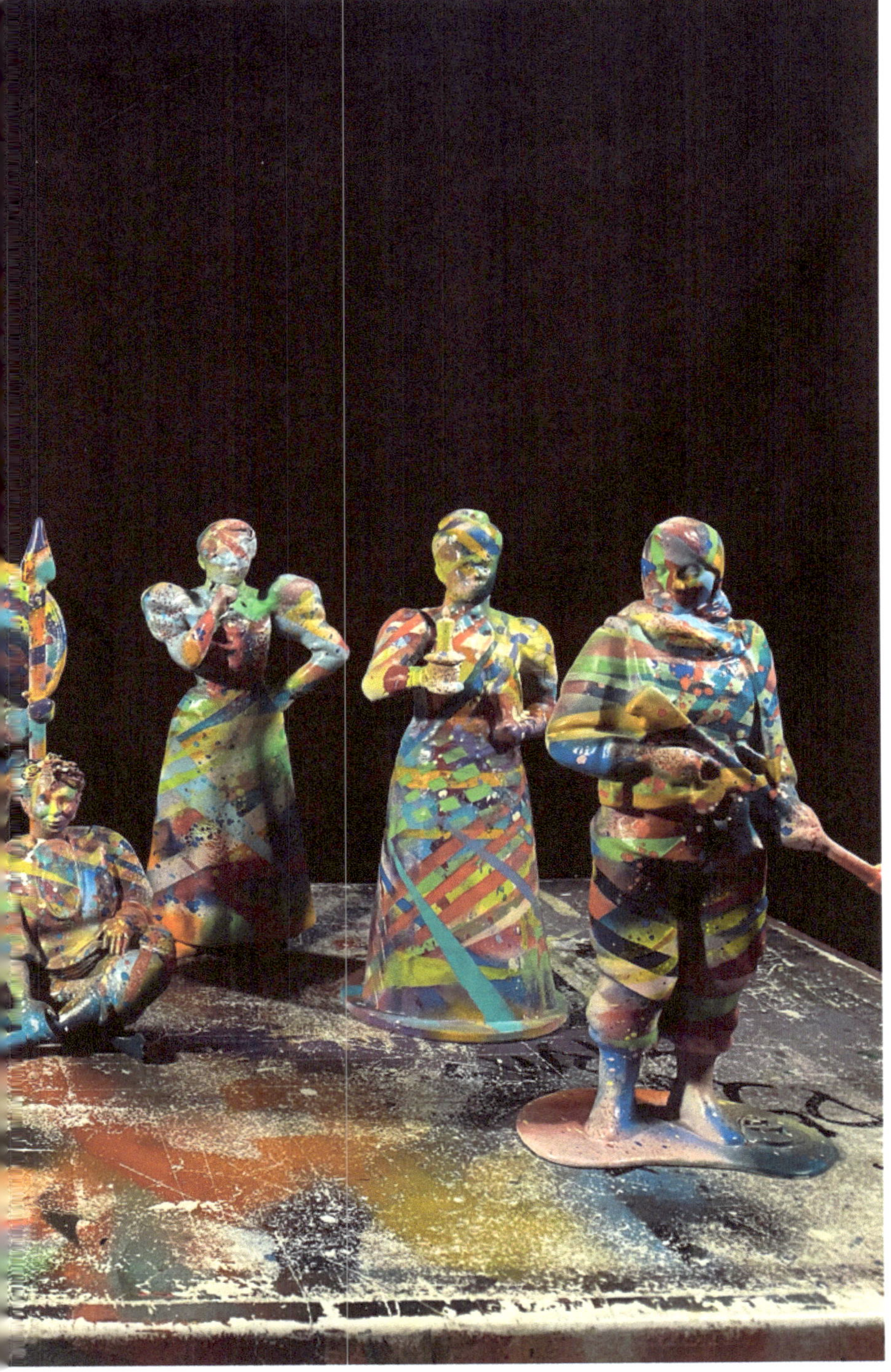

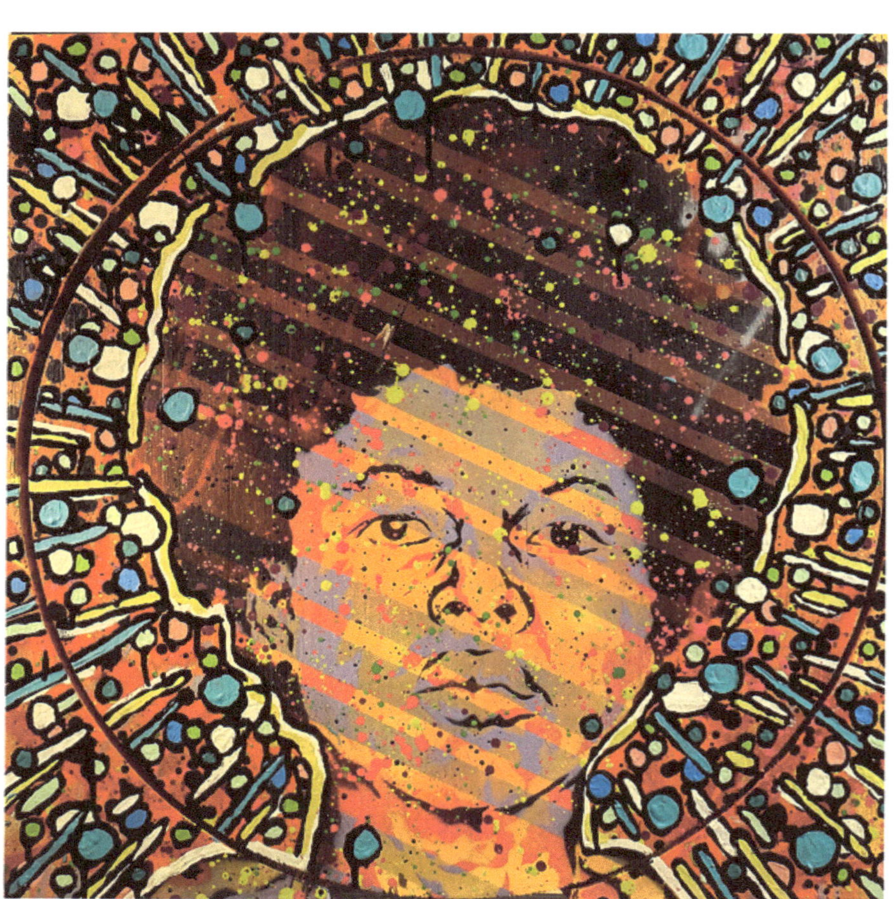

ASSATA SHAKUR - R/EVOLUTION

Somewhere in the spring of 2025, a new coworker joined our team. I had been bartending for a few months. On our first interaction I was terrified to learn that her first name was the same as my most recent X. I had gone through a terrible breakup a year prior and was still recovering. Even hearing that name made me shrink. Aside from that initial wince she seemed cool.

She had a tattoo on her arm: r/evolution. It was in the same spot as my text tattoos, running down her forearm. What did that mean?

She told me that it came from a poem by Assata Shakur. I knew nothing about her, but I was excited to share my project idea with my new like-minded friend… and I was excited to look into Assata. My work for Time Again was already in full swing and another figure seemed to have just waltzed into my life.

In a true act of synchronicity, Paul had already been working with Assata and I read her biography straight away. Assata was involved with the Black Panther Party and later the Black Liberation Army. She was a poet, a revolutionary and an activist. She was a political prisoner in the United States who somehow escaped, living out the rest of her life in Cuba until her passing just a few months after I painted her.

The synchs kept coming as the work Paul and I did kept overlapping. He sent a figure of James Baldwin. Baldwin has been one of my heroes for years. In my reading I came across Ida B. Wells. Paul was also working with her image.

My new coworker would eventually end up going to jail for helping someone, who she thought was innocent, escape from custody. I don't know all of the details, but I have a lot of respect for her for standing up for what she thought was right, and for accepting the consequences.

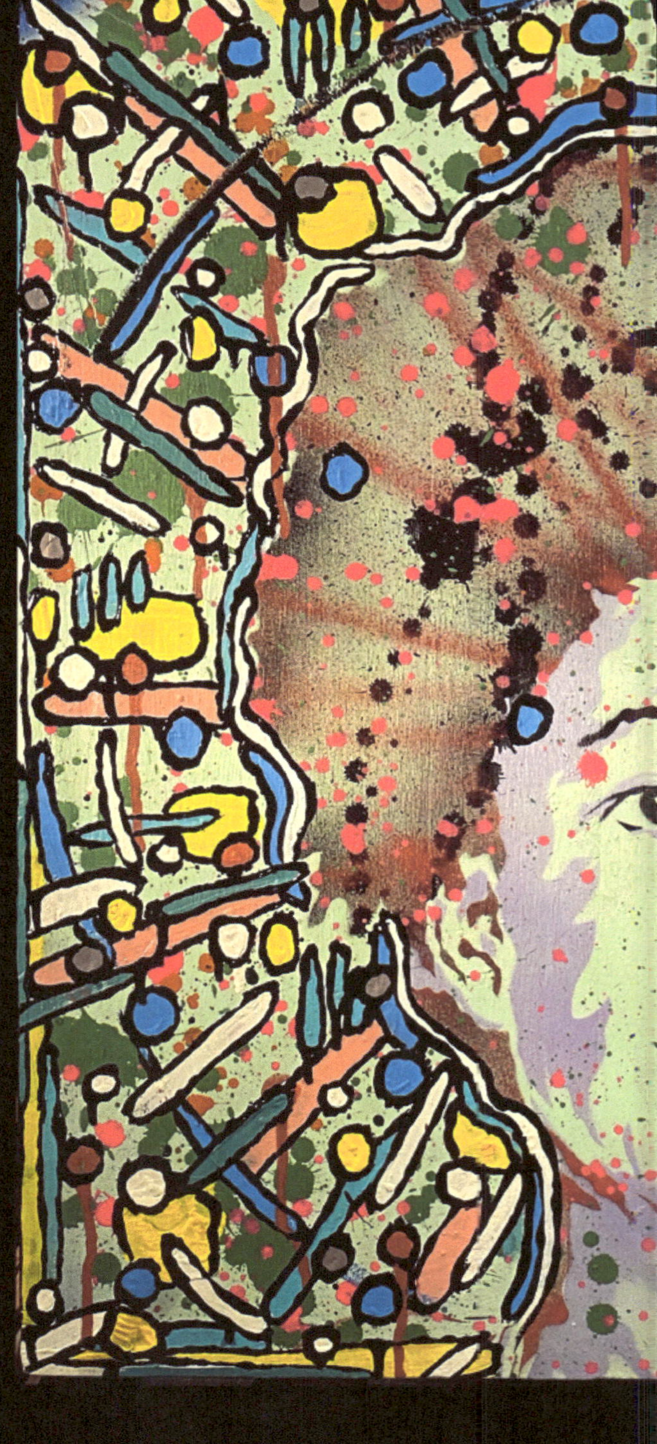

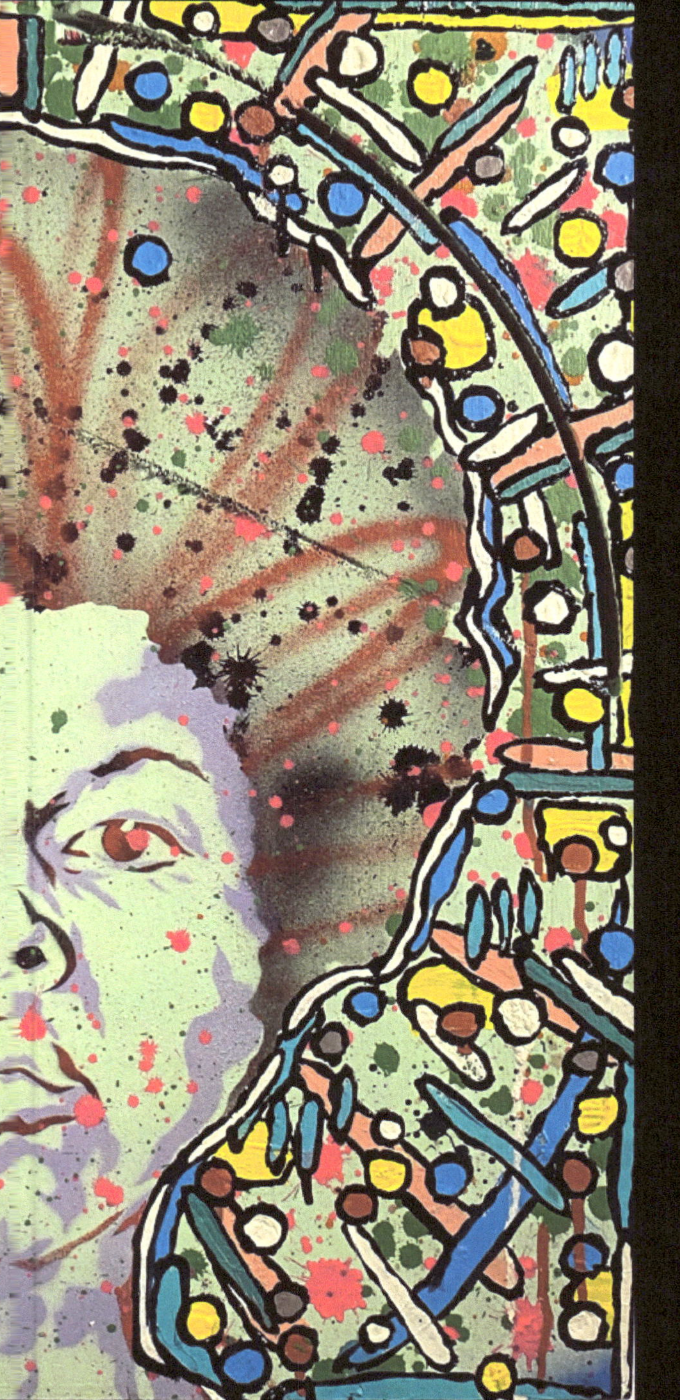

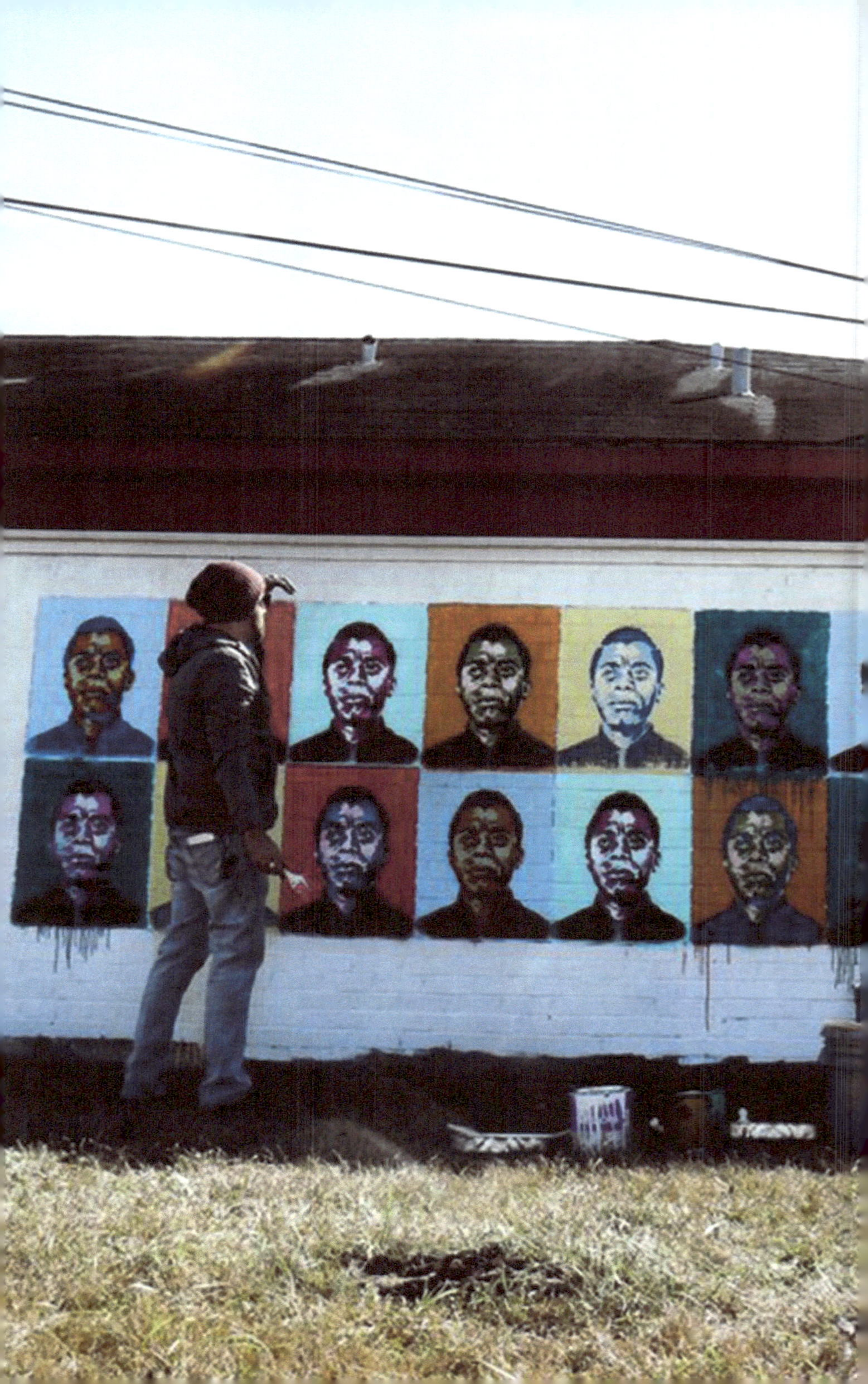

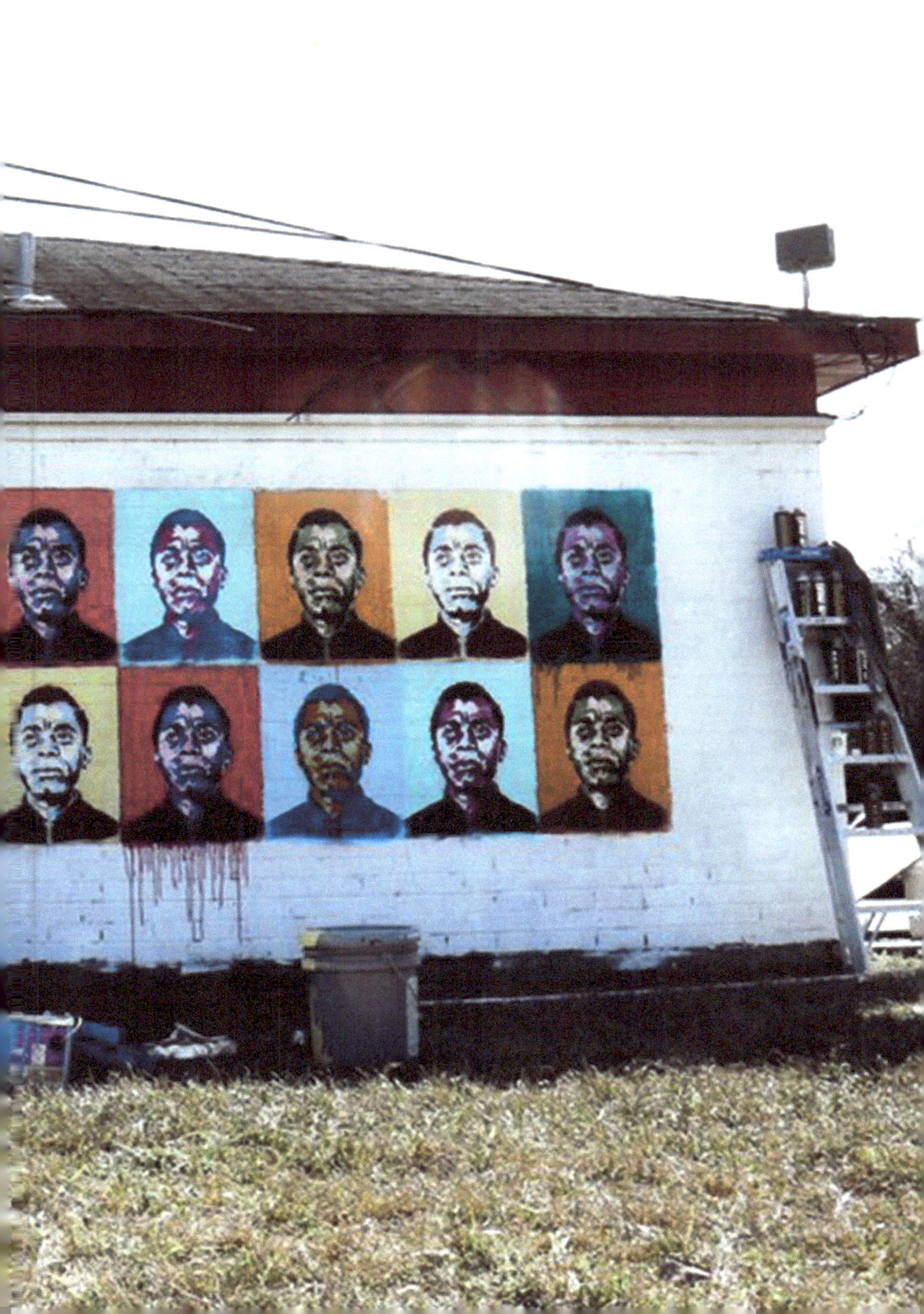

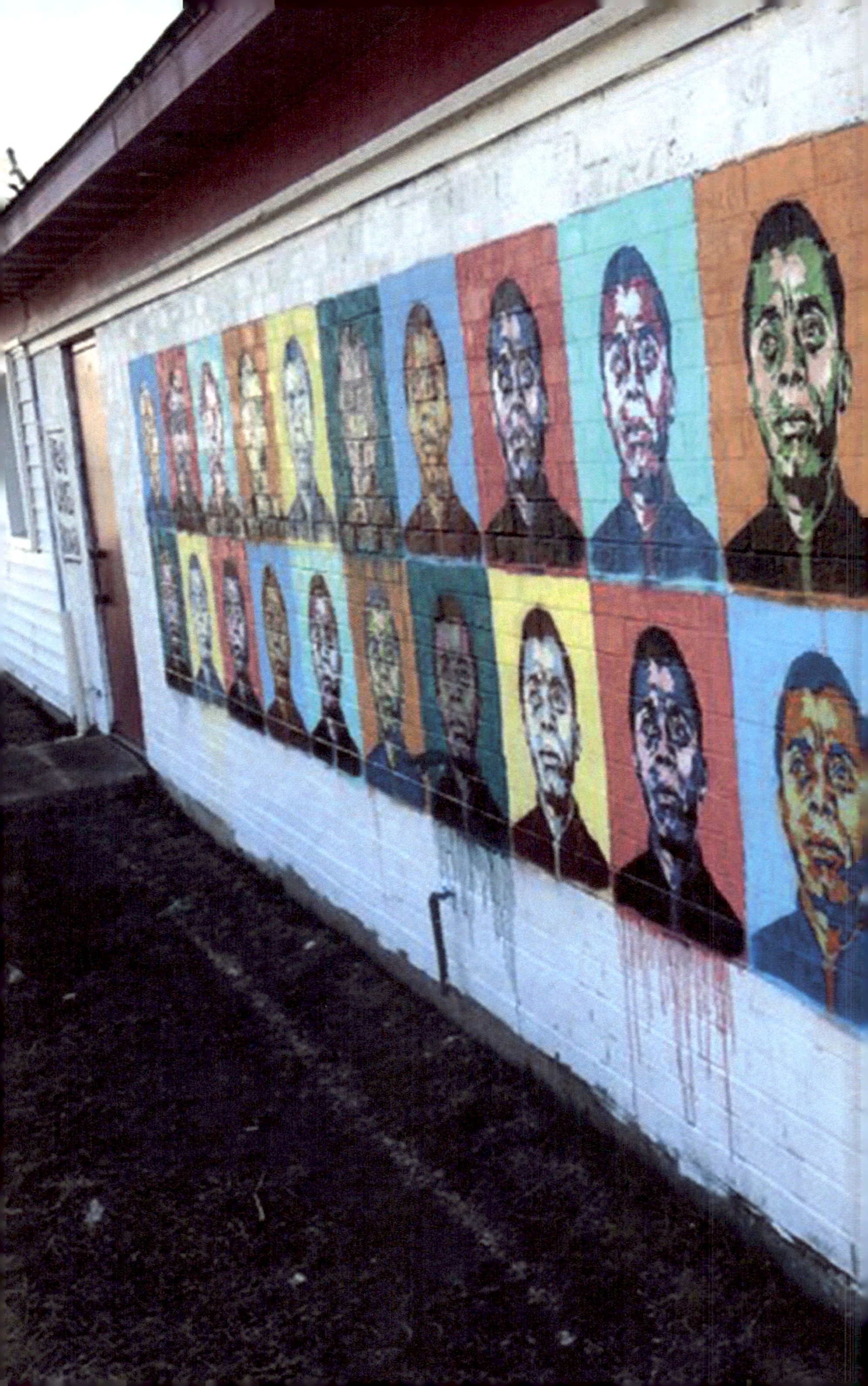

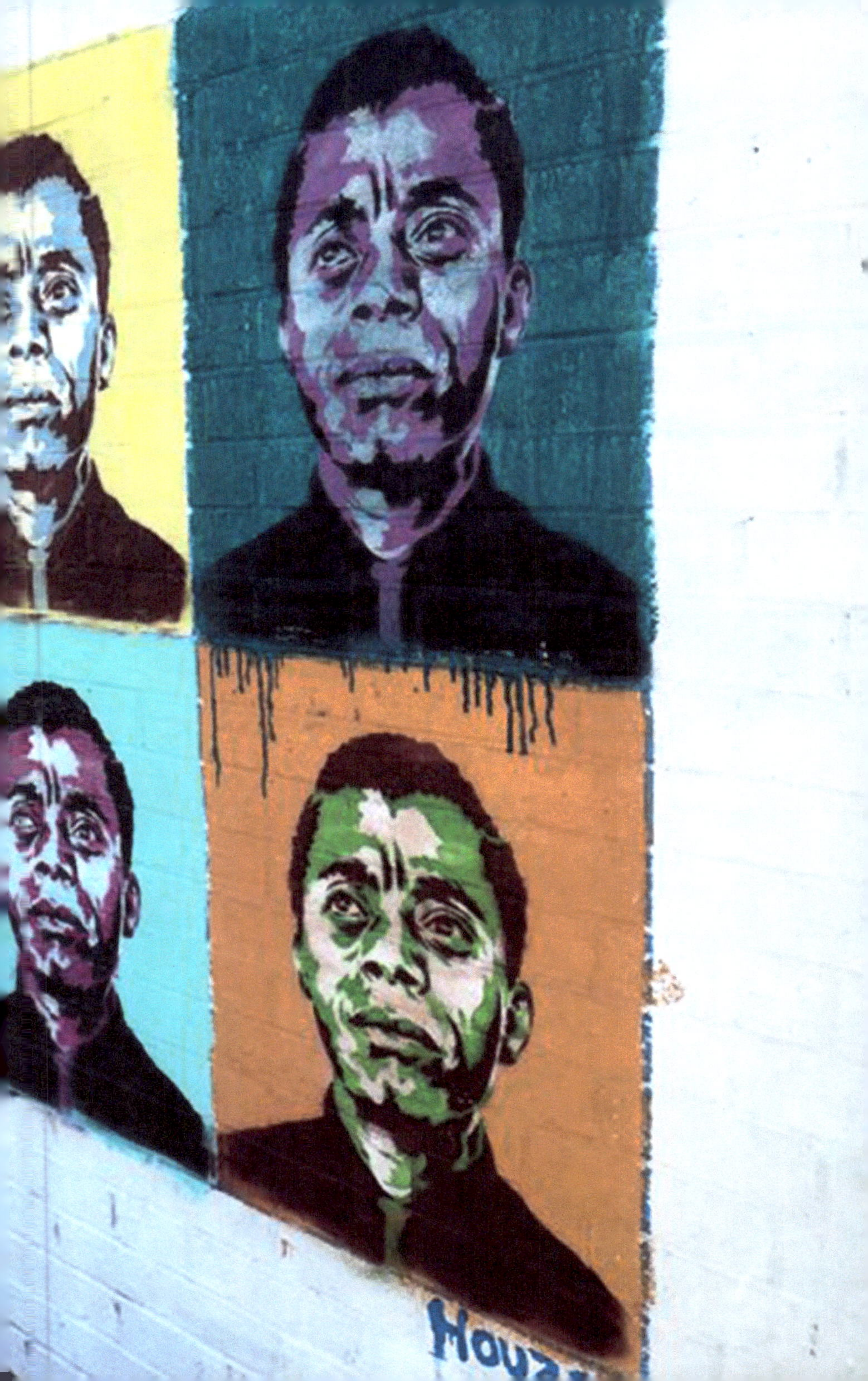

Hous

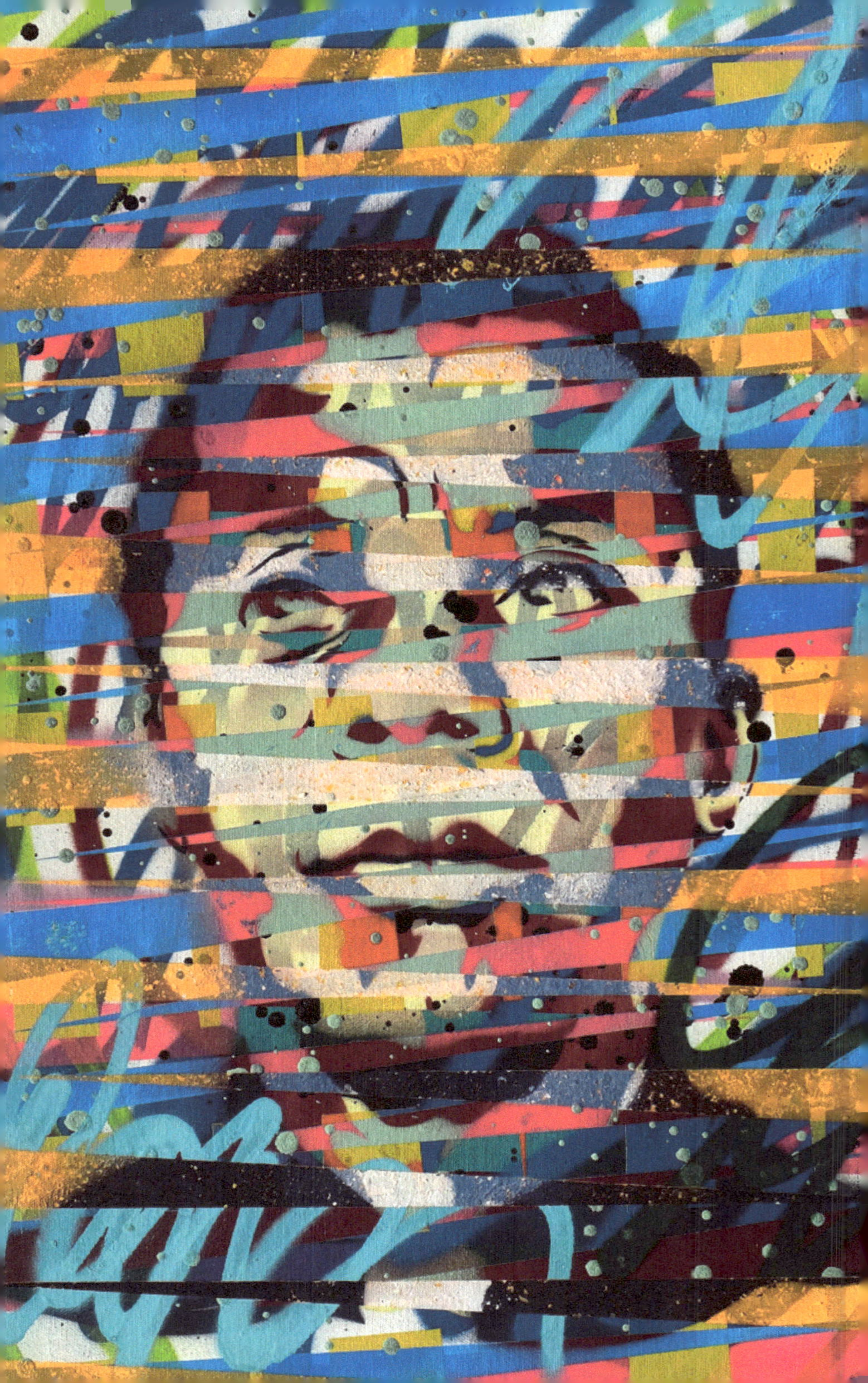

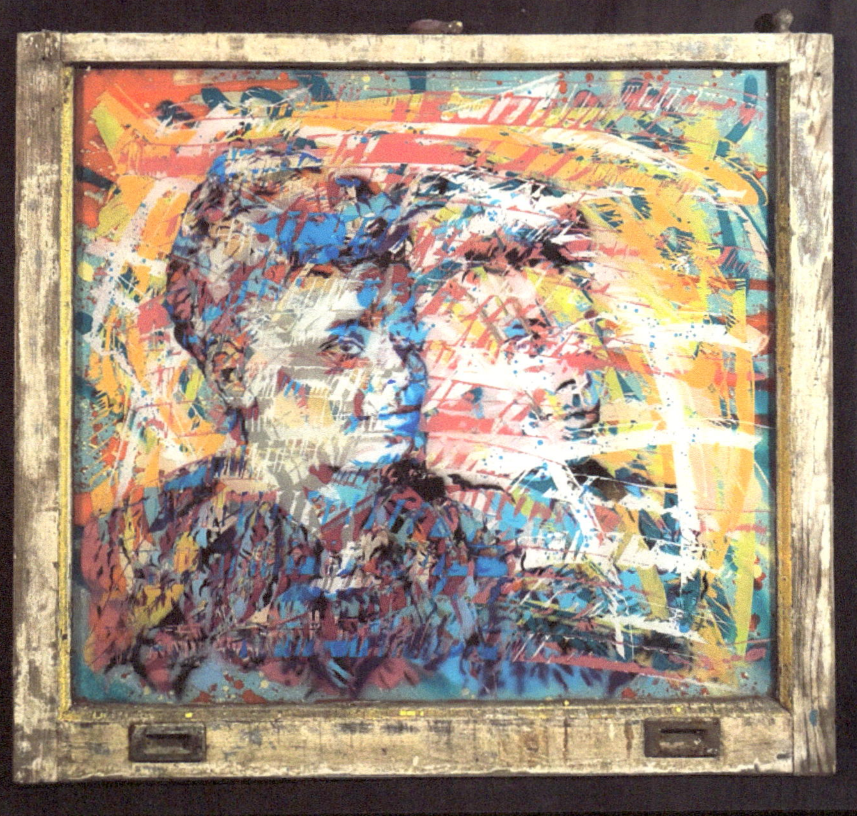

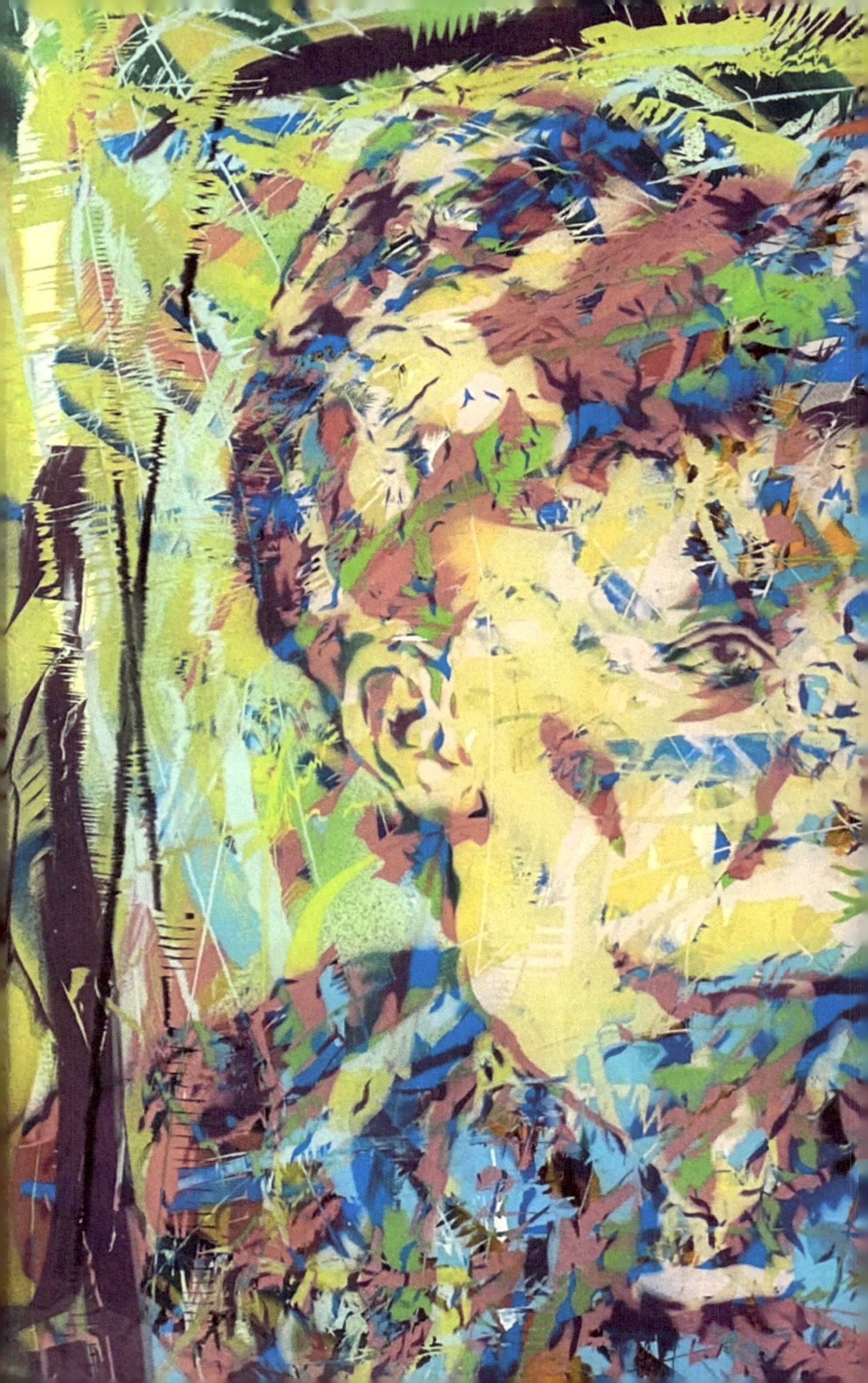

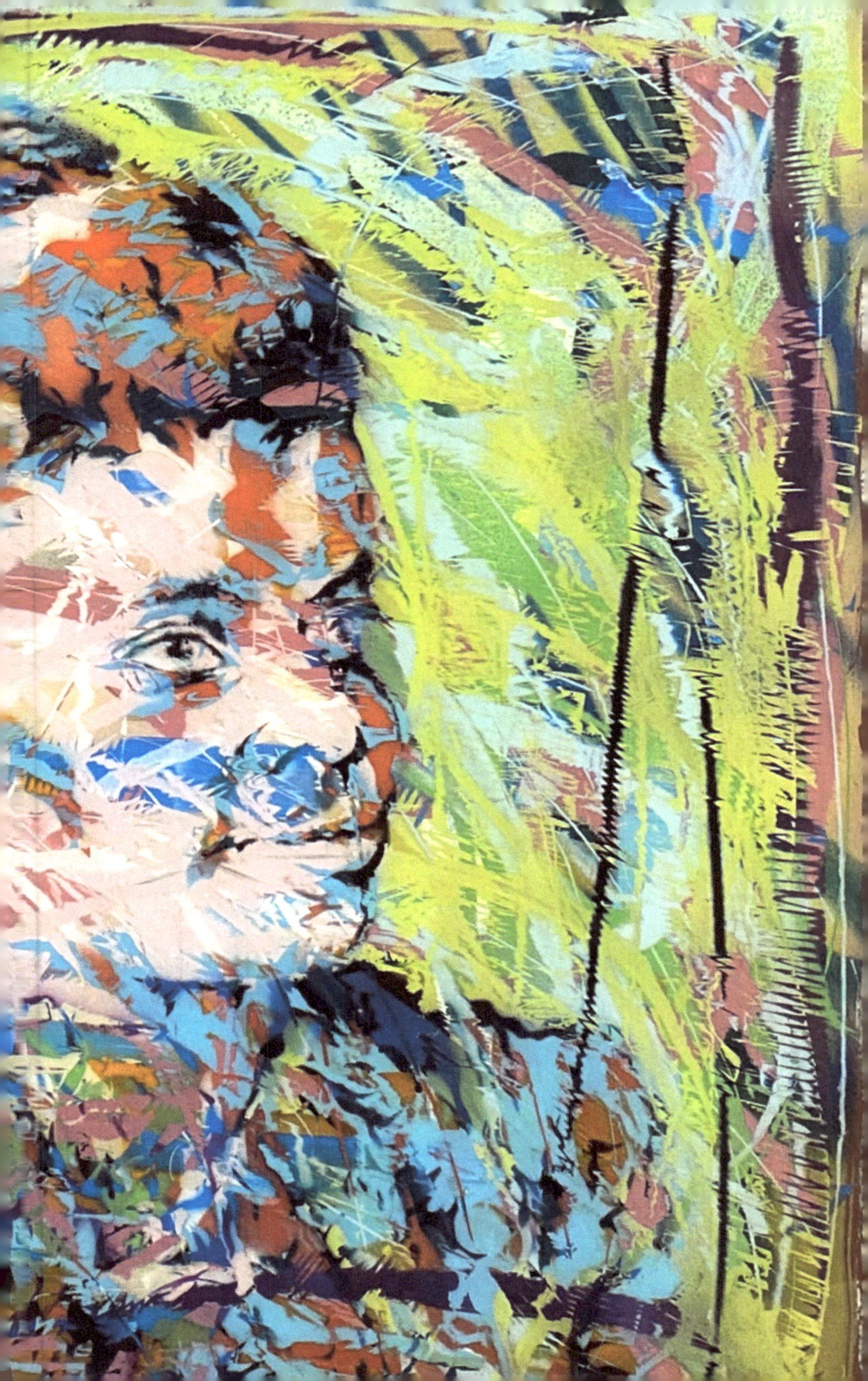

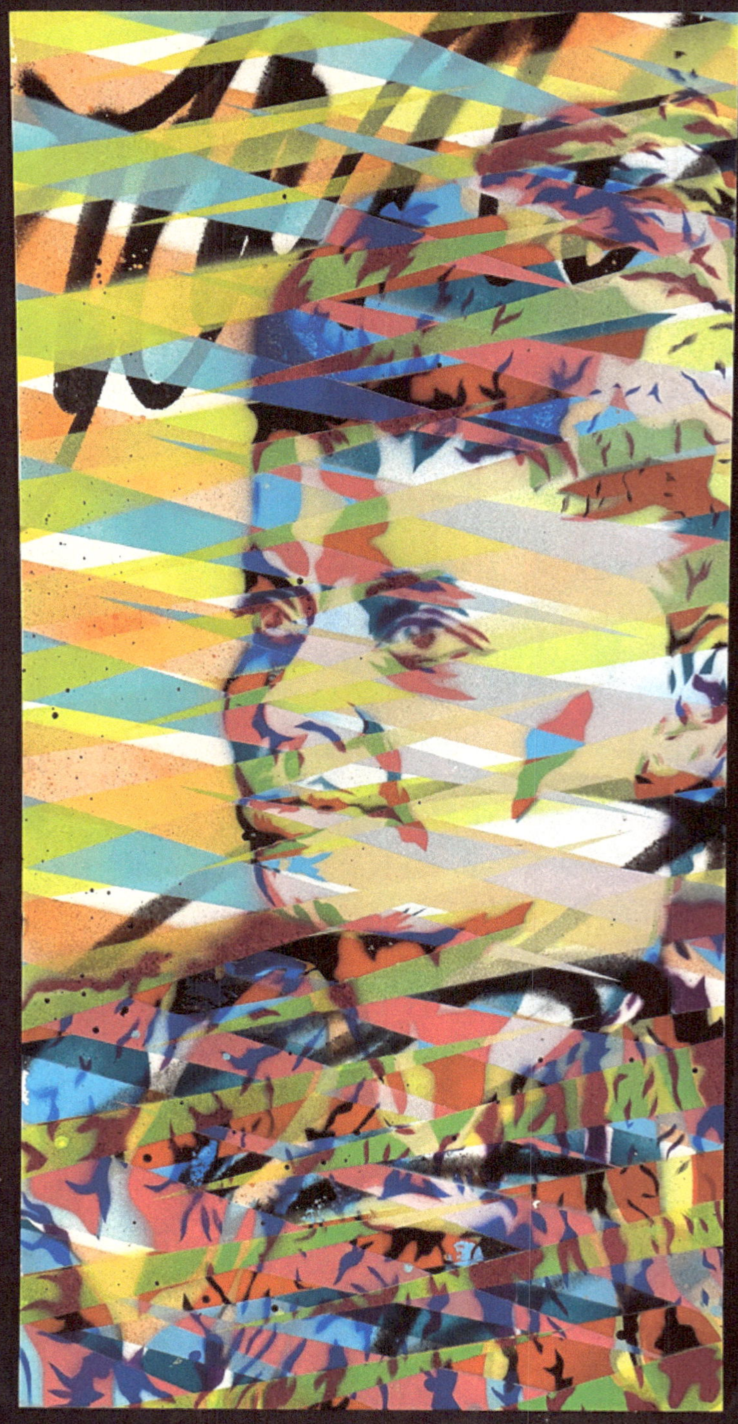

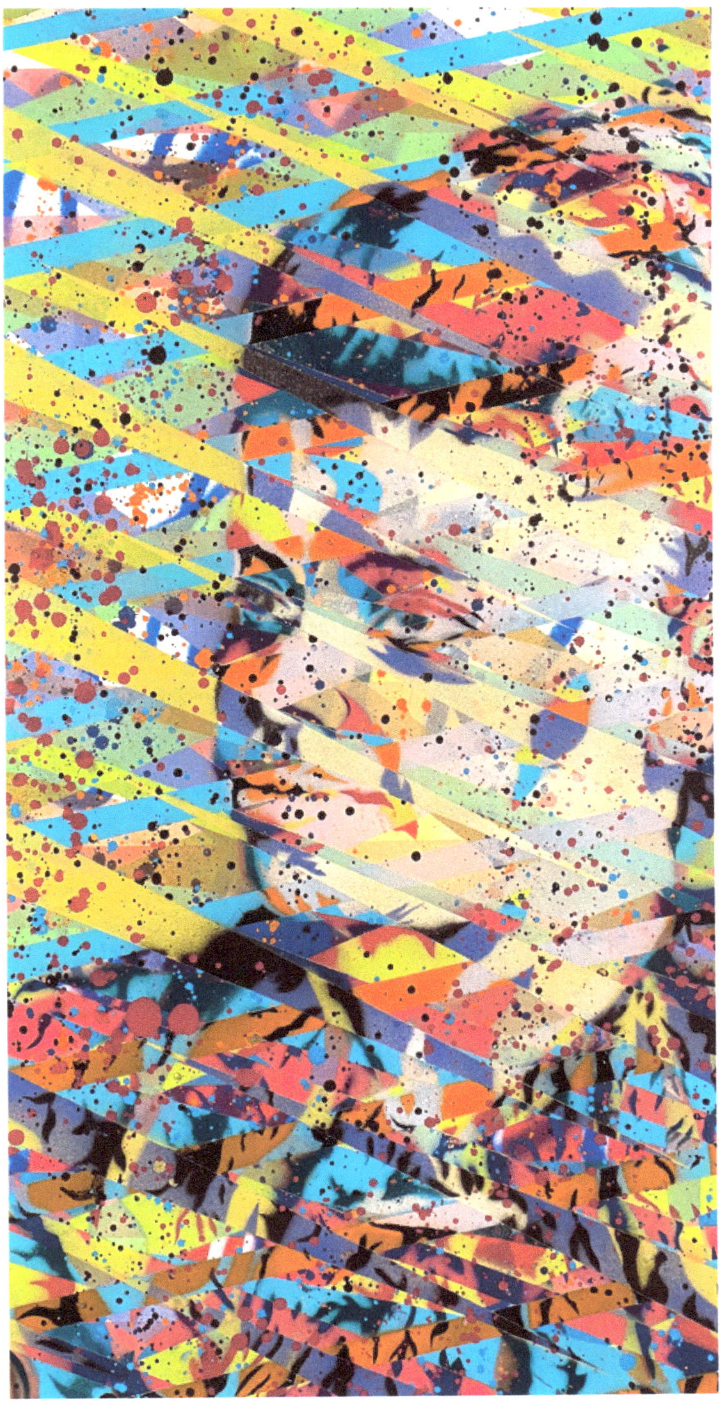

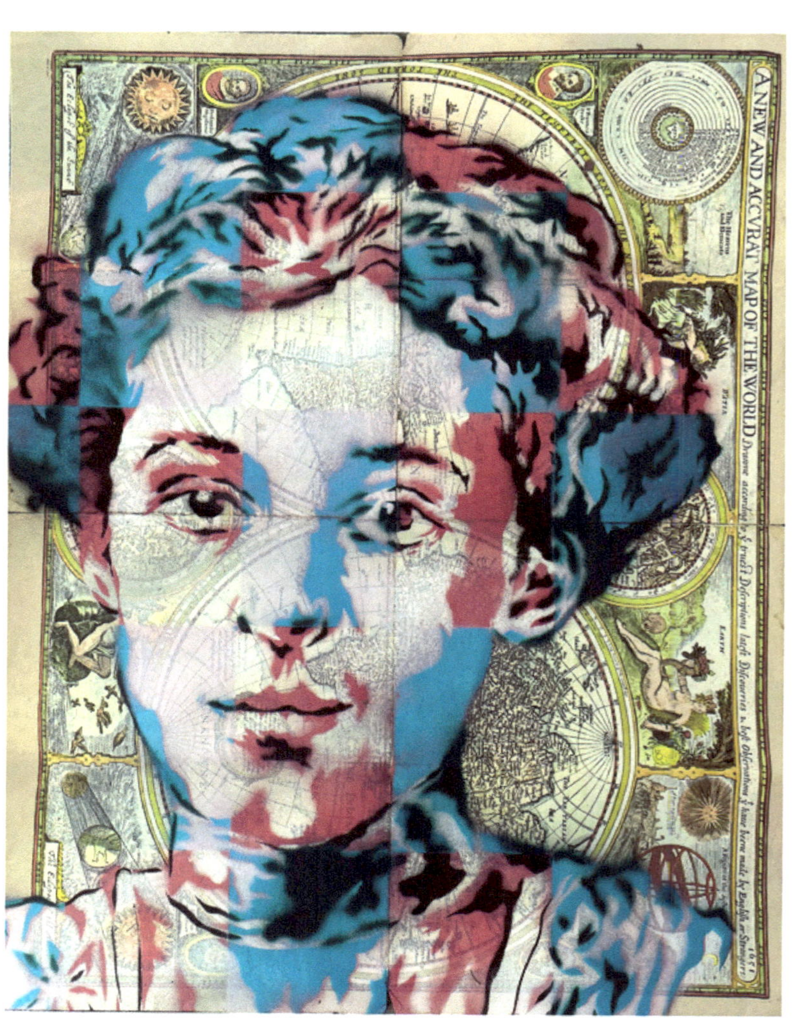

A NEW AND ACCVRAT MAP OF THE WORLD Drawne according to y truest Descriptions latest Discoveries & best Observations y have beene made by English or Strangers 1651
The Heavens and Elements
WATER
EARTH

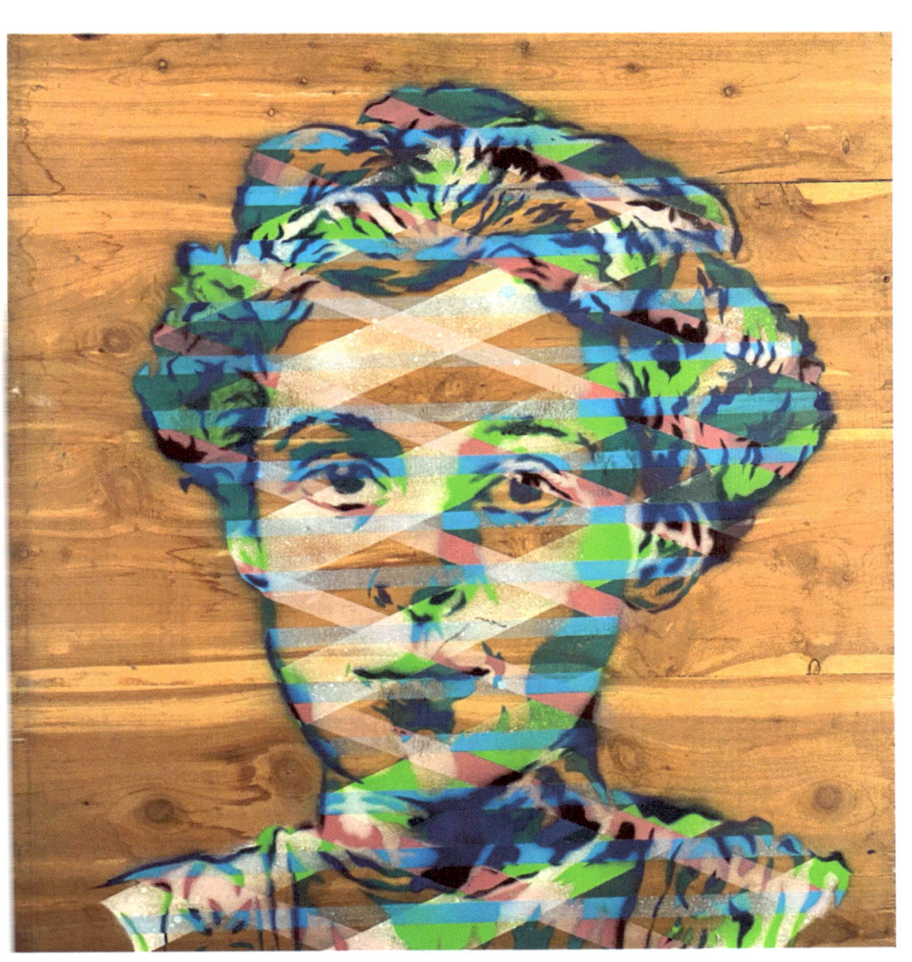

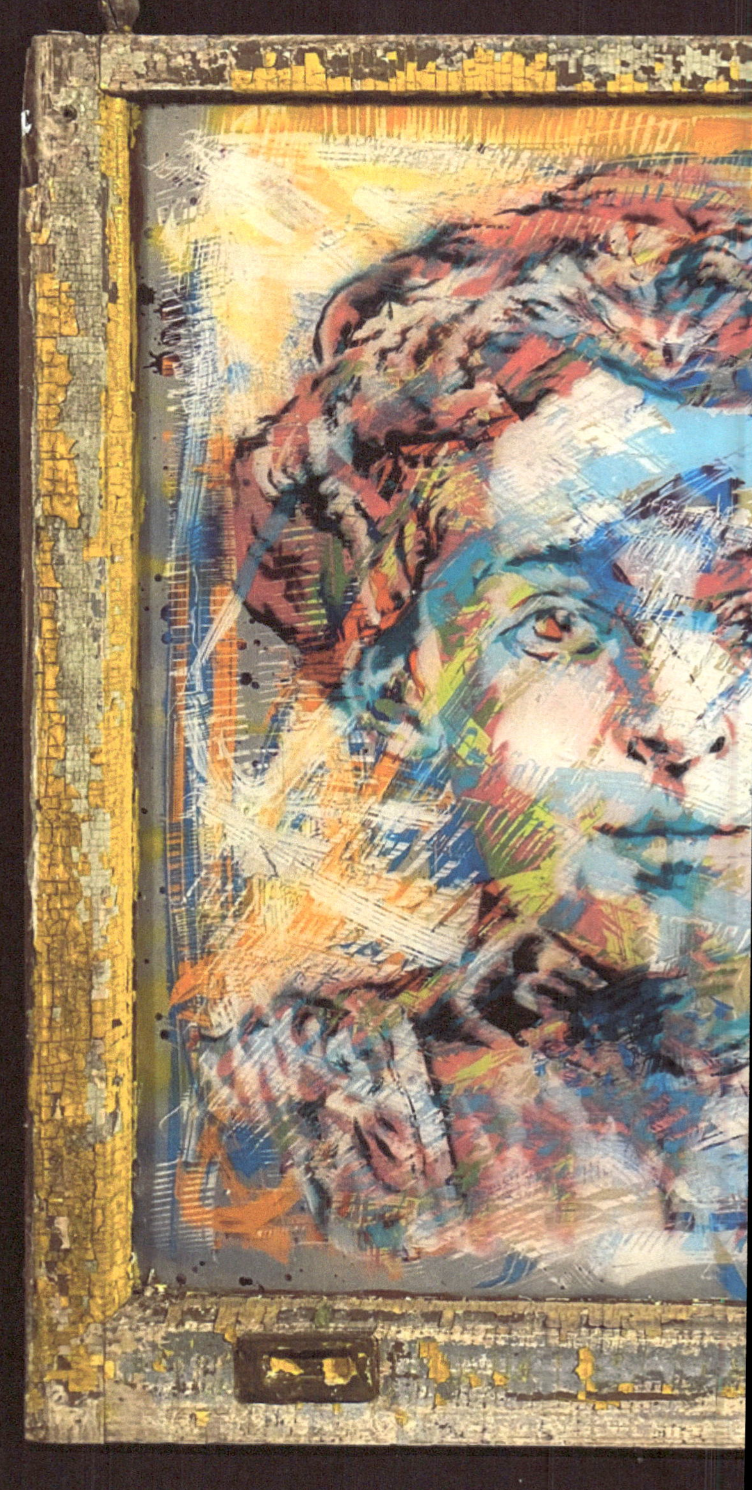

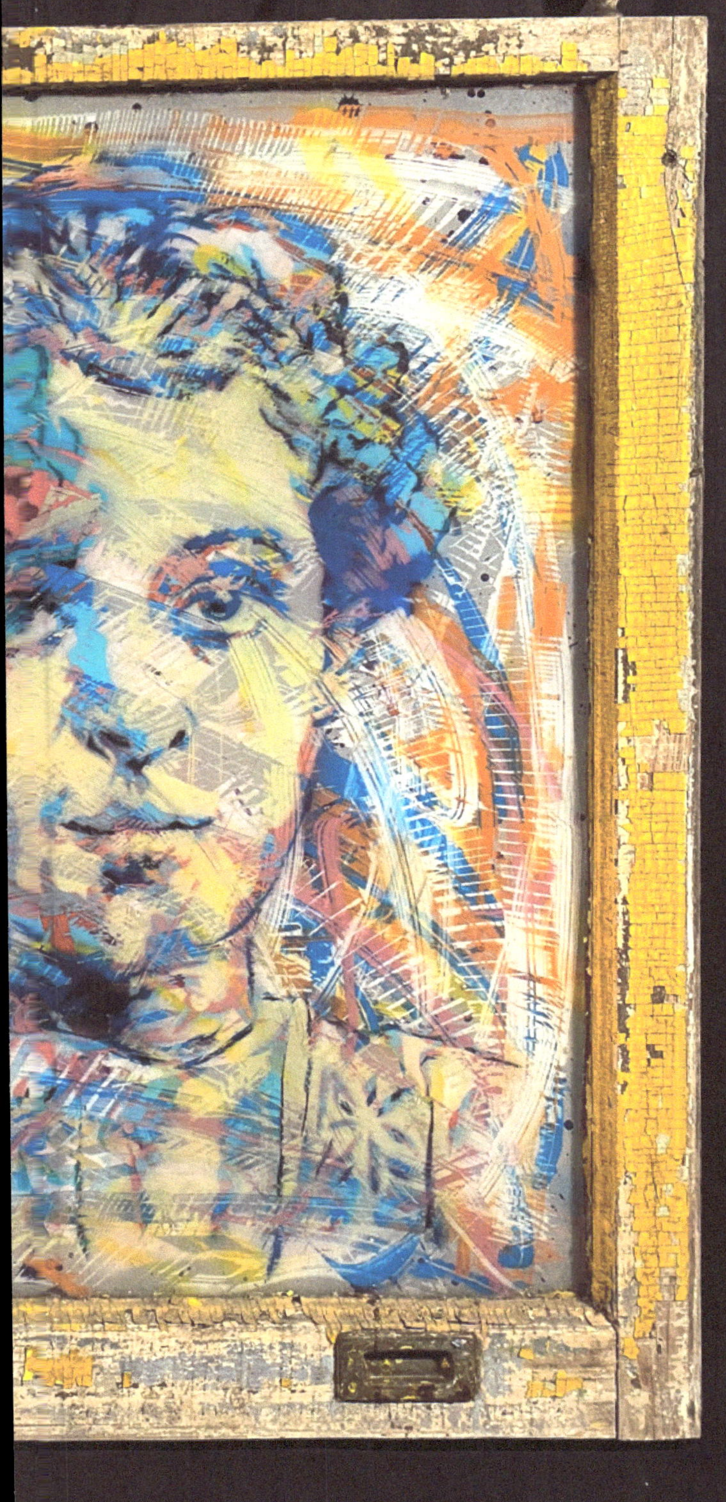

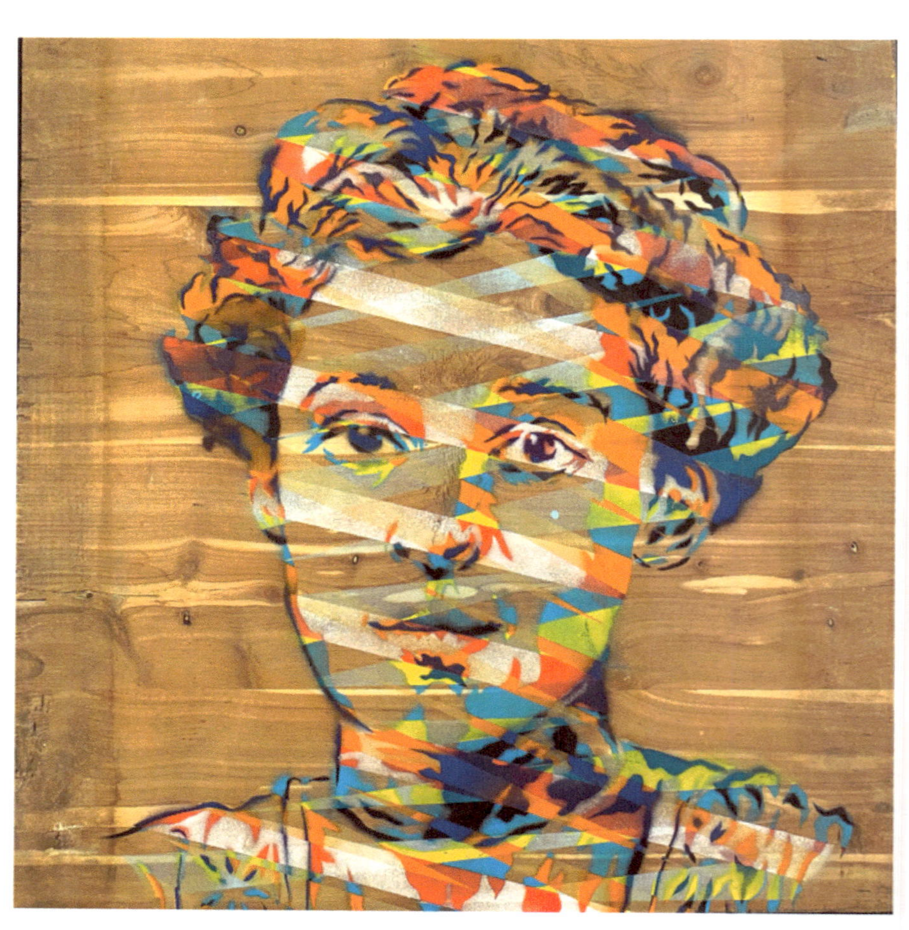

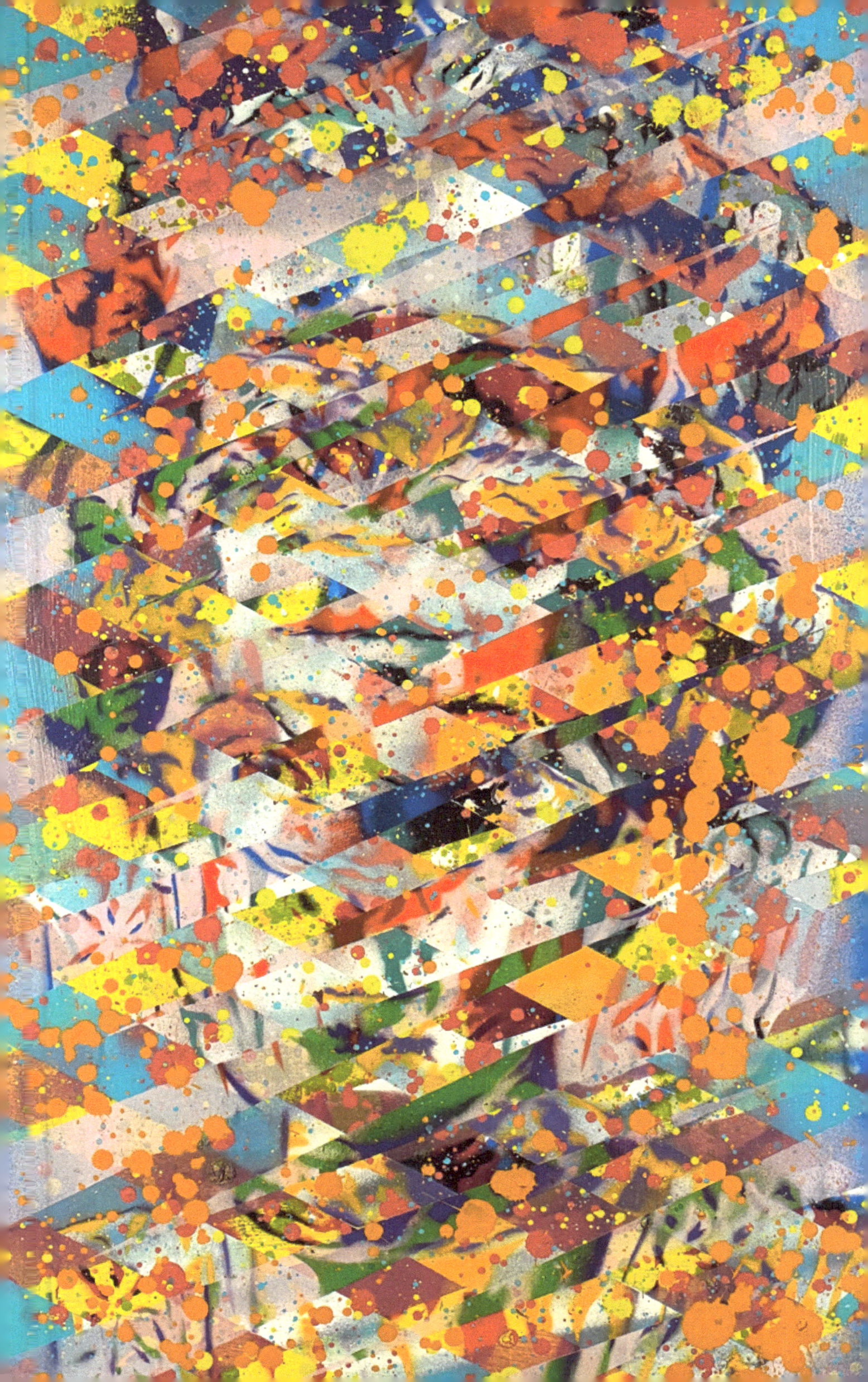

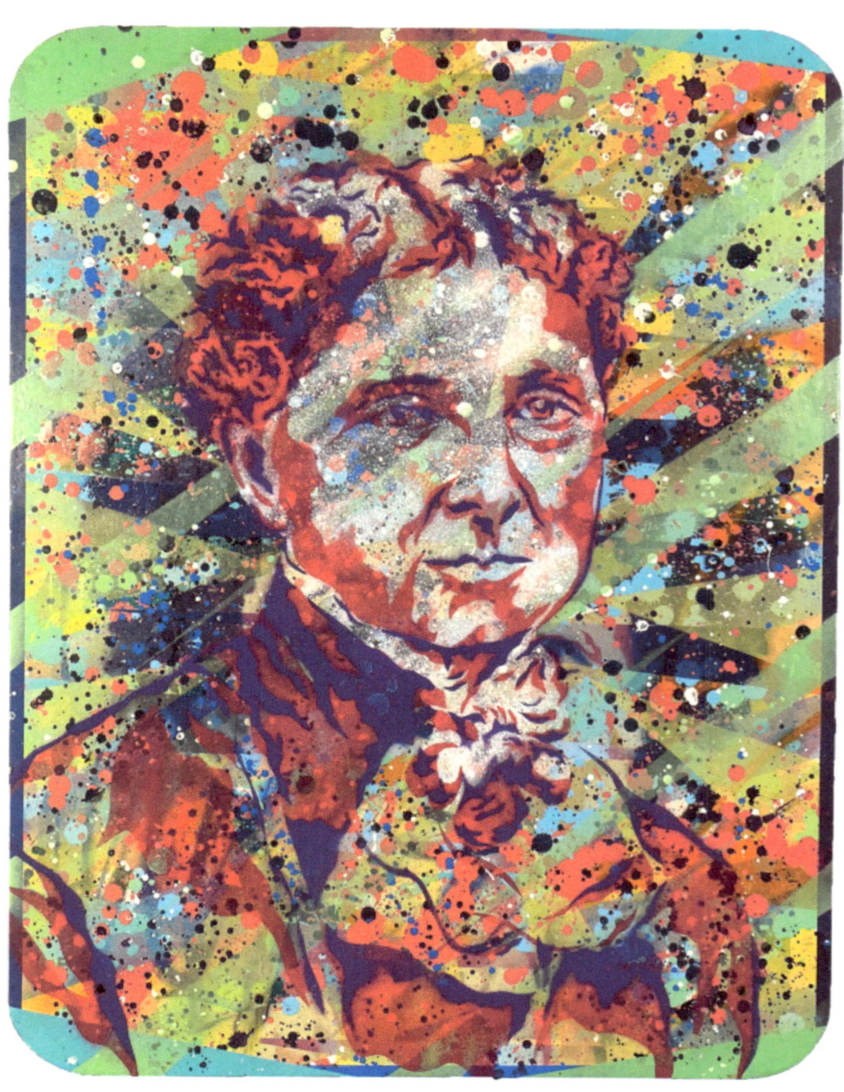

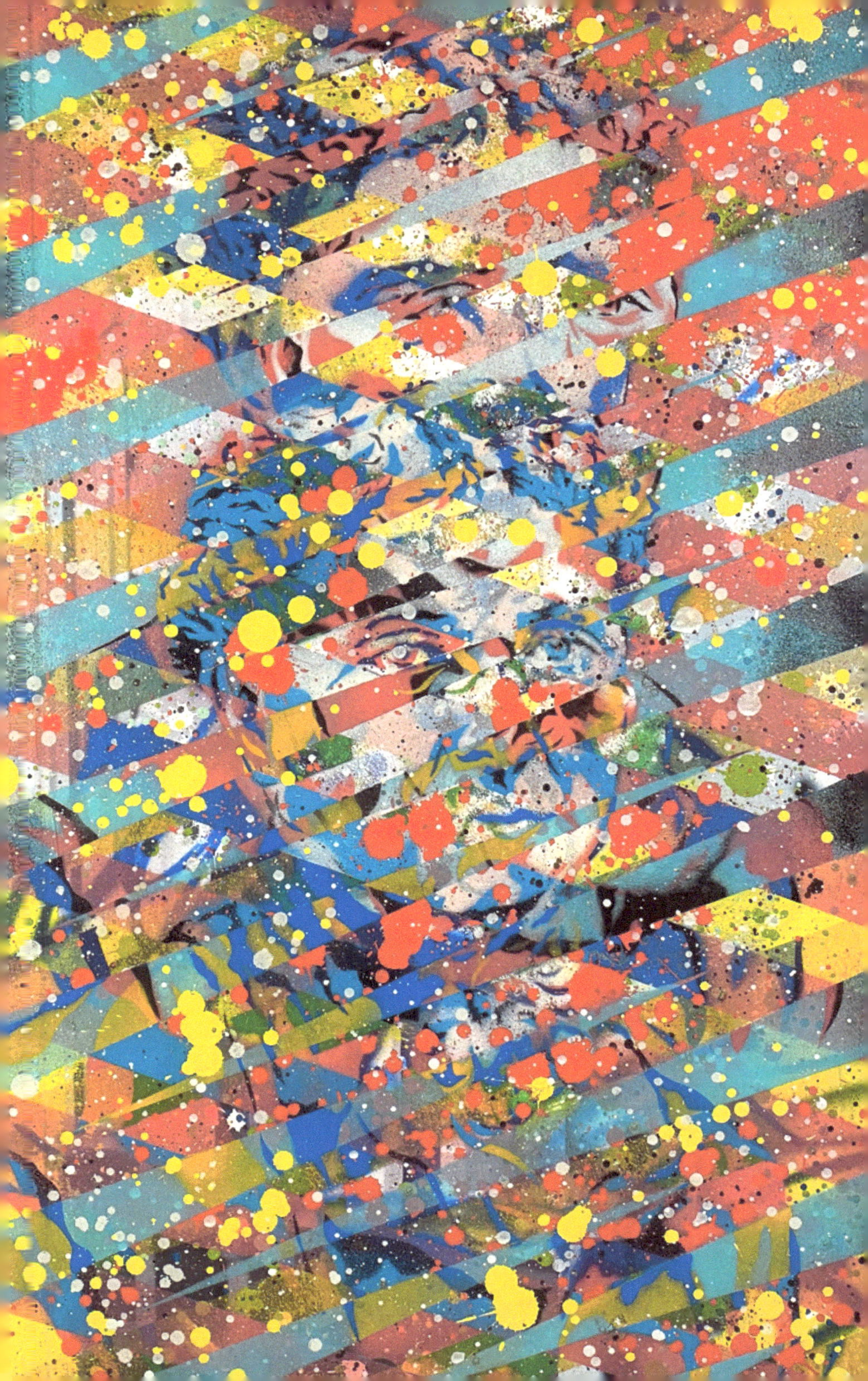

DEDICATION

Many of the people depicted in this volume were able to get their message out to the masses because they had a platform through their writing and speeches. What they were saying connected with how people were feeling. This is why we are able to learn so much from and about them, but that doesn't mean they were the only ones. The stands that they took also happened on many levels, many of them undocumented.

This book is dedicated to anyone who has ever taken a stand. To anyone who has ever stood up for themselves or their communities. To anyone who has ever fought for what they thought was right. This is the push and pull of history; it is a story that persists throughout all of time.

This is by no means a complete list, it is not even an attempt at one. These are the stories that came to me once my awareness started to become in tune with this subject. Many individuals and collectives throughout history—and I'm sure well into our future—will stand for the same ideas expressed here.

Oppression happens on so many levels. It's not just something the government does. It's not just something that happens at work or at school. It's not just your boss or your teacher. All forms of oppression stem from the fact that we separate ourselves from each other and the universe. Maybe at some point, in that future utopia that some dream about, everyone will have a better understanding and unity will be possible. Until then, we fight. It's Time Again.

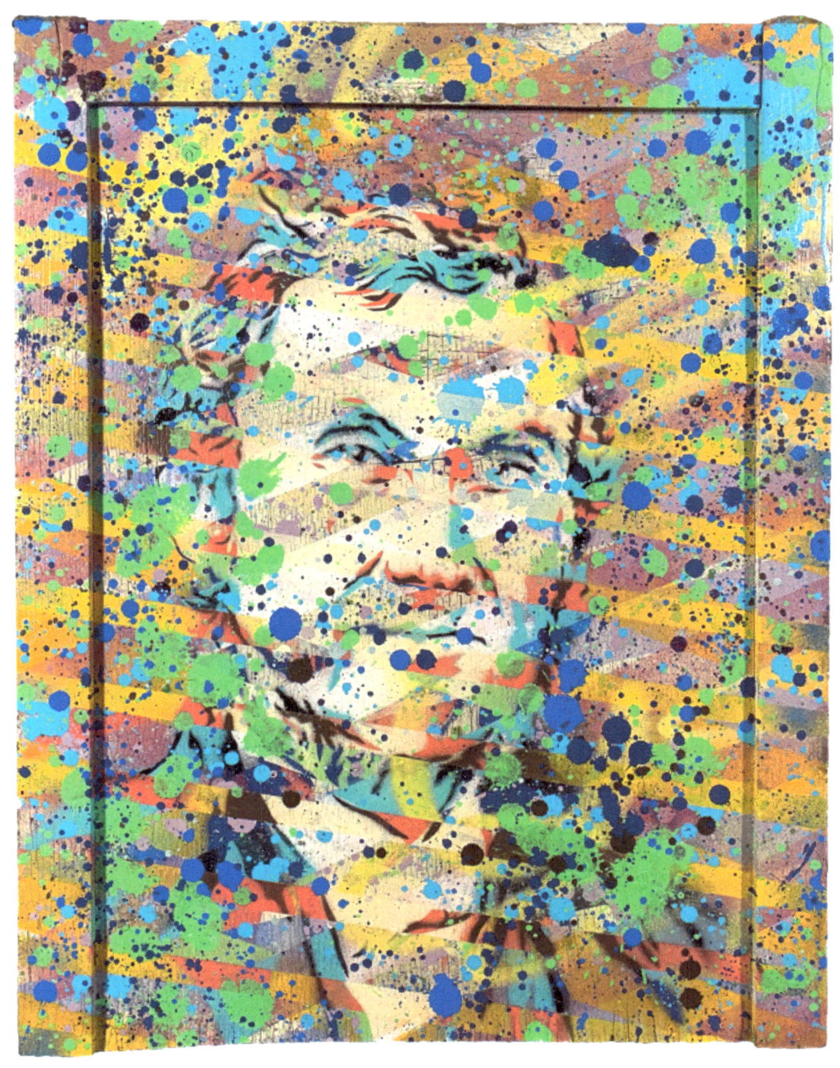

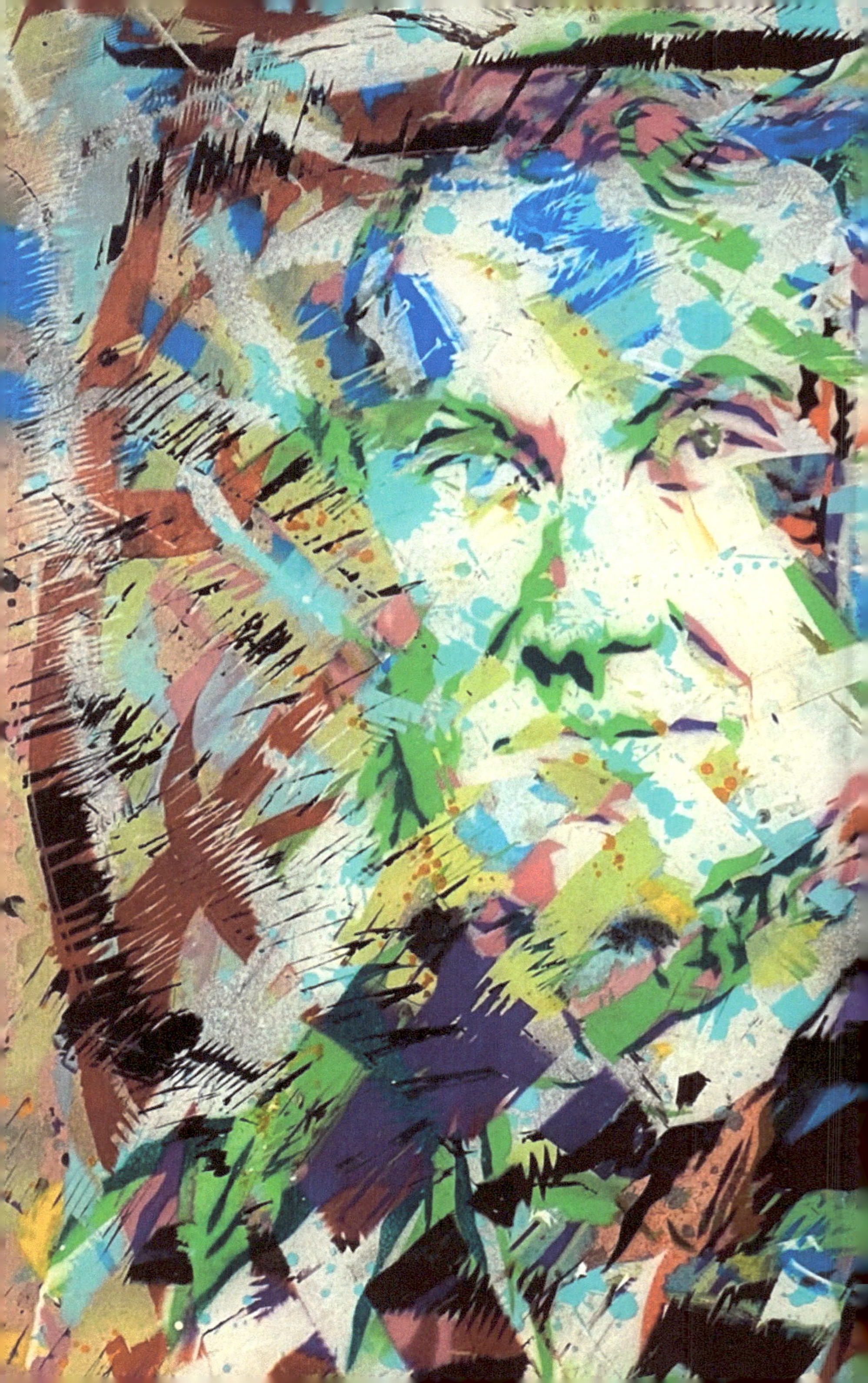

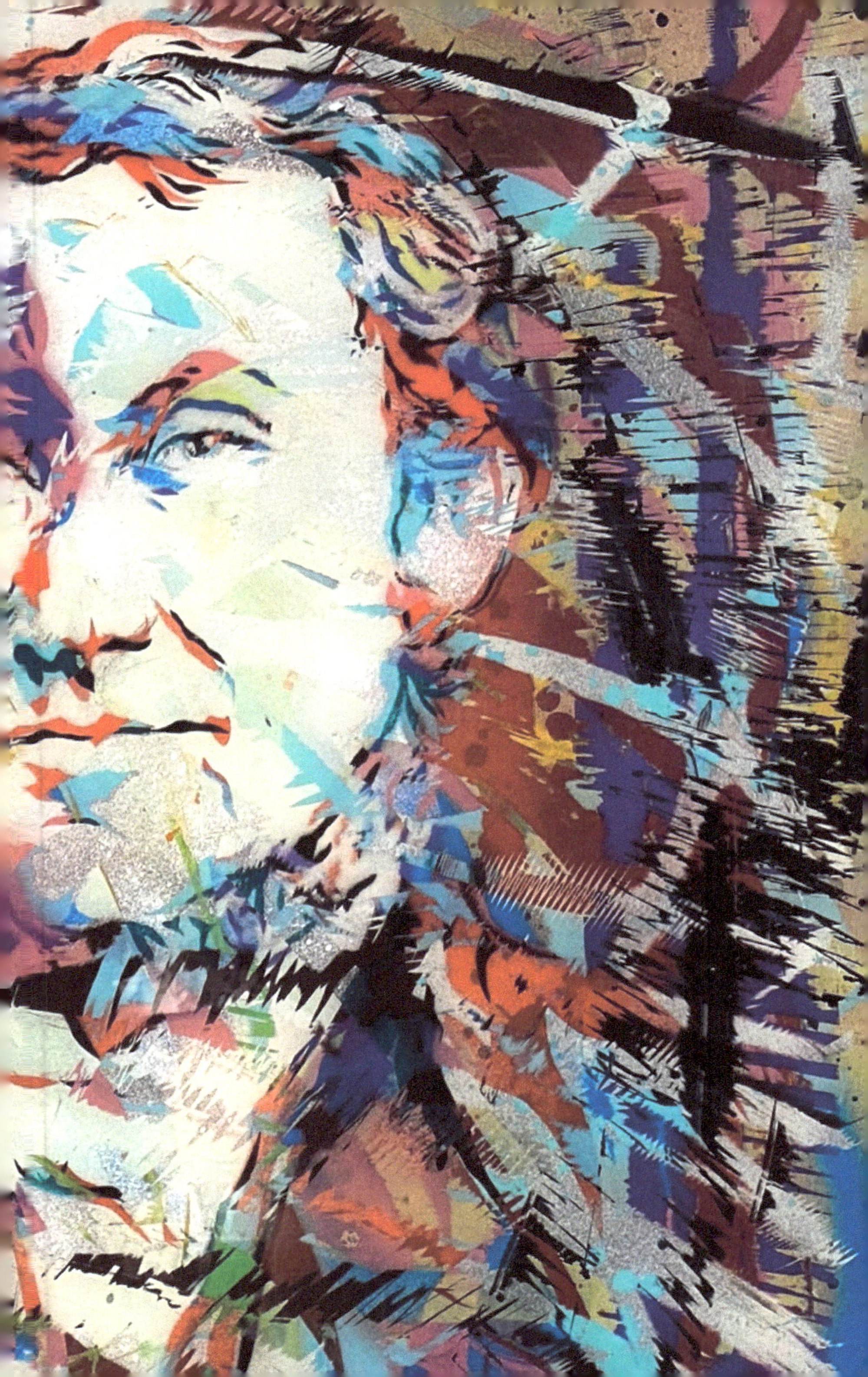

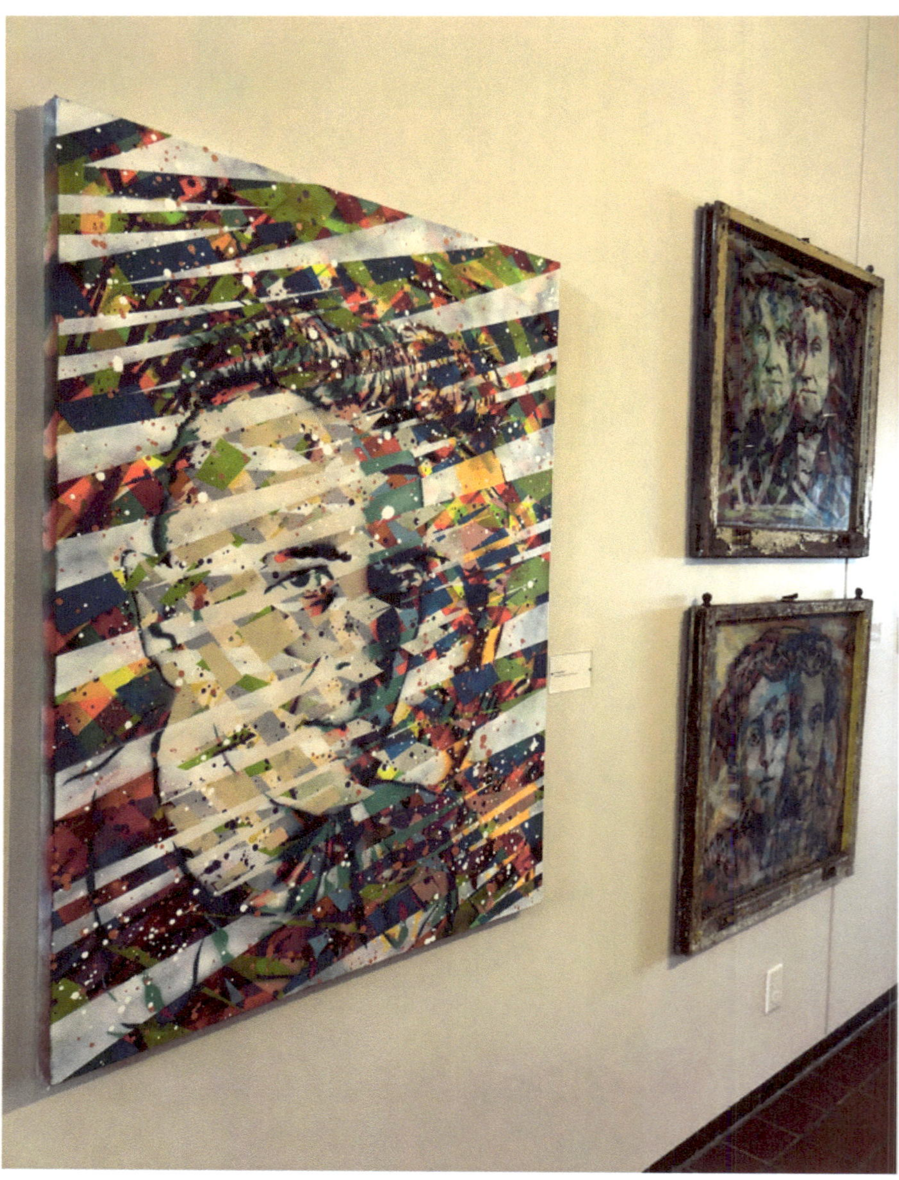

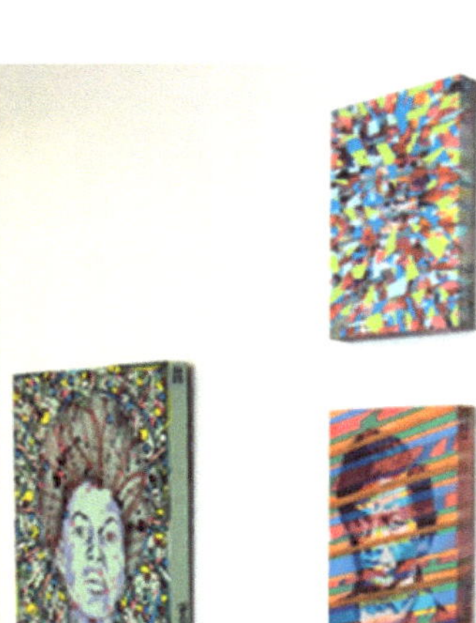

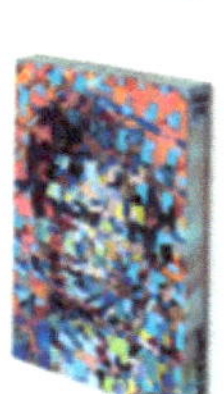

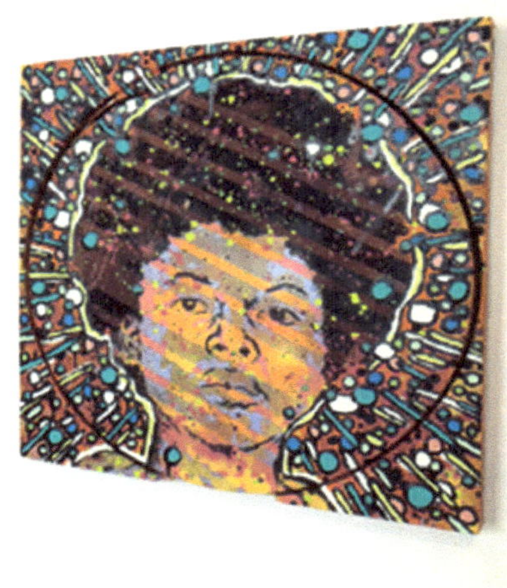

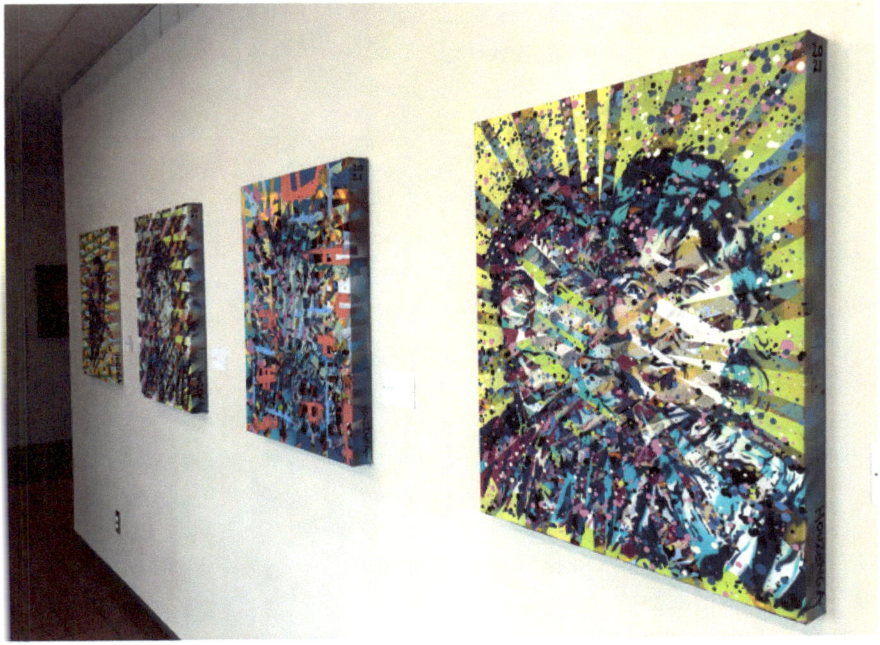

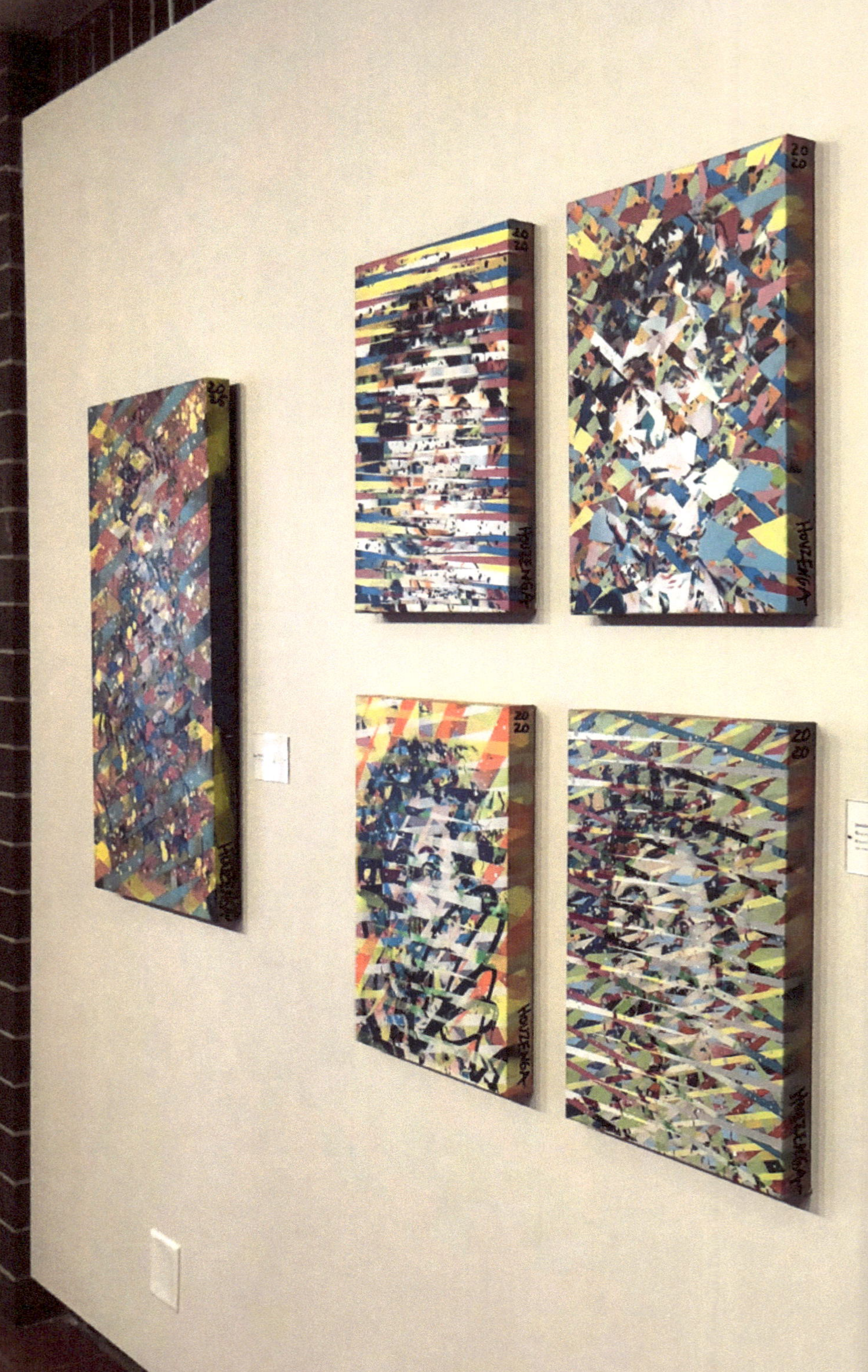

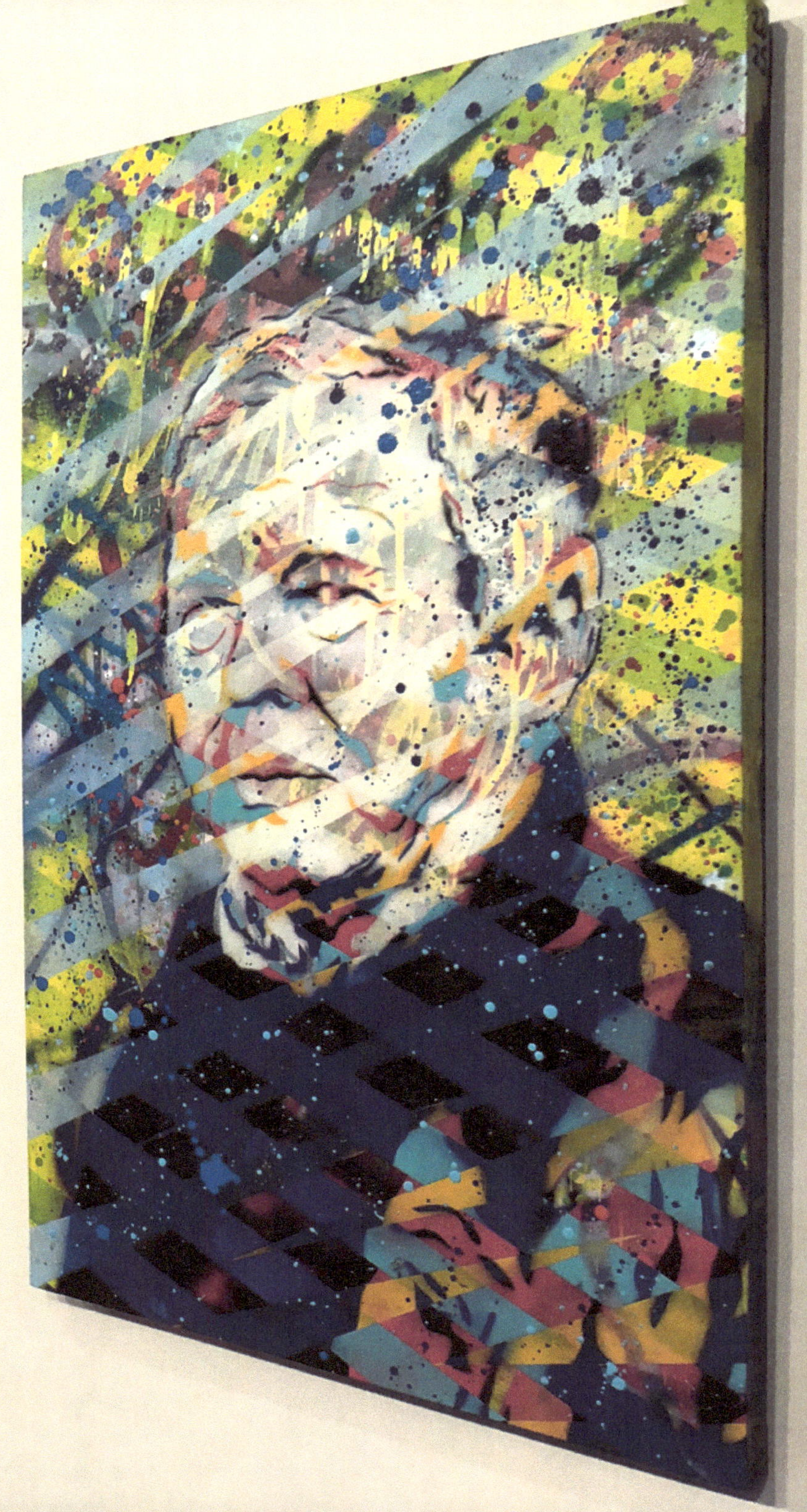

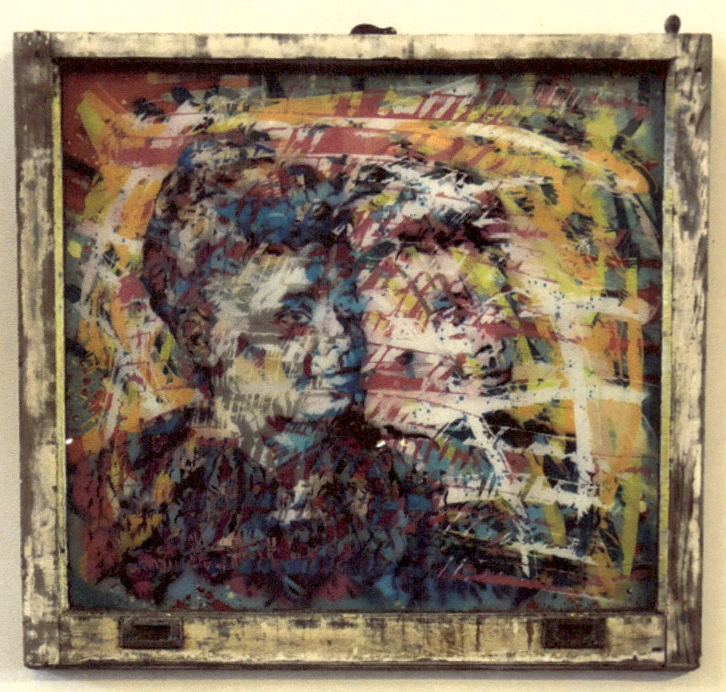

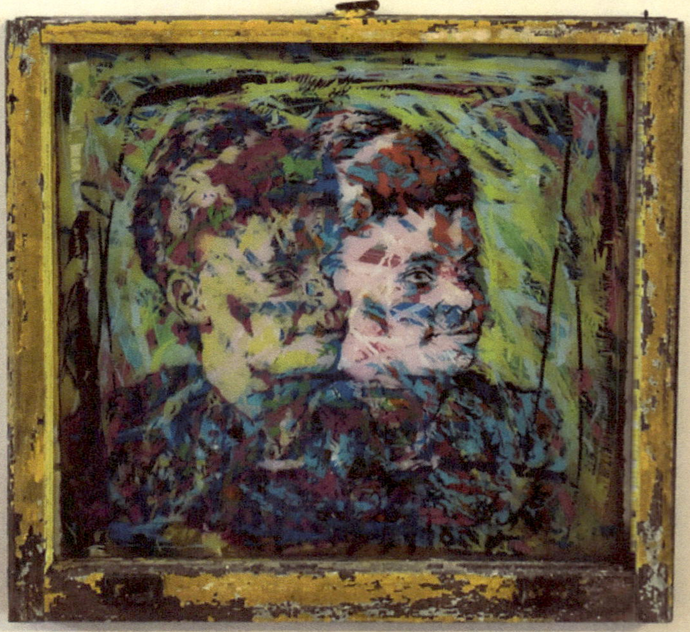

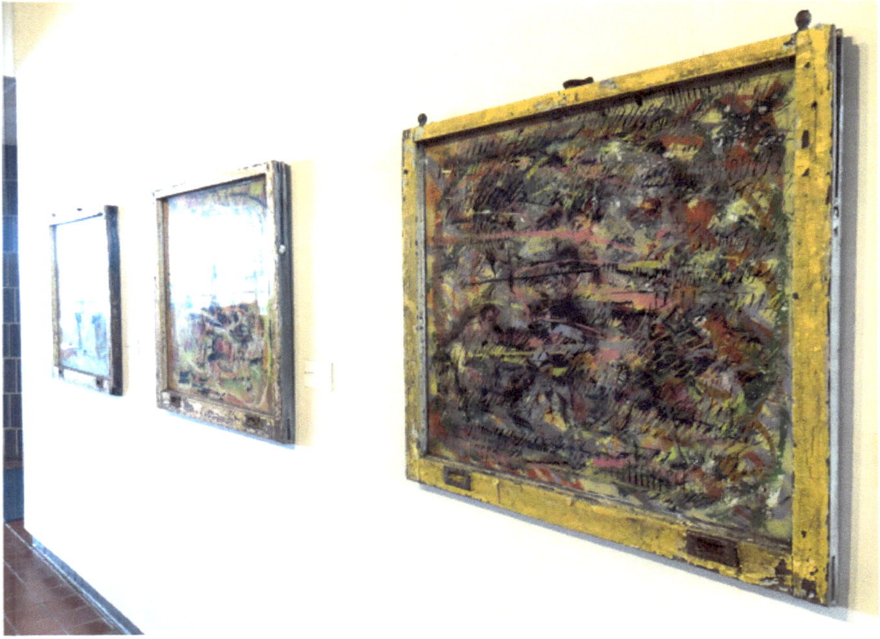

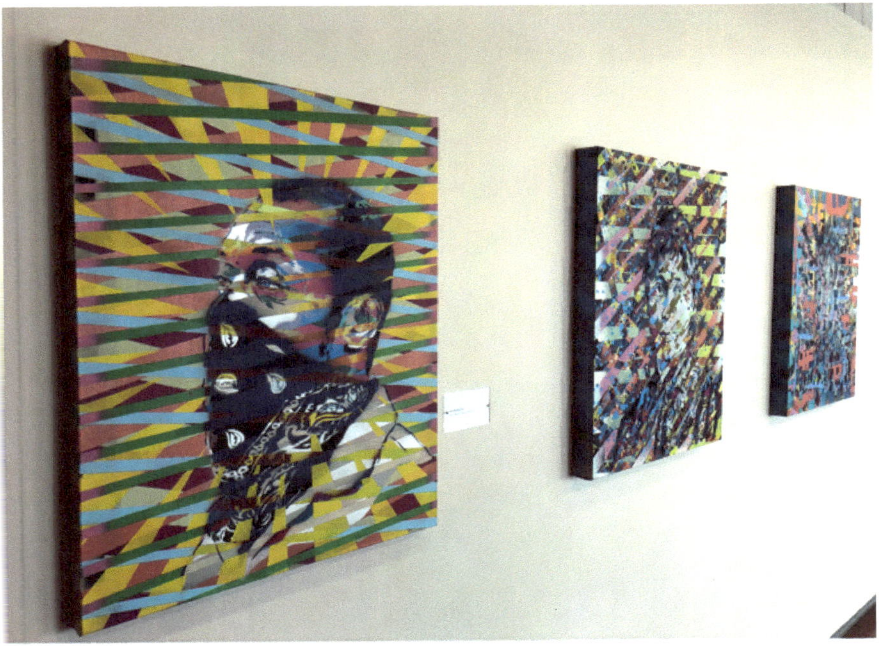

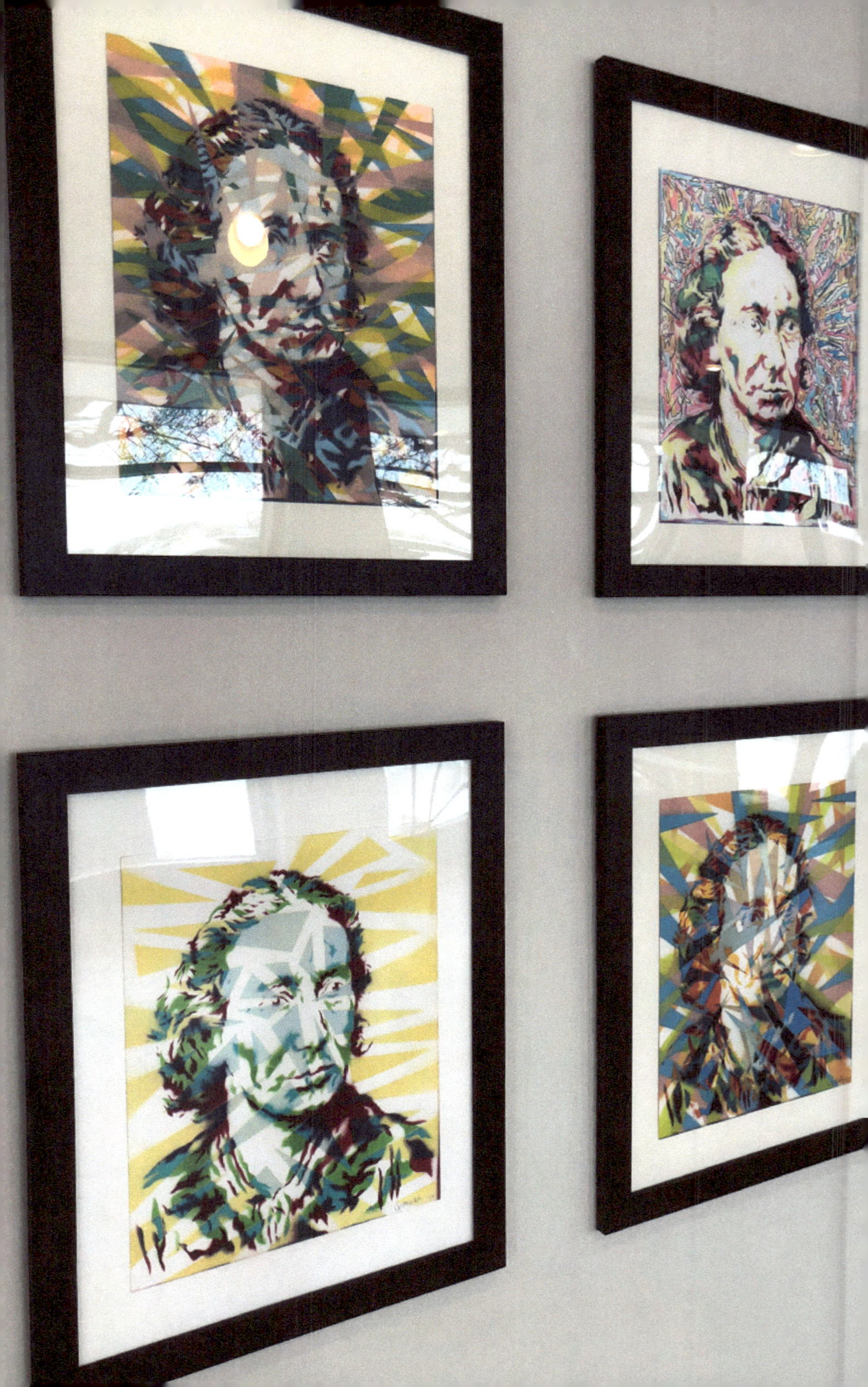

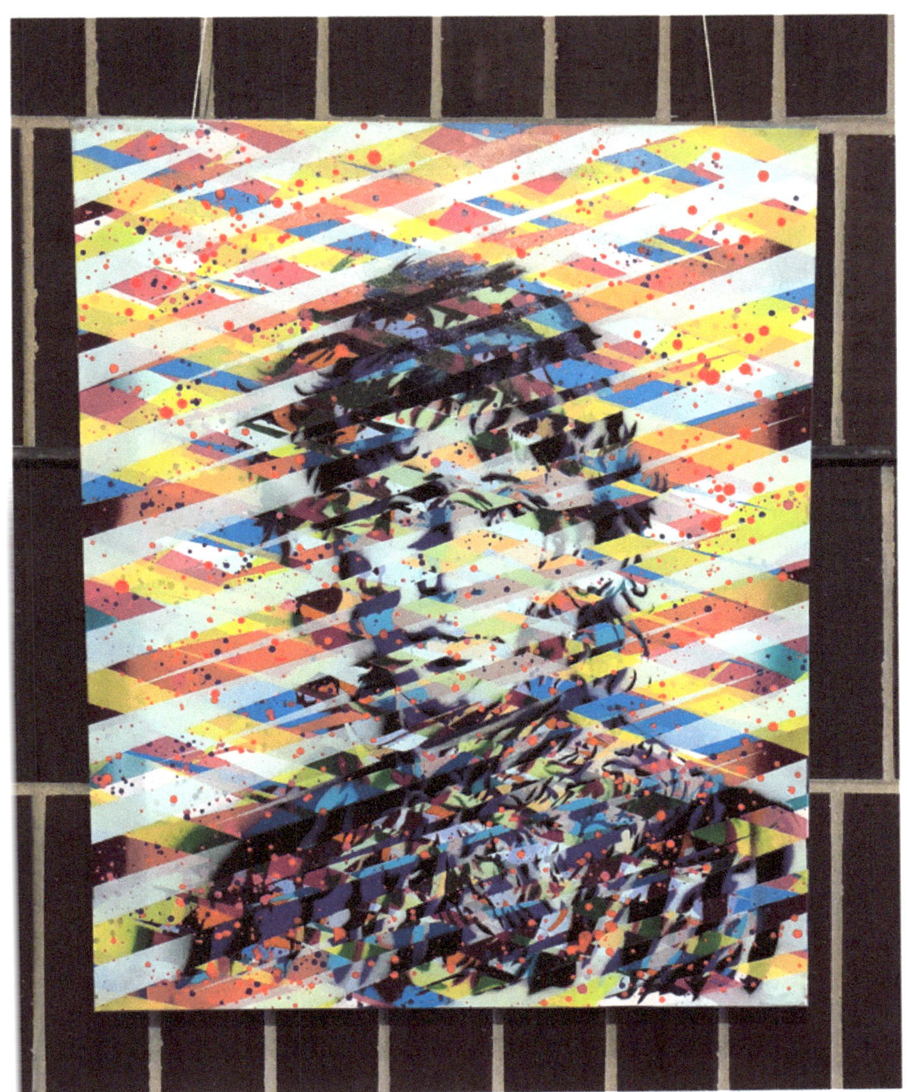

FIGURES PICTURED

Maude Adams
Joe Strummer
Philip K. Dick
Frederick Douglass
Emmeline Pankhurst
Lucy Parsons
Thomas Garrett
Henry David Thoreau
George F. Johnson
Louise Michel
Edward Bellamy
Charlotte Perkins Gilman
Emma Goldman
Leila Khaled
Huey P. Newton
Marsha P. Johnson
Assata Shakur
Che Guevara
James Baldwin
Ida B. Wells
Virginia Brooks
Amelia Bloomer
Joseph A. Dugdale

New Orleans in 2020:
The Nurses - Feed The Front Line
Penny Favalora Spiers and Leslie Green
Based on a photograph by Katie Sikora

Queen Tahj - Feed The Second Line
Based on a photograph by LaNitrah Hasan

The Hoppers On Strike
D'Artanion "Conversations" DeJean and Anthony Perkins
Based on photographs by Katie Sikora

All custom action figures modeled and 3D printed by Paul Garner

Portrait of the artist by Ryan Hodgson-Rigsbee

Brent Houzenga is New Orleans-based artist originally from Fulton, IL, a small midwestern town. Like many children of the 80's, he got an early taste for art and creativity through television and toys. Later, the record and comic book shops would play an important role. Even later, punk rock, skateboarding, and DIY culture would solidify his life as a creative.

Houzenga earned his B.A. in printmaking and graphic design from Western Illinois University in 2006 and his MFA at the University of New Orleans in 2017. Houzenga's art has been exhibited all over the country and world and resides in many private and public collections. He is an accomplished muralist, installation artist and educator.

Houzenga's work has been featured in publications such as *Time Out Chicago, Art and Art Galleries of the South, Art+Design New Orleans*, as well as the Rizzoli book *Stickers: From Punk Rock to Contemporary Art*. In 2021, his work appeared on the cover of the Image Comics book *Primordial*. In 2024 his work appeared on the cover of the dreampunk anthology *Somniscope* published by Fractured Mirror. He is the subject of the independent documentary film *Brent Houzenga: Hybrid Pioneer*.

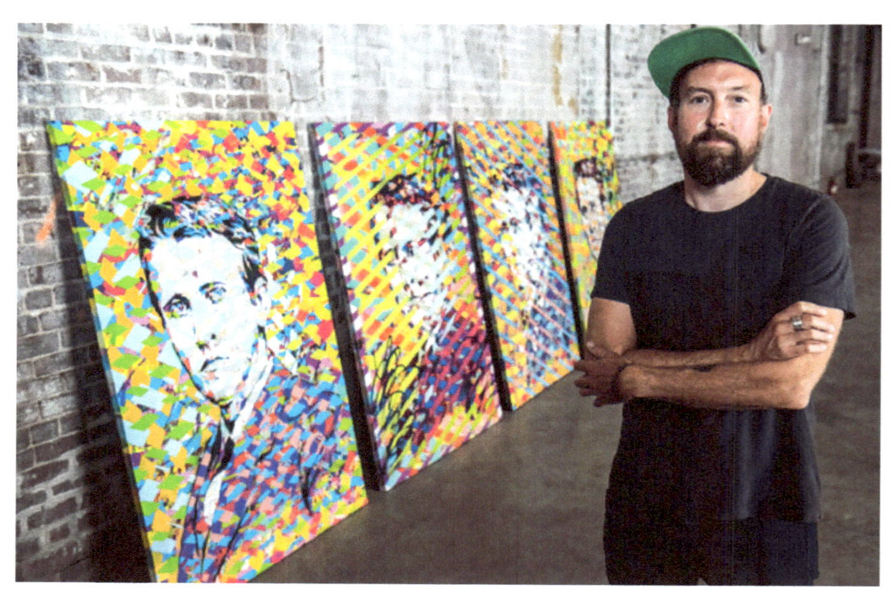

Houzenga.com

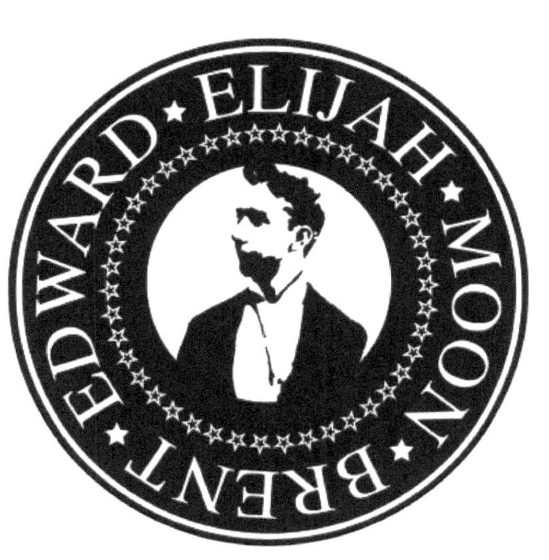
EDWARD * ELIJAH * MOON * BRENT

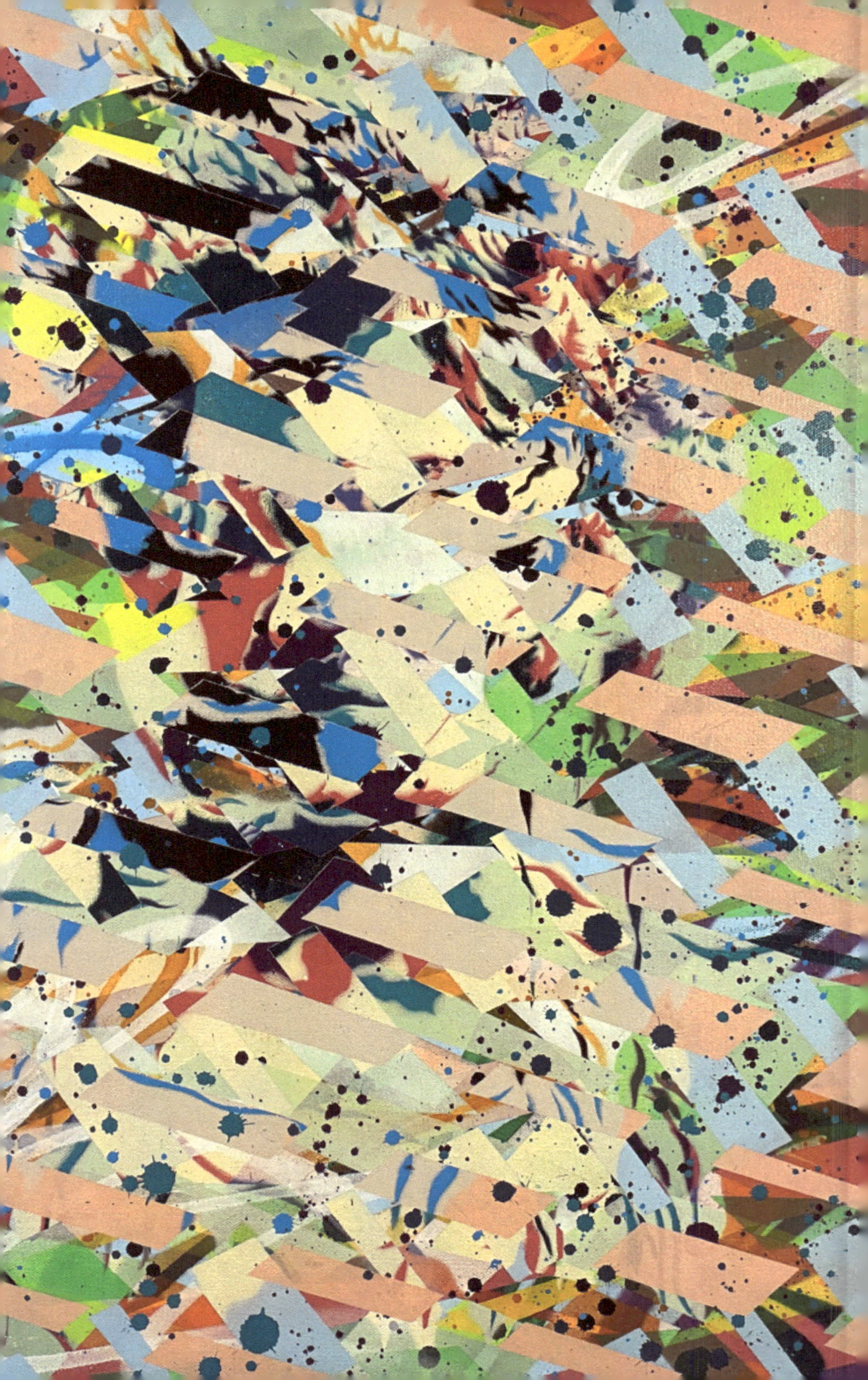